P9-EMN-451

# Survey Research

# Survey Research
## A Decisional Approach

*Donald S. Tull* • *Gerald S. Albaum*
University of Oregon

*INTEXT EDUCATIONAL PUBLISHERS*
*New York and London*

**Library of Congress Cataloging in Publication Data**

Tull, Donald S
    Survey research: a decisional approach.

    (The Intext series in marketing research)
    Includes bibliographies.
    1.  Marketing research.  2.  Market surveys.
3.  Decision-making.  4.  Social science research.
I.  Albaum, Gerald S., joint author.  II.  Title.
HF5415.2.T84                 658.8′3                 73–5994
ISBN 0-7002-2436-X

Intext Educational Publishers
257 Park Avenue South
New York, New York 10010

*To E.E.A., E.V.T., R.E.T., and the late L.A.*

# Contents

# Preface

Survey research problems may usually be categorized as either *decisional* or *basic* in nature. Decisional problems are, as the name implies, those for which a survey is conducted to provide information for making a decision. Basic research problems are primarily concerned with advancing scientific knowledge. The findings of such projects may of course be used to help make decisions at some future time. But they will be used by persons unknown and for decisions not now anticipated by the investigator.

This book has a decisional orientation, which represents a departure from most books on the subject. The essential methodological difference between the two types of research lies in the admissibility of investigator judgment as a factor in the collection and analysis of data. In the properly designed basic survey research project every effort is made to collect data that are objectively verifiable. The only sampling errors should be random in origin and stochastically predictable; systematic errors are measured and nonjudgmental means of analysis are employed. Competence in research design and care in its implementation are relied upon to realize these objectives.

In the properly designed decisional-research project, investigator judgment is used to supplement and in some cases supplant nonjudgmental procedures. The principle involved, applicable both to the research project as a whole and to its constituent elements, is to weigh value versus cost of information.

Relaxing the constraints of basic research opens up an entirely new range of design alternatives. If the investigator concludes that the added cost incurred by a random sample is unwarranted, a nonrandom sample will be taken and the sampling error estimated. The saving in sampling cost may be allocated to other areas of the project—the measurement of systematic error, for example—but only if it is believed that such an allocation will contribute substantially in value of new information obtained.

Written for the *user* of survey research as well as the *doer*, this book can be used by itself or in conjunction with more traditionally oriented texts. Because it is methodological rather than discipline oriented, it can be used in any areas in which decisional research is conducted.

As all authors, we are indebted to a sizable group of people who have contributed to the final product. We should especially like to thank Professors James Reinmuth of the University of Oregon, Charles Lillis of Washington State University, Ben Enis of the University of Houston, and Ralph Day of the University of Indiana, who read and made many suggestions for improving the manuscript. We are also grateful to our students at the University of Oregon who suffered through and wrote critiques of the early drafts. We are indebted to the Literary Executor of the late Sir Ronald A. Risher, F.R.S., and to Oliver and Boyd, Edinburgh, for their permission to reprint Tables of the $t$ and $\chi^2$ distributions from their book *Statistical Methods for Research Workers*.

While we in no way wish to diminish the contributions of those who provided assistance to us, we do ask that they be absolved from responsibility for any errors of omission or commission that remain.

# *Survey Research*

# Decision Making

# and Survey Research

Behavioral scientists have an immense advantage that natural scientists do not—the option to ask as well as to observe.

This book deals with *survey research,* the art and the science of asking questions and/or observing behavior to obtain information. The practice of conducting surveys extends back to at least the eleventh century (the Domesday Book). The widespread use of surveys is a product of the twentieth century, however. Investigators of social conditions were the early developers and primary users of survey research. While this continues to be an important sponsoring source of surveys, the recognition by governmental agencies, political candidates, and marketers of their need for information has provided the major impetus for the growth in survey use. Marketing research is now the largest single private sponsor of survey research projects.

This book has a *decisional* orientation. In this respect it departs from the tradition of authors of books on survey research to deal almost entirely with basic research. The implicit assumption contained in such books is that basic-research methodology is directly applicable to applied research problems. This assumption is only partially true, as we shall see, and may be a costly one for the researcher who needs information to help in making a decision.

This chapter opens with a discussion of the nature of survey research. It continues with a consideration of basic and decisional research and the differences in the two in terms of design objectives. The value versus cost orientation of decisional research is then discussed. The chapter concludes with a consideration of problem formulation.

## The Nature of Survey Research

*Survey research* is a term that is susceptible to a variety of interpretations. As most often used, it connotes a project to get information from a sample of people by use of a questionnaire. The questions may be designed to obtain information that is retrospective, concurrent, or projective with regard to time. They may be asked in a personal interview, by telephone, or sent to the respondent by mail. A survey may involve observation of respondent behavior,[1] or evidence of such behavior, in conjunction with or separately from the asking of questions. Observations may be made personally or by devices that record some aspect of behavior. The sample may be discarded after a single use, or it may be used over successive time intervals.

Despite the diversity of forms survey research may take, there are elements that remain common to all. The method of gathering information is always *systematic,* regardless of the form of collection used. There is always a *population* of interest that is represented by the sample or, in the occasional case, by the census of respondents.[2]

Survey research projects are always concerned with the behavior of the members of the population of interest. It may be the voting behavior of an electorate or the buying behavior of a group of consumers; in either case, it is *behavior* that is being investigated.

Further, we may observe that it is for the purpose of understanding or predicting behavior, or both, that the investigation is being made. The sponsor of the research on consumer behavior may be a university bureau of business and economic research that is interested in furthering the understanding of buying behavior, or it may be a marketing manager who is interested in both understanding and predicting behavior because he must make decisions for which such information is necessary.

This observation is an important one. In a decisional setting there is often a tendency to emphasize prediction at the expense of understanding.

1. The word *respondent* is used here to refer to members of the sample (or census) who supply information actively through answering questions and/or passively by being observed. It is used in this sense to avoid the word *subject,* a term that is widely used in experimental research to refer to rats, sophomores, people, and other objects.
2. In general, a *population* is any identifiable set of units of interest to the researcher, whether they be individuals, groups, events, or units of time. A *sample* is a part of the population.

After all, decisions involve choices among alternative actions, and these choices must be made in terms of some sort of prediction of the outcome of each of the alternatives. Judging which is the best of the alternatives, therefore, tends to be equated with decision making.

The important element that is overlooked in such a view is the development of the alternative actions from which to choose. This is a creative rather than a judgmental act, one which requires an understanding of the process involved if it is to be done well. It may be preferable to choose even the worst of a superior set of alternatives to the best of an inferior set; development of admissible alternatives is at least as important in decision making as choosing among them. The relationship of the two to understanding and prediction is shown in Table 1-1.

We have now reached a point where a definition of survey research can be stated:

> Survey research is the systematic gathering of information from (a sample of) respondents for the purpose of understanding and/or predicting some aspect of the behavior of the population of interest.

## *Decisional Research and Basic Research*

For the purpose of this book, the need for "understanding and/or predicting some aspect of behavior" is to provide information *to make a better decision.* This is to say that this book is concerned with decisional rather than basic research.

*Decisional research,* as the term is used here, is synonymous with applied research. Decisional research is always conducted to provide information for a pending decision. The information generated by basic research may be used for decision making at some future time, but not necessarily so. Its purpose is rather to increase the level of knowledge in a given area, with no necessary application to existing problems.

No one is likely to quarrel with this distinction, as it is based upon a commonly observed difference in usage of the information provided by the

TABLE 1-1   Understanding and prediction in decision making

| Analytic focus | Development of alternatives | Choice among alternatives |
|---|---|---|
| Understanding | X | |
| Prediction | | X |

Source: Adapted from Robert Dubin, *Theory Building.* (New York: The Free Press, 1969), p. 10.

research. These questions may well be asked, however: "Granted that there is a difference in usage of the information, what effect does it have on the way the research is conducted? For a given problem, why shouldn't the survey research project that is going to be done to investigate it be the same irrespective of whether it is basic or decisional in purpose?"

An answer to these questions lies in an examination of the determinants of survey research design. Reflection suggests that there are essentially four such considerations: the nature of the problem, the researcher, the respondent, and the client. It is not difficult to think of basic- and decisional-research projects dealing with the same problem, being conducted by the same researcher, and using the same respondents to provide information. A consumer-motivation study or a voting behavior study are potential examples. These projects would have different clients, however, and it is there that we must look for the source of design difference requirements.

It is clear that all clients, regardless of whom they may be, would *like* information whose errors are small but *need* information whose errors or potential errors can be measured with reasonable accuracy. Information of unknown accuracy may be worse than none at all. Similarly, it is apparent that all clients would like to have objective measures of the potential error.

It is the differences in the level of allowable error of basic- and decisional-research clients and the ways in which they go about assessing the level of actual error that give rise to design differences in the two types of research. The "client" of a basic survey research project is the scientific community to which it is reported. It is typically a large group of people who might more properly be referred to as a "clientele" than as a "client." It normally will not have commissioned the research nor, as a group if not as individuals, will not be affected personally by the outcome. The researcher may or may not be known to the majority of those to whom the results of the project is reported.

Scientists historically have insisted upon elimination of as much error as possible and obtaining objectively verifiable measures of the remaining potential error. Ideally, the research must have been conducted with full disclosure of procedures that provide for investigator independence. The capability of replication of the project by other investigators from the report is a means of ensuring that these requirements are met.

The client of the decisional-research project would always choose as little error as possible and objective measurement of the residual potential error if these options were available at no additional cost. However, as the financial sponsor of the research as well as the user of it, he may find that beyond some point added accuracy is not worth the cost of obtaining it. He may also reach the same conclusion about objective measurement of residual error.

The decisional-research client also has an added means of assessment of research information not generally available to his basic-research counterparts. He will typically have been closely associated with the project from the inception, in many cases even to the point of having chosen the principal researcher or researchers involved. He will, therefore, have had many opportunities to assess both the general competence of the researchers and the manner in which the project has been conducted. The need for objective measurement of error and for investigator independence in procedures may have become less as a result.

Finally, there is rarely a need for replication in decisional-research projects. Most survey research projects conducted for decision-making purposes are concerned with problems that are essentially unique and non-recurring. A new product to be evaluated before deciding whether or not to introduce it, or the determination of the proportion of the electorate who favor a political candidate may require decisions at a later date, but the circumstances will inevitably have changed. Including features in the design that incur added costs solely to permit replication are, therefore, seldom reasonable design objectives in decisional projects.

These differences in client requirements thus often give rise to different design requirements in basic- and decisional-research projects. The value versus cost orientation of decisional research is an outgrowth of these differences. Discussion of this area is, therefore, appropriate at this point.

## Value versus Cost of Information

A decision maker always has the choice of "decide now" versus "get more information." The marketing manager of the company contemplating changing the price of a product may decide that it would be prudent to get consumer reaction to the price change before making it. He may, in fact, make a similar decision again even after he has conducted the test and obtained this additional information from consumers.

It is clear that information has value in a decisional situation. The addition of information to a decisional situation can be thought of as resulting in a change in the probability of a particular course of action being taken. This may occur through the information being the source for suggesting new alternative courses of action or through changing the evaluation of existing ones.

A formal means for evaluating the expected value of information has been developed and is now in use. It is a part of *Bayesian decision analysis.* Very simply stated, the expected value of information is the difference between the expected value of a situation requiring a decision with prospective additional information and the expected value without the additional information. Readers who are not familiar with the principles involved will find it profitable to read one of the many books on this subject.[3]

By whatever means he chooses to do so, the decision maker must determine whether it is worthwhile to seek additional information. This evaluation must normally be made by considering separately each possible means of obtaining additional information and assessing its value against its cost. The information given by market testing different prices, for example, may be the best means available of predicting consumer reaction, but the cost may be prohibitive. At the same time, the information to be provided by consumer survey may be judged to be worth considerably more than its cost.

Survey research should be used as an information-providing medium in decision making only when two conditions are met:

1. When the expected value of the information to be provided by the survey research is greater than the estimated cost
2. When the *difference* between the expected value and the estimated cost of the survey research information is greater than that for any other prospective research design

# Formulation
## of the Survey Research Problem

### PROBLEM SITUATION MODELS

Reread the last paragraph above. Note in the introductory sentence that the statement "Survey Research should be used as an information providing medium only when . . ." is a *normative* or *prescriptive* statement. It states that one should do something only when certain conditions are met.

Also note that a measure of an outcome is specified by the conditions. The conditions stipulated are that the expected value of the survey research must be greater than its estimated cost, and that the net difference for the survey research project should be greater than that for any other prospective research design.

This is the outcome portion of a model for making a decision about whether to conduct a survey research project to get more information before making a decision. The measure of the outcome is not very clearly defined

3. The original development is given in Robert Schlaifer, *Probability and Statistics for Business Decisions* (New York: McGraw-Hill, Inc., 1959). A concise treatment is given in Ben M. Enis and Charles C. Broome, *Marketing Decisions: A Bayesian Approach* (Scranton: International Textbook Company, 1971). This topic is also treated in Paul E. Green and Donald S. Tull, *Research for Marketing Decisions,* second edition (Englewood Cliffs: Prentice-Hall, Inc., 1970).

here (what exactly does "expected value of information" mean?), nor are the variables which determine it made fully explicit.[4]

We define a *problem situation model* as

> a conceptual scheme which specifies a measure of an outcome (or outcomes) desired and the related variables and their functional relationship to the outcome(s).[5]

Suppose we ask the marketing manager faced with a pricing decision what effects he believes a price change may have. His response might well be something on the order of "I think that if nothing else changes, we will sell about 1,000 gross per year at $5; 1,100 gross at $4.50; and 1,250 gross at $4." It is clear that this is not a full disclosure of the variables he believes to be operative in the price change decision. It is also clear, however, that he has related a set of variables (price plus others) with an outcome (sales); in every sense of the word, he is using a *model* in reaching a decision on price.

The definition of a problem situation model may be expressed symbolically (with some added specification of types of variables) as

$$V = f(A_1, A_2 \ldots A_i, E_1, E_2 \ldots E_j)$$

where

> $V$ is a measure of the outcome or outcomes of interest,
>
> $A_i$ is a measure of the actions that can be taken that (it is hypothesized) will affect the outcome,
>
> $E_j$ is a measure of one or more environmental variables that affect the outcome, and
>
> $f$ is the functional relationship of the variables to the outcome(s).

We agree with Simon[6] that decision making is so nearly coextensive with management that we can treat it as if it were fully so. For marketing management, the set of controllable variables that is most widely accepted is the revenue determinants *product* $(A_1)$, *price* $(A_2)$, *promotion* $(A_3)$, and *distribution* $(A_4)$. These jointly define the marketing mix of the firm. The cost variables may be considered to be the controllable marketing costs $(A_5)$ and controllable manufacturing costs $(A_6)$. Any one or all of these variables may be changed by management in an attempt to improve the "profit" position of the firm.

Survey research problems, as well as those for which other designs are used, will necessarily be formulated in terms of some combination of the

---

4. This model is fully explicated in each of the references cited in footnote 3.
5. This definition follows that used in Green and Tull, *op. cit.*, p. 6.
6. See Herbert A. Simon, *The New Science of Management Decision* (New York: Harper & Row, 1960), p. 1.

$V$, $A_i$, $E_j$, and $f$ elements of the problem situation model. A discussion follows of the role of each of these elements in the formulation of problems.

## DETERMINATION OF OBJECTIVES—$V$

Two aspects of the determination of objectives need to be considered: identification and measurement.

*Identification.* The identification of objectives sometimes appears deceptively simple. The request for a pricing study of the new product may seem all that is required in the way of identifying the objectives of the person making the request. Reflection indicates that this is not the case at all; the reason for the possible change could be to improve the short term profit position for the company, to improve dealer relations, to maintain price leadership, or to serve some other purpose that may even reduce profits during the short term.

Where multiple objectives are involved, a solution reflecting all of the outcomes must, of course, be sought. If price stability and short-term profit improvement are both objectives, for example, a different set of variables and relationships are involved and a different model comes into use.

Successful research for decisional purposes requires that the project provide the information that the decision maker needs. Two approaches are useful in insuring that as complete communication as possible takes place between researcher and manager.[7] The first is for the researcher to explode the problem into potentially useful sub-problems and question the manager about them. Does "pricing study" here refer only to final price to the consumer, or is the concern about the amount of discounts received by the distributors? Are potential entrants of concern? Is the "price" to be considered as delivered price, or is the amount of freight absorption a problem?

The second approach is to ask, "What actions would be taken conditional on different results of the study?" Would price to the distributors be lowered if it were found that they were unhappy with the present discount they receive? Would price be lowered if it were determined that two other companies were considering adding a similar product? Would a new warehouse be added if it were discovered that carload rates offer enough of a saving over less-than-carload rates to make a new distribution point feasible?

This process may have beneficial effects other than improving communication; new alternatives may be suggested as well. The research may contribute to the soundness of the decision by this means before the project

7. These approaches are those suggested in Ralph Westfall et al., "Problem Definition," *Marketing Research Technique Series No. 2,* American Marketing Association (1958).

is even started. In this event, the identification of objectives goes beyond clarification to the researcher; it helps both the client and the researcher to identify them.

*Measurement.* It is always necessary to establish a criterion (or criteria) for measurement of the objectives. This is essentially what is referred to when it is stated that the researcher must "convert the manager's problem to a research problem."

A first matter that must be settled is the time period for which the measurement is applicable. In predicting the effect of a price change on relationships with dealers, for example, how long should the forecast period be—a week, a month, a year, or longer? How long should the planning period be for adding a distribution point? What period is the applicable one for the planning of a price stabilizing move?

The second aspect that is of importance is the unit of measurement to be used. Is the health of the company–distributor relationship to be measured by the salesman's report of cordiality of reception? By proportion of shelf space devoted to the product? By proportion of distributor sales? Is net profit by distributor a preferable measurement?

All measurements involve abstraction from reality; they are at best a surrogate for what they represent. It is the task of the researcher to find measures of the objective or objectives that are acceptable by the client. He should do this before the collection of data is begun; not to do so is to invite either additional work later or problems in implementing the research findings.

*Development of Alternatives.* This seldom is the sole purpose of a survey research project but often turns out to have been the most important result. Roberts has stated his belief that this is the case as follows:

> Research is probably more effective in unearthing new possibilities for action than in predicting the response to existing ones. Research focuses attention on possible actions that probably would not have been recognized in the absence of research. The new ideas that turn up as an unexpected by-product of research are frequently more valuable than the objectives originally sought.[8]

Additional alternatives are usually sought during the design phase of the research by an *experience survey.* This typically consists of discussions with a selected sample of persons who are knowledgeable in the problem area. Both addiional alternatives and evaluation of existing ones are sought in this phase of the project. It is hoped that the major alternatives to be considered will all have been identified by the time the design of the formal

8. Harry V. Roberts, "The Role of Research in Marketing Management," *The Journal of Marketing,* vol. 22, no. 1 (July, 1957), p. 28.

data collecting instruments and procedures is started so that they may be considered at this stage. It is not unusual, however, for more alternatives to be discovered during the collection of the data.

## UNDERSTANDING OF ENVIRONMENTAL VARIABLES—E

A reasoned choice among alternatives cannot be made without some understanding of the environmental setting. In a pricing problem, for example, one must have some understanding of market size, present and prospective prices of competitive and complementary products, consumer tastes and income, and consumer expectations in order to predict the effect of a price change on the sales volume of consumer product. Research projects whose purpose is to identify and describe relevant environmental variables are known as *descriptive studies.*

Decision making in marketing invariably requires the prediction of behavior of one or more sets of market participants. The behavior of customers, or distributors of competitors, or in some cases of all of these, must be present. Behavior is in turn forecast from past behavior, intended behavior, socioeconomic attributes, attitudes and opinions, level of knowledge, or some combination of these kinds of information. All can be obtained using survey research techniques.

## FUNCTIONAL RELATIONSHIPS
## OF VARIABLES TO OBJECTIVE(S)—f

It is of little value to know the variables that affect an outcome unless we know how they affect it. Research projects designed to investigate these relationships are known as *causal studies.*

The usual normative model for deciding on individual levels of the marketing mix variables (product, price, promotion, and distribution) is to set them where the marginal revenue response is equal to the marginal cost of the change. Forecasting the actual effects of changes in these variables is a more difficult and demanding task than deriving normative rules for optimizing. Still, intelligent decisions cannot be made without some estimation of response rates. Measures of actual response rates over past periods and a projection of them into the future is the most common method of prediction. This involves a time series analysis and is subject to all of the problems of confounding of effects that is inherent in the time series design.

Survey research supplies the basic data for most of the time series analyses run for this purpose. The most widely used method is to obtain continuous panel data to monitor and to analyze changes in sales following changes in the mix variables of the company and/or of competitors. The panels consist of a sample of retail stores or of consumers from which information is obtained on a regularly recurring basis.[9] Continuous panel or single sample surveys are also used to determine viewing and reading audiences for advertising.

A second widely used approach (for consumer products) is to conduct a *market test* in a sample of sales areas and deliberately vary one or more of the mix variables to obtain a measure of the relation. This design is experimental in nature in that it involves a deliberate manipulation of variables. It is a cross-sectional design in that it provides more accurate information than time series analysis but is also much more expensive. Surveys are usually not required in this type of design.

## Summary

In this chapter we have been primarily concerned with the nature of survey research and its role in decision making.

We first examined survey research, emphasizing as its purpose the understanding and/or prediction of some aspect of behavior. We then considered the two generic types of research, basic and decisional. The difference in design objectives of these two research types stemming from the level of allowable error and the ways of assessing residual error were discussed.

Research as a cost-incurring but value-producing activity was then considered. The general decision rule offered for deciding whether research should or should not be conducted was whether the expected value exceeds the estimated cost.

We then turned to a consideration of problem formulation. Problem situation models occupy a central role in problem formulation. The generic types of formulations involve the development of alternatives, the description of environmental variables, and estimating functional relationships of variables to objectives. The survey research project will always include at least one of these types of problems, and the usual project more than one of them.

In the next chapter we consider the basic methods of inquiry available for testing hypotheses. In a decisional context, hypotheses are always concerned with alternative actions. Tests of hypotheses, therefore, are the basis for choice among alternatives. They are the final steps in the decision-making process.

9. The A. C. Nielsen Co. provides panel data on retail stores audited every two months. Data are available for both grocery and drug stores. The Market Research Corporation of America provides consumer panel data purchases by brand in product classes of interest.

## SELECTED BIBLIOGRAPHY

Ackoff, Russell L. et al. *Scientific Method: Optimizing Applied Research Decisions.* New York: John Wiley & Sons, Inc., 1962. An excellent book on method and measurement in research.

Enis, Ben M. and Charles L. Broome. *Marketing Decisions: A Bayesian Approach.* New York: Intext Educational Publishers, 1970. A concise and lucid treatment of Bayesian decision analysis and its application to marketing problems.

Kotler, Philip. *Marketing Decision Making: A Model Building Approach.* New York: Holt, Rinehart and Winston, 1971. A well-written book, which serves both as a compendium of relevant models and an authoritative guide to their application in making marketing decisions.

Palda, Kristian S. *Economic Analysis for Marketing Decisions.* Englewood Cliffs: Prentice-Hall, Inc., 1969. A book on economic analysis of marketing variables. Every student of marketing should read it.

Selltiz, Claire et. al. *Research Methods in Social Relations* New York: Holt, Rinehart & Winston, 1959. A book that is perhaps the best single work on research methodology.

Simon, Herbert A. *The New Science of Management Decision.* New York: Harper & Row, 1960. A brief book that treats decision making in a concise and lucid manner.

## QUESTIONS AND PROBLEMS

1.1. In neoclassical economic theory, the number of units of a product demanded is assumed to be a function of the price of the product, the price of competitive products, the price of complementary products, tastes, and income.

    a. This statement can be viewed as a problem situation model. Write it as such in symbolic form.

    b. Do you view this statement as a useful one for, say, a marketing manager who is considering changing price? Would the addition of other variables make it more useful? Explain.

1.2. It has been suggested that the distinction between basic and decisional research is that the purpose of the former is to answer a question and the purpose of the later is to solve a problem. Comment.

1.3. Is it possible for one to understand without being able to predict? Is it possible to be able to predict without understanding? Explain.

1.4. There are a number of generic problem formulations.

    a. Identify them.

    b. Write a short problem statement for each of them for decisional research projects that might reasonably be conducted for the president of a company that manufactures bicycles.

1.5. Give several examples of research projects dealing with human behavior that might be either basic or decisional in nature, depending upon who the "client" of the project is.

# Methods of Inquiry
# and Survey Design

In establishing investigative methods in the behavioral disciplines, it was only natural for the early behavioral scientists to turn to those that had worked the most successfully in other fields. The greatest advancements in knowledge had been made in the natural sciences. The method of inquiry used in the natural sciences was, therefore, borrowed and, with as little change as could be managed, applied to the behavioral sciences.

The name *scientific method* was borrowed along with the procedures. While this method was never the only one used, it quickly became accepted and entrenched as the standard against which other investigative methods were to be measured. The hallmark of a scientific methodist, whom we shall refer to as an *objectivist* in the behavioral sciences, is to run an hypothesis test using publicly stated procedures which are investigator independent. Other investigators differ in kind or degree of requirement with respect to these criteria. The *subjectivist* requires an hypothesis test but is not as strict in the requirement for publicity of procedures or investigator independence. The *Bayesian* also tests hypotheses, using either objectivist or subjectivist methods in addition to his prior judgments. He, therefore, will insist that procedures cannot be either fully publicly available or investigator independent. The *phenomenologist* has been insisting for the past seventy-five years that hypotheses not be tested, that the procedures for inquiry need not be public, and that the process of inquiry cannot be investigator independent.

The purpose of this chapter is to review these four methods of inquiry and to relate them to survey research design. Each of them is considered in turn. The chapter is concluded with a discussion of design determinants for basic versus decisional research.

## The Objectivist Method

Objectivism may be described as consisting of the following steps:

1. Formulating a problem
2. Developing an hypothesis
3. Making predictions based on the hypothesis
4. Devising a test of the hypothesis
5. Conducting the test and
6. Rejecting or failing to reject the hypothesis based on the test results.

While the terminology used is that associated with basic research, the reader will recognize that the process described is analogous to that of decision making. Substitution of the word *alternative* for *hypothesis* accomplishes most of the rephrasing required to transpose it to a decisional context.

Each of these stages is considered subsequently, both as steps in a generalized procedure and as they apply in an example. We shall use the same example to illustrate the application in other methods of inquiry as well.

The situation to be posed as the example is that information is needed by the officers of a bank who are considering making available an extra reserve plan for depositors. Such a plan would permit depositors to overdraw their checking accounts up to some stated maximum amount. The overdraft is to be paid, along with interest and carrying charges, in monthly installments. The officers of the bank feel that they need certain information to aid them in making their decisions. Such information includes the use of credit by depositors, the purposes for which it is used, how often money is borrowed, and the amounts borrowed each time.

After a literature search and discussions with several persons knowledgeable in this area, it is decided that a survey of depositor families will be necessary to provide all the necessary information. This decision is made with the full understanding that there will be difficulties in obtaining the information desired; the bankers understand that most people view their financial matters as being personal and private and are, therefore, reluctant to discuss them.

### FORMULATING THE PROBLEM

This initial step of an investigation is discussed in the last chapter. It should be noted here that, in a decisional setting, a problem arises either when a performance standard is not being met or when an opportunity for performing beyond the level of presently accepted performance is recognized. In the credit problem, for example, the impetus for examining an extra reserve form of lending may have arisen either as a result of there being funds available for loan or the recognition of a needed service which could also be profitable to the bank.

## DEVELOPING AN HYPOTHESIS

It is usually more difficult to ask good questions than it is to answer them; by the same token it is often more difficult to develop good hypotheses (alternatives) than it is to test them (choose among them).

Hypotheses are always concerned with some measurable characteristic of the population of interest. This characteristic is called a *parameter*. Hypotheses are then formed about the value of the parameter. In our example, the hypothesis that is to be tested will be of the general form that a mean amount of money that would be borrowed by individual depositors through the extra reserve plan, if it were available, would be less than X dollars per year.

Hypotheses are invariably based on a model held by the investigator concerning the problem area to be investigated. As we have already seen, the model may be public or private, but in either case it is the basis for any hypotheses that are proposed. The existence of such a model implies a prior judgment concerning the outcome of the test. Kaplan refers to this judgment as an *antecedent probability*,[1] and the Bayesians call it a *prior probability*.

We shall examine the arguments concerning the admissibility of prior judgments in the form of a probability statement when we consider the investigative method of the Bayesians. It is sufficient at this point to emphasize that in the objectivist method, the prior judgment held by the investigator may not properly influence the design or the procedure used in the investigation after the hypothesis has been developed. This is the central point of difference between objectivism and the other methods of inquiry.

## MAKING PREDICTIONS

Predictions must involve only behavior that can be observed, including verbal behavior. Moreover, the behavior that is to be recorded must be specified as a part of the prediction. Ad hoc decisions to record incidental behavior are not permitted.

This latter requirement is an effect of insistence upon investigator

1. Abraham Kaplan, *The Conduct of Inquiry* (San Francisco: Chandler Publishing Co., 1964), p. 17.

independence in the outcome of the test of the hypothesis in the design or conduct of the test. To permit the investigator to decide what should be recorded while the test is being conducted is to admit the possibility of inter-investigator differences in findings.

In survey research projects, this means that the only questions that may be asked are those that are prepared before the survey is begun. A structured questionnaire with *direct* questions (questions that are not intended to elicit answers that are to be analyzed for indirect or disguised meanings) is the only means of obtaining verbal information that is allowed. Verbal probes, such as those used in depth interviews, are strictly forbidden unless they appear on the questionnaire.

## DEVISING THE TEST

A test of an hypothesis using objectivist methods can be made only by observing and recording overt behavior, using a recording procedure that has been fully and publicly prespecified. The test is not necessarily restricted to actual behavior; a simulation of the behavioral process may be developed and the behavior resulting from trials of the simulating process recorded. Whether the behavior is actual or simulated, however, it must consist of overt behavior that is related directly to the subject of the hypothesis.

Testing methods commonly in use for the objectivist design include controlled experiments, survey research using random samples, fully structured questionnaires, and simulations. Survey research methods are, therefore, permissible if suitably restricted to prevent the data being affected by the subjective judgments of the investigator once the survey is underway.

Tests of hypotheses may be conducted using either a census or a sample of the population of interest. When a census is taken, a direct test of the hypothesis is available; the test results may be used directly as a measure of the parameter of interest or as descriptive of the relationship being investigated. In the extra reserve problem, one might conduct a survey of all depositors in the bank to determine the amount of non-mortgage borrowing, for example. The usual situation in survey research is that a sample of respondents is taken, however. Even the number of bank's depositors is large enough that a census may be prohibitive in terms of cost.

An hypothesis test using objectivist procedures and based upon data from a sample of elements of the population requires that four elements be specified:

1. A probability distribution of the sample statistic to be tested
2. A null and alternate hypothesis which contain predictions of the population value against which the sample statistic is to be tested

3. A test statistic
4. A rejection region in the probability distribution

Each of these elements is considered below.

*The Probability Distribution.* Each sampling procedure generates a probability distribution, known as a *sampling distribution,* of the test statistic. When the sampling procedure is *random* in nature, the probability distribution can be derived by mathematical methods. When *nonrandom* sampling procedures are employed, the probability distribution of the test statistic cannot be determined by objective methods. Random sampling is, therefore, a requirement for sample surveys conducted using objectivist procedures.

The test is conducted using the probability distribution to draw inferences about the probability of the sample statistic varying from an hypothesized value by the observed amount as a result of sampling variation. In Figure 2-1, for example, so long as the distribution shown is known to be the probability distribution of $\overline{X}$ values, we may conclude that there is a probability of $\alpha$ that an observed $\overline{X}$ value will be equal to or greater than $\overline{X}_c$ as a result of sampling variation.

*Specification of the Null and Alternate Hypotheses.* The *null hypothesis,* designated here by the symbol $H_o$, typically is the hypothesis that, if not rejected, leads to a continuation of the status quo. In a basic research investigation, the usual result of a test that does not lead to rejection of the null hypothesis is that existing theory and/or previous findings are supported. In a decisional context, a test resulting in the null hypothesis not being rejected usually results in a contemplated change *not* being made.

The null hypothesis for the extra reserve plan, for example, might be:

> $H_o$: The mean amount of dollars which would be borrowed per year by depositors through the extra reserve plan if it were available would be no more than the amount required by the bank to break even.

If we let $\mu$ be the hypothesized mean amount borrowed by depositors and $\bar{\mu}$ be the mean amount required for the plan to break even, the null hypothesis may be written as

$$H_o: \mu \leq \bar{\mu}$$

There is a wide range of mean amounts of dollars borrowed per year per depositor which would be insufficient to support the extra reserve plan. The specific value of $\mu$ chosen is one from this range, concerning which the investigator is willing to run a specified level of risk of concluding that it is not the true mean. This type of error is called a *Type I error* and is represented notationally as $\alpha$.

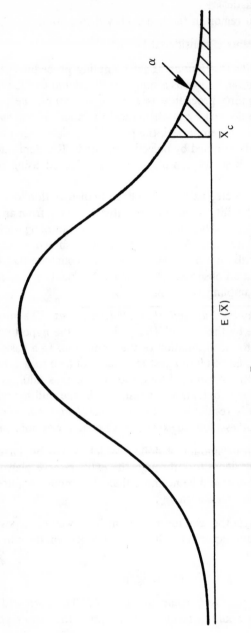

FIGURE 2–1 Probability distribution of $\bar{X}$ values when random sampling procedure is used

The alternate hypothesis in a decisional context is a statement of the condition under which the alternative being considered will be chosen. In the example, the alternate hypothesis may be stated as:

$H_1$: The mean amount of dollars per year that would be borrowed by individual depositors through the extra reserve plan is greater than that required to break even.

$$H_1: \mu > \bar{\mu}$$

The value of $H_1$ is determined as the mean amount of dollars borrowed concerning which the investigator is willing to incur only some specified probability of concluding that $\mu$ is the true mean when $\bar{\mu}$ is, in fact, the true mean. An error of this kind is known as the *Type II error* and is denoted by $\beta$.

*The Test Statistic.* In the example we are, of course, concerned with the sample mean as the test statistic. However, the test statistic in other problems may be a measure of any population parameter. The usual statistics tested are the mean, proportion, the differences in two means, the differences in two proportions, the $F$ ratio, $X^2$, and the coefficient of correlation.

*The Rejection Region.* The range of values which the sample statistic may assume is divided into two regions, an *acceptance* and a *rejection* region. The test is conducted by determining into which region the test statistic falls. If it falls within the rejection region, the null hypothesis is rejected, and the alternate hypothesis is accepted. If it falls within the acceptance region, the alternate hypothesis is rejected.[2]

The rejection region is determined by the level of $\alpha$. As a practical matter, however, one will always be interested in both $\alpha$ and $\beta$ risks. Ideally, the investigator will have some specific value in mind for the null hypothesis which it is of practical importance that he detect. In the example, the bank officials would not want to discard the extra reserve plan if the average amount borrowed through it per year were greater than some specified amount, say $\mu + \$50$. While the rejection region will still be determined by the specified value of $\alpha$, the sample size will be adjusted to give an acceptable value of $\beta$ for the specified alternate hypothesis value. Here we assume a fixed sample size and so deal explicitly only with the $\alpha$ risk.

The critical value, $c$, which separates the rejection and acceptance region is some number of standard errors away from the value of the parameter in the null hypothesis. The level of $\alpha$ specifies the number of

2. To be technically correct, we should refer to the two regions as the *nonrejection* and the rejection regions. One never actually accepts a null hypothesis; he just fails to reject it.

standard errors. In our example, a large random sample (a random sample of, say, thirty or more depositors) will yield a normal probability distribution of sample means. If, for example, $\alpha$ is set at .10, the number of standard errors (for a single tailed test) is 1.28. The critical value of $\overline{X}$, denoted as $\overline{X}_c$ and the acceptance and rejection regions for an $\alpha$ of .10 are shown graphically in Figure 2–2.

## CONDUCTING THE TEST

It is apparent that the objectivist test procedures have been devised to exclude the possibility of investigator judgment influencing, once the test has begun, the collection of data or the interpretation in findings. The test procedure must be specified in its entirety in advance of the actual conduct of the test.

The procedures for conducting the test must be made fully public. The results of the test must be investigator free to the extent that they can be replicated by other investigators within the bounds of sampling variation.

## ANALYZING TEST RESULTS

The analysis of the test consists of determining the value of the conditional probability $p$ (observed sample statistic | population value in hypothesis under test) and comparing it with the previously specified level of $\alpha$. This conditional probability is also known as a *likelihood*. That is, the researcher is drawing an inference of the probability of having obtained the sample statistic given an assumed true population value. If the probability is *greater* than $\alpha$, the test will fall in the acceptance region and he will not reject $H_o$. If the probability is *less* than $\alpha$, he will reject $H_o$.

It is apparent that the true objectivist investigator has no opportunity to influence the conclusions drawn from the test. He must, as one writer describes it, conclude the test by "humbly accepting that hypothesis singled out by the data."[3]

# The Subjectivist Method

The philosophic position of the subjectivist has been stated clearly by Diesing:

> The subjectivists have argued that the essential unique characteristic of human behavior is its subjective meaningfulness, and any science which ignores meaning and purpose is not a social science. Human action is governed by

3. Robert Ackerman, *The Philosophy of Science* (New York: Western Publishing Company, 1970) p. 28.

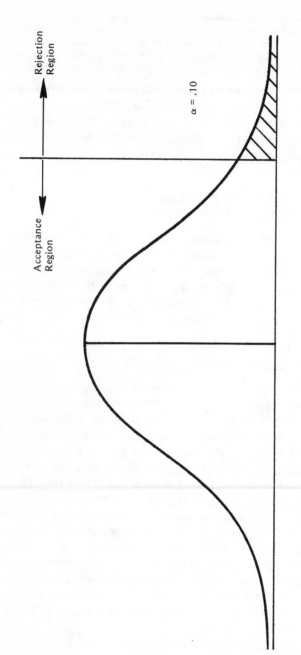

FIGURE 2-2   Normal probability distributi^ $\mu$ ^ sample mean with
hypothesized value of population mean and . ∩tance and rejection regions

subjective factors—by images, not stimuli, by reasons, not causes, consequently an adequate science of man must understand action from the standpoint of the actor, as a process of defining the situation, evaluating alternatives in terms of goals, standards and predictions, and choosing to act.[4]

A more humanistic view of man as the subject of inquiry is reflected in the methods used by the subjectivists. The essential difference, as one might logically expect, is the allowance for use of subjective judgments while both collecting data and analyzing it. We may note these methodological differences by comparison of subjectivist and objectivist methods.

## FORMULATION OF THE PROBLEM AND DEVELOPING OF HYPOTHESES

There are no substantive differences between the objectivist and subjectivist approaches in formulating problems or developing hypotheses. Some differences in extent of usage of kinds of hypotheses may be observed, however. The subjectivist is less inclined to attempt to quantify attributes or relationships, and so the hypotheses he wishes to test are more likely to be qualitative in nature than are those of the objectivist.

## MAKING OF PREDICTIONS

Predictions need not be limited to overt behavior if the researcher is using subjectivist methods. Interpretation by the investigator is permitted.

In our research on the extra reserve plan, one might give each respondent one of two lists of financial transactions and ask him to characterize the head of a household making such transactions. The two lists might include such items in common as "deposited $25 in savings account," "paid automobile insurance premium for 3 months," and so on through several items. The lists would vary only with respect to a single item dealing with the purchase of, say, a new refrigerator; on the one list an item such as "withdraw $200 from savings to buy a refrigerator" and on the other "borrowed $200 from the bank to buy a refrigerator." In a subjectivist design, the investigator would be free to make an interpretation of the differences in characterizations of the fictitious household head with respect to the revealed attitudes toward borrowing of money. Such an interpretation would not be allowable in an objectivist design, and so an instrument of this sort would not be used.

The behavior to be recorded need not all be specified in advance in a subjectivist design. Depth interviews are commonly used, wherein probing

4. Paul Diesing, "Objectivism vs. Subjectivism in the Social Sciences," *Philosophy of Science*, vol. 33 (March–June, 1966), p. 124.

questions are formed as a consequence of the direction and content of earlier responses. There must then be ad hoc recording as well.

## DEVISING OF TEST

The test consists of observing overt behavior (including verbal behavior) but, as already discussed, the investigator may be allowed to interpret indirect behavior. The test may be partially ad hoc in nature conditional on the results of earlier stages. In some cases the nature of the test is revised enough that the criteria for rejection of the hypothesis must be established on an ex post basis.

The testing methods advocated and used include a priori deduction, participant observation, uncontrolled experiments, and survey research using probability or non-probability samples and structured or unstructured questionnaires.

## CONDUCTING OF TEST

Procedures often cannot be made fully public and findings may or may not be capable of being replicated since they may be investigator dependent.

## ANALYZING TEST RESULTS

Analysis is conducted using methods of descriptive and inferential statistics. A likelihood is obtained of the form described earlier, namely, $p$ (observed sample statistic | population value in hypothesis under test).

However, several assumptions are usually required to be able to make this calculation, and some of them tend toward the heroic. Not the least of these is the assumption that the sample was random when, in fact, it was purposive. The conclusion is then reached to reject or not to reject the hypothesis depending upon the likelihood.

## The Bayesian Method

Implicit in the objectivist and subjectivist designs are the assumptions that (1) the likelihood obtained from the test is the only probability statement that is to be included in the test and (2) costs of errors are adequately reflected in the significance levels chosen.

Bayesians disagree with both of those assumptions. The Bayesian believes that prior judgments, expressed as probabilities, should be included as a part of the test. He believes that a client who has ordered a study and an investigator who has reached the point of developing hypotheses for the study each have reasonably well-developed judgments about the alternatives to be investigated. The everyday process of utilizing additional information to revise prior judgments should be incorporated and revised in the formal testing process.

The Bayesian also believes that the test should be in terms of the expected payoff of the alternative rather than on the probability of its occurrence. *Expected payoff* is the weighted average of the possible payoffs of an uncertain quantity, the weights being the probabilities of the possible payoffs. A contract that is worth $100,000 in additional profits to the firm if it receives the award, no profits if it does not receive the award, and a probability of 0.25 of getting the award has an expected value of $25,000. ($EV = \$100,000 \times .25 + \$0 \times (1.0 - .25)$.) The costs of errors are explicitly introduced into the Bayesian designs through this means.

The Bayesian design incorporates the prior judgments of the investigator as a part of the information to be used for the test. These judgments are expressed either as *prior probabilities* or as a *prior probability density,* depending upon whether one wishes to conduct the test using discrete or continuous data. This information is revised by combining it with the information obtained from the research through the use of Bayes' Theorem.[5] For the discrete data case, Bayes' Theorem may be expressed as

$$\text{posterior probability} = \frac{(\text{prior probability})(\text{likelihood})}{\Sigma[(\text{prior probability})(\text{likelihood})]}$$

and, for the continuous case, may be stated as

$$\text{posterior density} = \frac{(\text{prior density})(\text{likelihood})}{\Sigma[\text{prior density})(\text{likelihood})]}$$

It is important to note that the likelihood referred to in the two formulae is precisely the same likelihood obtained in the objectivist and subjectivist testing procedure. The difference in its use, of course, is that in those two designs the likelihood is the only information used for the test, whereas in the Bayesian design it is used to revise the prior probability (or density) to the posterior probability (or density) which is used in the test. A summary of the objectivist, subjectivist, and Bayesian methods of inquiry is given in Table 2–1.

5. So named after the Rev. Thomas Bayes, who developed the theorem in the eighteenth century. See Thomas Bayes, "An Essay Toward Solving a Problem in the Doctrine of Chance, *Biometrika*, vol. 45 (1958), pp. 293–315.

TABLE 2–1   The objectivist, subjectivist, and Bayesian methods of inquiry in the behavioral sciences

| Stage | Objectivist | Subjectivist | Bayesian |
|---|---|---|---|
| 1. Develop hypothesis | The hypothesis is based on a model held by the investigator concerning the subject to be investigated. The model may be private or public. The existence of such a model implies a prior probability attached to the truth of the hypothesis by the investigator. This prior probability is ignored. | Same as objectivist. | Same as objectivist/ subjectivist except that prior probabilities are recognized and expressed formally when the hypothesis is formulated. |
| 2. Make prediction(s) | Predictions must involve only behavior that can be observed. The behavior to be recorded must be specified. | Prediction need not be limited to observable behavior. The behavior to be recorded need not necessarily be specified in advance. | May be objectivist, or subjectivist or a combination of both |
| 3. Devise test | The test must be made by observing and recording overt behavior (real or simulated) by specified method. Criteria for acceptance or rejection of hypothesis are specified.<br><br>Testing methods commonly in use include controlled experiments, survey research using random samples, structured interviews, and simulations. | The test must be made by observing overt behavior, but the investigator has at least some freedom of selection of behavior to be recorded. Test may be partially ad hoc in nature conditional on results in early stages. Criteria for acceptance or rejection of hypotheses are sometimes established on ex post basis.<br><br>Testing methods advocated and used include a priori deductions, participant observation, uncontrolled experiments, and survey research using population samples and unstructured interviews. | May be objectivist or subjectivist or a combination of both |

25

TABLE 2-1    (Continued)

| Stage | Objectivist | Subjectivist | Bayesian |
|-------|-------------|--------------|----------|
| 4. Conduct test | Procedures must be public. The findings must be investigator free in that they are capable of being replicated by other investigators. | Procedures often cannot be made fully public and findings may or may not be capable of being replicated since they may be investigator dependent. | May be objectivist or subjectivist or a combination of both. |
| 5. Analyze test results | Analysis is conducted using methods of descriptive and inferential statistics. Hypothesis is rejected or not on the basis of the criteria specified earlier. | Analysis is conducted using methods of descriptive and, where applicable, inferential statistics. Hypothesis is rejected or not based on specified or ex post criteria. | Analysis may proceed initially along either objectivist or subjectivist lines. If the initial analysis is objectivist in nature, the prior probability that the hypothesis should be rejected is revised formally by the use of specified mathematical procedures. If the initial analysis is subjectivist in nature, the prior probability that the hypothesis should be rejected is revised informally. |

## Phenomenology as a Method of Inquiry

The method resulting in the greatest degree of investigator dependence is that of *phenomenology* (often referred to as the *phenomenalist method*). The dependence of observation of an observer using any method of investigation is a basic proposition held by the phenomenalists. In investigations of physical phenomena, they point out that an object can only be viewed by a subject. While it may be intersubjectively observed and viewed, it can only be perceived and conceived in each case as a part of the phenomenal field.

Even a thoroughgoing objectivist is not likely to deny that there is some possibility of differences in selection of data to be recorded or even of bias in the recording due to perceptual distortion by the investigator. The difference lies in the perception of the degree of the distortion that is likely to be present.

A difference of kind in belief between the objectivist-subjectivist-Bayesian on the one side and the phenomenalist on the other is with respect to the role of the explanatory hypothesis. The discussion to this point has emphasized the centrality of the hypothesis and the testing of it to each of the three methods of inquiry. The phenomenalist is opposed to the use of explanatory hypotheses. Hypotheses represent preconceived ideas of the phenomenon and, as such, are viewed by the pheonomenalist as leading to selective perception and distortion of measurement.

A legitimate question is, then, "What *is* the method of phenomenology?" An answer is that, while there is no one universally accepted "method" as such, four steps are recognized by enough phenomenalists to qualify as representative of the approach generally followed. They are:

1. Suspension of prior conceptions
2. Description of the phenomenon
3. Determination of universal elements
4. Apprehending of relationships

We shall not discuss these investigative steps. We do want to observe, however, that they collectively comprise one specification of procedures for constructing a model. Once articulated, such a model is a source of hypotheses for testing in precisely the same way as those suggested by a comprehensive model obtained by any other procedure. The significance of this observation goes beyond the recognition that phenomenolists construct models; it is more important to observe that they do *not* test hypotheses. The arguments with respect to method of the objectivist versus the phenomenalist as representing the extremes of investigator independence do not meet but pass each other by. The objectivist has never argued, in fact could not argue, that the model which is the source of the hypotheses he tests must be investigator independent. He is only concerned that the test of the hypothesis be as investigator free as possible. The phenomenolist is concerned only with the pre-hypothesis investigative stage; he does not test hypotheses at all.

## Selection of Methods of Inquiry for Sample Surveys

The basic normative view held by the authors concerning the selection of methods for sample survey is that expressed earlier in this chapter, namely, that a method should be used which results in the greatest excess of expected value of research information over the estimated cost of acquiring it. This no doubt has a familiar ring to those versed in the Bayesian approach to the economics of information acquisition. To those who are not, it may sound like a pious but impractical pronouncement. To this latter group we can only urge that you acquaint yourself with the analytic procedures that have been developed for determining the expected value of information in problem situations. The selected bibliography at the end of this chapter has references for this purpose.

Given this kind of position, our preferences with regard to methods of inquiry are essentially ecumenical. We veiw the determinants of method as being the nature of the problem and the constraints imposed by the client, the researcher, and the respondents The method of inquiry which most nearly satisfies these determinants will also result in the highest net expected difference in value and cost of information. We have no prior methodological preferences that we wish to impose or even to urge on others, except that they also accept the value-cost orientation.

However, for reasons developed in the last chapter, it seems to us that there is generally less reason for using objectivist methods on decisional- than on basic-research problems. The client in decisional research is the decision maker. Only a limited audience receives the findings, and each has the opportunity to review both methods and findings with the researcher. The personal credibility of the researcher plays an important role in client assessment of information validity. There is substantially less need for full explication of procedures, for these reasons. In addition, replication is the exception for decisional research.

## Summary

This chapter has been concerned with a typology of basic methods of inquiry and a consideration of each. The methods of the objectivist, subjectivist, Bayesian, and phenomenalist were discussed in terms of their position on the continuum of investigator dependence as well as the procedures identified with each. The cost-value tradeoff for more highly investigator dependent methods is often a favorable one for decisional research problems. When it is, such methods should be used.

### SELECTED BIBLIOGRAPHY

Ackerman, Robert. *The Philosophy of Science.* New York: Western Publishing Company, 1970. A concise, readable treatise on the methodology of science.
Diesing, Paul. "Objectivism vs. Subjectivism in the Social Sciences," *Philosophy of Science,* vol. 33 (March–June, 1966), pp. 124–33. An excellent review article of the positions of the objectivists and subjectivists.

Enis, Ben M. and Charles L. Broome. *Marketing Decisions: A Bayesian Approach.* New York: Intext Educational Publishers, 1970. Annotated earlier.

Helmer, Olof and Nicholas Rescher. "On the Epistemology of the Inexact Sciences," *Management Science,* vol. 6, no. 1 (October, 1959), pp. 25–52. Another outstanding review article on the methods of inquiry in the social and other inexact sciences.

Kuhn, Thomas S. *The Structure of Scientific Revolutions.* Chicago: The University of Chicago Press, 1962. A book which documents the effects of paradigms on scientific investigations. It is written about the natural scientist but should be read by social scientists as well.

Meehl, Paul E. *Clinical Versus Statistical Prediction.* Minneapolis: University of Minnesota Press, 1954. An account of a study of the relative accuracy of the diagnoses of mental ailments by psychometricians (objectivists) and clinicians (subjectivists).

Popper, K. R. *Conjectures and Refutations.* London, 1963. An evolutionary view of the development of science is presented and elaborated upon.

Raiffa, Howard. *Decision Analysis—Introductory Lectures on Choices Under Uncertainty.* Reading: Addison Wesley, 1968. An excellent exposition of the Bayesian analysis.

Spiegelbug, Herbert. *The Phenomenological Movement,* Vols. 1 and 2. The Hague: Martinus Nijhoff, 1969. Perhaps the definitive work on phenomenology. Section five of Vol. 2 summarizes the phenomenological method and provides a good starting point for the casual reader.

## QUESTIONS AND PROBLEMS

2.1. It has been argued by Milton Friedman and others that the only relevant test of the validity of an hypothesis is by comparison of its predictions with experience. Do you agree with this position for tests of hypotheses in basic research? In decisional research? Explain.

2.2. In your judgment, are decision makers inclined to be more subjectivist than objectivist, informal Bayesians, or informal phenomenologists? Explain.

2.3. In this chapter, four methods of inquiry were discussed. Which methods are more appropriate for basic research and which are more suited for decisional research? Explain.

2.4. What criteria are available for judging the superiority of any one technique or research method vis-à-vis any other in a given situation? Explain.

2.5. Survey researchers who practice strict observance of objectivist procedures are often criticized sharply by those who prefer subjectivist procedures, and vice versa.

    a. Prepare an argument to defend the proposition that objectivist methods are preferable to subjectivist methods for survey research.

    b. Prepare an argument for the reverse of the proposition in (a).

2.6. "Subjectivist procedures should be used to suggest hypotheses and objectivist procedures to test them." Comment.

# Sampling for

# Survey Research

As pointed out in Chapter 1, survey research involves techniques designed to acquire information from a group of people or population for the purpose of understanding and/or predicting, either directly or indirectly, behavior of the members of the group. Specification of a population involves identifying *which* units (in terms of kind) are included, as well as *where* and *when*. For example, a bank considering making available an "extra reserve" plan for depositors might acquire information from any or all of the following groups:

| Which Units? | Where? | When? |
| --- | --- | --- |
| All depositors | Designated bank | Last 12 months |
| Depositors who have borrowed money | Designated bank | Last 12 months |
| All people | Specified geographic area | Last 12 months |
| All people who have borrowed money | Specified geographic area | Last 12 months |

Each of these groups represents from a research point of view a distinct population with corresponding implications for the interpretation of any information obtained.

The desired information may be obtained from all members of the population (that is, a complete enumeration or census) or from only a part or subset of the population (that is, a *sample*). *Sampling* is the process of selecting a sample, and includes everything that is involved in the selection. Since the collection of all relevant information is not always possible and often is very costly, samples must be used in survey research.

In this chapter, we first discuss in a general way the nature of sampling and samples and present a discussion of traditional sampling theory. The major emphasis of the chapter is on traditional approaches to planning the sample, the alternative types of sample design that are available, and determining sample size.

## Nature of Sampling and Samples

Since the use of a sample in a survey by its very nature means that only a relatively small number of the population members are to be queried, the results obtained are quite likely to be such that perfectly accurate inferences cannot be made for the population as a whole because of variations attributable to the sampling process itself. These variances constitute the variable error resulting from the chance specifications of population elements according to the sample plan—in short, the *sampling error*. Even if sampling error could be eliminated, perfect accuracy in all respects probably would never be possible to achieve because of the nonvariable or systematic errors that arise from the collecting, processing, and analyzing of information. That is, *nonsampling errors* (to be discussed in Chapter 4) are those that would be present even if a census were made.

Regardless of whether or not it is possible to get perfect accuracy in a survey, such accuracy is not necessary for decision making purposes.

All that is needed are results with a sufficiently high degree of accuracy *to be of practical value* [emphasis added]. In effect, surveys yield information on the probable limits within which the true, unknown values for the population lie. The specification of these limits is a practical problem, depending on the judgment of those who are going to use the results. The sampling problem is to determine what sample size and sample design will yield results within these limits as economically as possible.

Alternately, the sample size and design may be specified by other considerations, such as a desire to maintain comparability with previous studies, and the problem may be simply to measure the accuracy of the results.[1]

### SAMPLE VERSUS CENSUS

For every survey the question arises of whether the information being sought should be obtained from every member of the population or from

1. Robert Ferber and P. J. Verdoorn, *Research Methods in Economics and Business* (New York: The Macmillan Company, 1962), p. 237. © The Macmillan Company 1962.

only a sample of the population. In most instances, samples are used. The desirability and advantages of using a sample rather than a census depend upon the absolute size of the population as well as the relative proportion of the population that will have to be used as the sample so as to provide results sufficiently accurate for the purposes for which they are required.

Two of the major advantages of using a sample rather than a census are speed and timeliness. A survey based on a sample takes much less time to complete than one based on a census. Moreover, in certain instances a complete count may require such a long time that, because of changes in conditions, it becomes a historical record by the time it is completed and available for use.

Another consideration in deciding whether or not to use sampling is the *relative cost and effort* that will be involved. Although

> the amount of effort and expense required to collect information is always greater per unit for a sample than for a complete census . . . if the size of the sample needed to give the required accuracy represents only a small fraction of the whole population, the total effort and expense required to collect the information by sampling methods will be very much less than that required for a census of the whole population.[2]

Often, administrative considerations dictate that sampling be used, particularly when a census would necessitate the hiring, training, and supervising of a large number of people. In many situations, therefore, the use of a sample results in notable economy of effort. Of course, the overriding test that must be applied is cost versus value.

The use of sampling techniques is also indicated in those instances where measuring or observing an element in the population destroys it or impairs its future usefulness. This can be a serious problem in surveys of human populations when there is need for many different surveys to be conducted on the same population within a relatively short period of time. If such is the case and a census is used, there is a great risk that many of the individual members of the population will react negatively to being asked to participate in more than one study during a given time period. The chance that this can occur when sampling techniques are used is low if the sample is a small proportion of the total population and probability techniques are used for selecting the individual sample elements. When nonprobability techniques are used for selection, the problem can be protected against explicitly.

The use of a sample in survey research is also desirable in those instances when the quantity of measurement and observation will affect the quality. A census of some population may result in a more inaccurate

2. From Frank Yates: *Sampling Methods for Censuses and Surveys* third edition, p. 3, 1971. By permission of Charles Griffin & Co. Ltd., London.

description of the universe's characteristics than a more carefully controlled partial count, particularly when probability sampling techniques are used.

> Although the use of sampling necessarily introduces certain inaccuracies, owing to sampling errors, the results obtained by sampling are frequently more accurate than those obtained in a complete census. . . . The random sampling errors are always assessable. The other errors to which a survey is subject [i.e., nonsampling errors], such as incompleteness of returns and inaccuracy of information, are liable to be very much more serious in a complete census than in a sample . . . since far more effective precautions can be taken to see that the information is accurate and complete in a sample.[3]

Thus, the use of a sample may be better than a census in minimizing the total error that arises in a survey, because greater attention can then be given to nonsampling error, which often considerably outweighs variable sampling error alone.

Finally, a sample may be necessary simply because there is no other alternative available except to collect no information at all. The entire population may not be available for measurement at the time the survey must be made.

Sampling is not without its limitations, however, and there are some situations in which censuses possess special advantages.[4]

1. Data for small units can be obtained
2. Public acceptance is easier to secure for complete data
3. Public compliance and response may be better secured
4. Bias of coverage may be easier to check and reduce

In addition, if the subject of interest occurs only rarely in the population, then a census might be desirable, since a very large sample would be necessary to provide information that is statistically reliable.

## USES OF SAMPLES

Underlying all sample surveys are one or both of two broad objectives —*estimation* and *testing of hypotheses*. Each of these involves making inferences about a population on the basis of information from a sample. The process of estimation involves making inferences about the population from knowledge of the sample, while in hypothesis testing we take a deductive approach, proceeding from a hypothesis about the population to the behavior of samples.[5]

3. *Ibid.*

4. Leslie Kish, *Survey Sampling* (New York: John Wiley & Sons, Inc., 1965), p. 18.

5. E. Grebenik and C. A. Moser, "Statistical Surveys," in Dennis P. Forcese and Stephen Richer, eds., *Stages of Social Research: Contemporary Perspectives* (Englewood Cliffs: Prentice-Hall, Inc., 1970), pp. 192–193.

In estimation, we are interested in estimating the value of an unknown quantity from the information provided by a sample. This quantity represents a characteristic of the population (that is, a parameter), and may be a variable or attribute, for example, an average, a total, or a proportion. The population under study is most often described by its parameters. The reason for using such summary descriptors is based on the need for economy in description as well as the fact that it is usually some characteristic, not the individual per se, which the researcher typically is interested in measuring. Thus, samples provide estimates of the parameters describing populations. The value of a variable or attribute calculated from a sample is called a *statistic*. In the extra reserve problem, a bank might be interested in estimates of such parameters as the proportion of all depositors who have borrowed money during the past twelve months, the average amount borrowed by those who have borrowed, the average time loans have been outstanding, or any other characteristic that will have a bearing on the decision concerning whether the plan should be initiated.

In general, hypothesis testing is concerned with determining whether certain populations or sections of a population differ from one another in particular characteristics. The validity of sample-based inferences about the population is judged on the basis of statistical significance tests. We discussed hypothesis testing in the previous chapter, and we will discuss it in more depth in Chapter 8.

## ALTERNATIVE SAMPLING TECHNIQUES[6]

There are many ways in which samples can be selected, and these lead to differing sample designs. In the preceding discussion we have referred to *probability* and *nonprobability* methods of selection without stating how these differ. According to Kish

> *In probability sampling, every element in the population has a known nonzero probability of being selected.* This probability is attained through some mechanical operation of randomization. . . . Its value is determined in accord with the demands of the sample design. Probability samples are usually designed to be *measurable;* that is, so designed that statistical inference to population values can be based on *measures of variability,* usually standard errors, *computed from* the sample data.[7]

In "idealized" probability sampling, assumptions about the population distributions do not need to be made in order to make inferences. In contrast, nonprobability sampling is that in which the elements of the population do not have a known chance of being selected, and there is no

6. This section draws on material from Kish, *op. cit.,* pp. 17–21.
7. Kish, *op. cit.,* p. 20.

necessary provision that every element has some chance of being selected. This type of sampling must, therefore, be based on broad assumptions about the distribution of the survey variables in the population.

*Probability Sampling.* Our discussion of probability sampling is in terms of an "ideal." Such ideal samples, however, can be only approximated, because of certain types of systematic sampling errors that arise in the actual development of real world samples. Even so, there are ways in which these errors can be controlled, reduced, or eliminated in a specific situation.

The basic probability selection process is *simple random sampling.* All other processes represent variations of this basic process so as to allow more practical, economical, or precise designs. There are five major types of modifications that can be made to the basic selection process (see Table 3–1).

The first concerns whether the population elements have an equal or unequal chance of selection. It should be noted that simple random sampling is only a special type of the equal probability of selection method.

A second modification is based on whether the sampling unit is the individual element of the population or a group of population elements,

TABLE 3–1    Probability selection methods: alternatives that may be combined

| | |
|---|---|
| I. *Equal probability* for all elements<br>  a. Equal probabilities at all stages<br>  b. Equal overall probabilities for all elements obtained through compensating unequal probabilities at several stages | *Unequal probabilities* for different elements; ordinarily compensated with inverse weights<br><br>  a. Caused by irregularities in selection frames and procedures<br>  b. Disproportionate allocation designed for optimum allocation |
| II. *Element Sampling*: single stage, sampling unit contains only one element | *Cluster Sampling*: sampling units are clusters of elements<br><br>  a. One-stage cluster sampling<br>  b. Subsampling or multistage sampling<br>  c. Equal clusters<br>  d. Unequal clusters |
| III. *Unstratified Selection*: sampling units selected from entire population | *Stratified Sampling*: separated selections from partitions, or strata, of population |
| IV. *Random Selection* of individual sampling units from entire stratum or population | *Systematic Selection* of sampling units with selection interval applied to list |
| V. *One-Phase Sampling*: final sample selected directly from entire population | *Two-Phase (or Double) Sampling*: final sample selected from first-phase sample, which obtains information for stratification or estimation |

Source: Adapted from Leslie Kish, *Survey Sampling,* p. 20.

called *clusters.*[8] *Multistage sampling* is a result of the subsampling of clusters such that the choice of individual sample members results from selection of sampling units in two or more stages. Either all the elements in a cluster can be included or a sample of elements.

The third modification centers around whether or not the population is broken into relatively homogeneous subpopulations, called *strata,* with the resulting sample being comprised of elements selected from each strata. The basis for such stratification can be any relevant characteristic of the population, variable or attribute, that is correlated with the factor under study and results in the formation of homogeneous population segments. For example, in the extra reserve problem, a bank may feel that for a survey of all depositors the sample would be more representative if it was developed from the stratification of the population on the basis of annual income of depositors.

Fourth, the sample may be selected by random choice or by systematic selection. In the latter case, sampling units are selected in sequences separated on lists by an interval of selection. The interval *(k)* is determined by the relationship between the size of the population *(N)* and the sample size *(n)* as follows:

$$k = \frac{N}{n}$$

In short, the first unit is selected by random choice from the first $k$ units on the list, and then every $k$th unit after is included. In the extra reserve situation, for instance, a bank may decide to use this type of sampling to draw a sample of 500 depositors. If the total number of depositors were 10,000, then

$$k = \frac{10,000}{500} = 20.$$

The first sample member would be selected randomly from the first 20 depositors, and then every 20th one on the list after the first would be included.

The last major modification concerns the number of phases involved in the selection process. *Multiphase sampling* occurs when the final sample is selected from a preselected larger sample or samples, depending upon the number of phases of selection used.

Each of the above modifications can occur with any other. This inter-

---

8. More formally, sampling units are nonoverlapping collections of elements from the population. That is, every population element belongs to one and only one sampling unit, and the entire population is included in the total of sampling units.

relationship leads to the existence of many possible different sample designs. Using the modifications of Table 3–1, there are thirty-two distinct designs possible. It will be noted that simple random sampling has the following characteristics: equal probability, single element, unstratified, random choice, one phase.

*Nonprobability Sampling.* In general, there are three basic types of nonprobability sampling that may, under appropriate conditions, be useful in survey research. These are convenience, judgment, and quota sampling.

*Convenience sampling* refers to samples selected not by judgment or probability techniques but because the elements in a fraction of the population can be reached conveniently. There is no attempt made to have a representative sample. Thus, a survey by a bank contemplating an extra reserve plan may be conducted using as a sample the first 100 people to enter the bank on a given day.

A somewhat more representative sample may be provided through use of *purposive* or *judgment sampling.* The key assumption underlying this type of sampling is that, with sound judgment or expertise and an appropriate strategy, one can carefully and consciously choose the elements to be included in the sample so that samples can be developed that are suitable for one's needs. The intent is to select elements that are believed to be typical or representative of the population in such a way that errors of judgment in the selection will cancel each other out. One weakness of this approach is that without an objective basis for making the judgments or without an external check, there is no way of knowing whether the so-called typical cases are, in fact, typical.[9]

The third major type of nonprobability sampling is *quota sampling.* The basic goal of this sampling process is to develop a sample that is a replica of the population of interest. To accomplish this, the population is broken down on the basis of key demographic characteristics, and a sample is developed that is proportional to the population on these characteristics. Interviewers are then assigned a certain quota to be filled, and they are supposed to select representative individuals. Quota samples are not necessarily representative. Yet, for practical purposes, they may be suitable, if relatively quick and somewhat crude results will suffice. In addition, it has been shown that quota sampling is quite close to traditional probability sampling under certain conditions.[10]

*Combinations.* Our discussion of probability and nonprobability sampling has been such as to imply an "either or" situation. Generally, this will

9. Claire Selltiz et al., *Research Methods in Social Relations* (New York: Holt, Rinehart and Winston, revised edition, 1959), p. 521.

10. See Seymour Sudman, "Probability Sampling With Quotas," *Journal of the American Statistical Association,* vol. 61 (1966), pp. 749–771.

be the case. However, if the sampling is to be directed in a series of stages, it is possible to develop a sample design that combines features of both approaches; one or more stages can be carried out using probability sampling and the rest by nonprobability techniques. For example, the researcher may choose clusters by probability techniques but select the individual elements from each cluster that are to be included in the sample as a quota sample. Such a design is often practical for area sampling, a special type of cluster sampling in which the researcher selects a probability sample of geographic areas, such as counties, census tracts, blocks, etc., and within each of the selected areas uses a quota sample controlled for such demographic variables as age, sex, and/or occupation.

## Precision and Accuracy

The basic ideas and theory of sampling are perhaps best made clear by limiting our discussion to samples drawn by the process of simple random sampling. It will be recalled from the discussion in the previous section of this chapter that surveys based on probability samples are subject to two types of error: (1) variable sampling error and (2) nonsampling, or systematic, errors. The difference between a result from a sample and the result from a census taken under the same conditions is measured by the precision, or reliability, of the sample result. This measure is based on differences in the estimates which would occur if repeated samples of the same size were taken from the population of interest using the same procedure. The average of samples estimates over all possible samples, that is, the *expected value* of a sample estimate, occupies a key position in sampling. Precision is reflected by the sampling error and, as we shall show later, is related to sample size and variability in the population. *Accuracy,* on the other hand, is the difference between the sample result and the true value of the parameter. The accuracy of a sample reflects both sampling and nonsampling errors. Moreover, because of nonsampling error, accuracy is largely independent of sample size, although it is related to size to the extent that the sampling error component is affected.

### SAMPLING DISTRIBUTIONS

A sampling distribution is a special type of probability distribution. It is a distribution of the population of values of a given sample statistic (for example, the sample mean, sample proportion, or sample variance) that could be generated from random samples of a given size drawn from a specified population. For ease in understanding, we limit our discussion to the sampling distribution of means and proportions.

Being a type of population, a sampling distribution itself has parameters. That is, the probability distribution of the sample mean or proportion has a mean and a standard deviation. The standard deviation of a sampling distribution is known as the *standard error*. In order to make an estimate of the population mean or proportion, we must be able to estimate the standard error of the sampling distribution ($\hat{\sigma}_{\bar{x}}$ or $\hat{\sigma}_p$). The following symbols will be used in deriving the relevant elementary formulas for these standard errors (for samples drawn by the process of simple random sampling):

$\mu$ = population mean
$\pi$ = population proportion
$\sigma$ = standard deviation of the population
$s$ = standard deviation of the sample
$\hat{\sigma}$ = estimate of the population standard deviation
$\overline{X}$ = arithmetic mean of a sample
$X_i$ = single observation from a sample
$\rho$ = sample proportion
$N$ = size of population
$n$ = size of sample

There are important properties associated with sampling distributions:[11]

1. The *expected value* of a sample estimate is the average of estimates for all possible samples drawn from the same population. For any given sample size, the arithmetic mean of the sampling distribution of means or of proportions—that is, the expected value of the sample mean or proportion—equals the corresponding population parameter value. Thus, $E(\overline{X}) = \mu$ and $E(p) = \pi$

2. The arithmetic mean of sample variances ($s^2$) is less than the population variance when calculated by the following formulas:

$$s^2 = \frac{\sum\limits_{i=1}^{n} [X_i - \overline{X}]^2}{n} \; ; s^2 = \frac{\sum\limits_{i=1}^{n} [p(1-p)]}{n}$$

This bias can be corrected by multiplying $s^2$ by

$$\frac{n}{n-1},$$

11. Paul E. Green and Donald S. Tull, *Research for Marketing Decisions* (Englewood Cliffs: Prentice-Hall, Inc., second edition, 1970), pp. 257–258.

which results in:

$$\hat{\sigma}^2 = \frac{n}{n-1} s^2$$

3. If the original population is normally distributed, then the sampling distribution of the means will be normally distributed. Moreover, even if the population is not normal, according to the *Central Limit Theorem* in statistical theory, the sampling distribution of means (of random samples) will aproach normality as sample size increases. The only restriction is that the variance of the original population be finite, a condition that is easily fulfilled in most practical surveys. The sampling distribution of the mean approaches normality quite quickly as $n$ increases.

4. When samples are large, say, $n \geq 50$, and when $\pi$ is close to 0.5, the normal distribution represents a good approximation to the binomial distribution for working with sample proportions.

## BIAS

When the expected value of an estimate does not equal the true value being estimated, we say that bias exists. That is, the difference between the expected value of a sample estimate and the population parameter is called *bias.* A sampling procedure that gives rise to this situation is called *biased,* and the estimate derived from the procedure a *biased estimate.* For example a sampling procedure which schedules interviews with housewives only in the daytime most likely would overestimate the number of children and underestimate the proportion of working wives. On the other hand, a sampling procedure that generates a distribution where the expected value of the estimate equals the population parameter is unbiased, and the estimate is termed an *unbiased estimate.*

Figure 3-1 illustrates the concept of bias and shows how it relates to sampling error. If simple random sampling is used, the sample average is an unbiased estimate of the mean regardless of the size of sample and the nature of the population from which the sample is drawn.

It is desirable, but not essential, that an estimate be unbiased. The choice between an unbiased and a biased estimator rests on the cost of each and the resulting value. We deal with the estimation of bias in Chapter 4.

## STANDARD ERROR OF THE MEAN

Although simple random sampling is unbiased, each sample estimate of the mean will differ from others and from $\mu$. Since, in practice, the

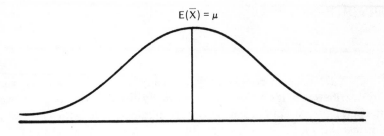

a. Unbiased distribution

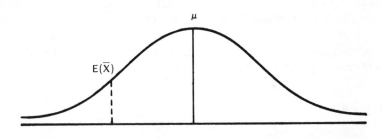

b. Biased distribution

FIGURE 3–1    An unbiased and a biased distribution of a sample mean

estimate of the population parameter is based on only *one* sample, what is needed is a measure of the extent to which the estimate derived from different samples of a given size drawn from the same population are likely to differ from each other. That is, we need to be able to determine the dispersion of the sampling distribution.

An estimate can be made from any randomly selected sample (if $n \geq 2$) of what the magnitude of these sampling fluctuations are likely to be on the average. The usual measure of the dispersion of the sampling distribution is its standard deviation.

As previously stated, the standard deviation of the sampling distribution of the mean is called the standard error of the mean. If the standard deviation of the population is known, the standard error of the mean is[12]

$$\sigma_{\overline{X}} = \frac{\sigma}{\sqrt{n}} \tag{3.1}$$

12. If $n < 30$ and $\sigma$ is unknown, $n-1$ is substituted for $n$ in Eq. (3.1), and the Student's "$t$" distribution is used instead of the normal distribution for estimating probabilities of error.

However, since in practice population parameters are seldom known, $\sigma_{\bar{x}}$ must be estimated from the sample as follows:

$$\hat{\sigma}_{\bar{X}} = \frac{\hat{\sigma}}{\sqrt{n}} \tag{3.2}$$

where, as previously shown,

$$\hat{\sigma} = \sqrt{\frac{n}{n-1} s^2} \tag{3.3}$$

When the formula for $\hat{\sigma}$ is substituted into Eq. 3.2, the estimate for the standard error of the mean becomes

$$\hat{\sigma}_{\bar{X}} = \frac{s}{\sqrt{n-1}} \tag{3.4}$$

## STANDARD ERROR OF A PROPORTION

The procedure for estimating the standard error of a proportion is much the same as that for the mean. When the population proportion is known, the standard error is[13]

$$\sigma_p = \sqrt{\frac{\pi(1-\pi)}{n}} \tag{3.5}$$

More realistically, $\pi$ is not known and must be estimated from the sample proportion as follows:

$$\hat{\sigma}_p = \sqrt{\frac{n}{n-1}} \cdot s \tag{3.6}$$

Since

$$s = \sqrt{\frac{p(1-p)}{n}}$$

the estimate of the standard error of a proportion becomes

$$\hat{\sigma}_p = \sqrt{\frac{p(1-p)}{n-1}} \tag{3.7}$$

13. The same substitution of $n-1$ for $n$ mentioned in footnote 12 is made in Eq. 3.5 when $n < 30$.

## FINITE POPULATION MUTLIPLIER

What we have said above concerning the standard error of estimates applies to sampling from infinite populations. It should be noted that the standard error of the mean depends upon sample size. The size of the population has been ignored, since it is presumed to be infinitely large.

When the population is finite and the sample size is some "significant" fraction of the population size, the standard error formulas should be modified by the finite population multiplier

$$\sqrt{\frac{N-n}{N}}$$

For example, application of the finite multiplier to the standard error of the mean (with $\sigma$ known) results in

$$\sigma_{\overline{X}} = \frac{\sigma}{\sqrt{n}} \sqrt{\frac{N-n}{N}} \tag{3.8a}$$

and application to the estimate of the standard error gives[14]

$$\hat{\sigma}_{\overline{X}} = \frac{s}{\sqrt{n-1}} \sqrt{\frac{N-n}{N}} \tag{3.8b}$$

The smaller the proportion of the population that is sampled, the less is the effect of the finite multiplier. Although there is no definite fraction that dictates when the multiplier should be used, it is traditionally used when the sample constitutes 5 percent or more of the population being studied.

## *Planning the Sample*

The precision and accuracy of survey results are affected by the manner in which the sample has been chosen. Consequently, strict attention must be paid to the planning of the sample. It must also be recognized that sample planning is really part of the total planning of the survey.

### STEPS IN A TYPICAL SAMPLE PLAN

Regardless of the type of survey to be conducted, the process of selecting a sample follows a well-defined progression.

14. Strictly speaking, one should use $N-n/N-1$ as the finite population multiplier when $s$ is used. However, the difference between this and the formula shown above is negligible. For example, in an extreme case where $N=50$ and $n=25$, the difference in multipliers when $N$ and $N-1$ are used in the denominator is .007.

The first thing that the sample plan must include is a definition of the population to be investigated. While seemingly an easy task, defining the population often is one of the most difficult things to do in sampling. The greatest difficulty that arises in population definition is due to imprecise research problem definition. Imprecision of problem definition in turn is often the result of the fact that the purpose or objectives of the survey, which are based on the decision problem of concern, are not clearly transmitted from the decision maker to the investigator.

Once the population has been defined, the investigator must decide whether the survey is to be conducted among all members of the population or only a subset of the population. That is, a choice must be made between census and sample. Obviously, this cannot be done before the population is specified, since the choice between the two depends largely upon the size of the population, and the size is determined by the precise boundaries of the population.

If it is decided that the desired information is to be obtained from a sample, then the investigator must determine what *sample design* is to be used. Specification of sample design, which includes the method of selecting individual sample members, involves both practical and theoretical consideration:

> The sample design is decided upon in light of what is practically feasible as well as what is theoretically desirable. Once decided, it in turn gives rise to numerous practical decisions of selection and organization. In considering these matters, due regard must be paid to the purposes of the survey, the accuracy desired in the results, the cost, time and labor involved, and other practical considerations.[15]

Typical questions to be answered include:

> What type of sample to use
> What is the appropriate sampling unit
> What frame (that is, list of sampling units from which the sample is to be drawn) is available for the population and what problems might arise in using it for the particular design and unit decided upon
>> How are refusals and nonresponse to be handled

Somewhat related to the sample design, but in many ways a separate decision area for the investigator is the determination of the sample size. In general, size of sample is directly related to precision. Thus, there are two general traditional approaches to determining the size of the sample to be used in any given survey. The first approach is where an arbitrarily or judgmentally determined size is selected. When the results of the study are

15. Excerpted from Chapter 1, "The Nature of Social Surveys and Some Examples" in *Survey Methods in Social Investigation,* second edition, by C. A. Moser and G. Kalton, © C. A. Moser and G. J. Kalton, 1958, 1971.

compiled, then, if a probability design were used, the precision could be measured by applying the appropriate standard error formula or formulas. The second approach involves the opposite procedure. That is, by specifying a desired precision in advance, and by applying the appropriate standard error formula, sample size can be arrived at. Determination of sample size will be discussed in more depth later in this chapter.

Finally, the sample plan must take into account the estimated costs of sampling. Such costs are of two types: (1) overhead costs, which are relatively fixed for a sampling procedure, and (2) variable costs, whch depend upon the scope of the study. In reality, it is difficult, and perhaps not even reasonable, to separate sampling costs from overall survey costs. Consequently, in a typical survey costs from all aspects of the survey are usually considered together.

There are two basic requirements for the sampling procedure to fulfill. A sample must be *representative* and it must be *adequate*. When it is representative, a sample will be a relatively small piece of the population that mirrors the various patterns and subclasses of the population. A sample is adequate when it is of sufficient size to provide confidence in the stability of its characteristics. This, in turn, requires a measure of precision, which requires the use of a probability-based design. From this discussion, one might conclude that the ideal sample is one obtained by a probability process. In general, this is preferable. However, it should be recognized that it is more important to avoid distorted samples than to be able to measure sampling error. Of course, probability techniques do not inherently lead to distorted or biased samples. The point is that there may be a tendency to ignore the existence of potential bias when using probability designs.

## Determination of Sample Size

Our discussion is limited to the more traditional approach to selecting sample size. As such it does not explicitly consider cost and value of information from sampling. The Bayesian approach, on the other hand, allows us to be explicit about both of these factors. By this approach, optimal sample size is determined by relating the maximum value to the cost. In addition, an upper limit on sample size can be specified somewhat easily by determining the expected value of perfect information (EVPI). Since EVPI is the maximum value that information can have, the cost of sampling cannot be greater.[16]

As previously stated, the size of sample can be arrived at in two different ways. Our concern here is with the approach that states a desired

16. For a more complete discussion of the Bayesian approach to sampling see Ben M. Enis and Charles L. Broome, *Marketing Decisions: A Bayesian Approach* (Scranton: Intext Educational Publishers, 1971), Chapters 5–6, or Paul E. Green and Donald S. Tull, *op. cit.*, Chapter 9.

precision and then determines size by applying appropriate standard error formulas.

In order to determine the sample size needed when sampling for a characteristic or value (for example, a mean) the following information is needed:

1. An estimate of the variance (or standard deviation) in the population

2. The necessary or desired precision

3. The tolerable error or permissible tolerance of variation in the sample statistic

With these data, the value of the standard error becomes a predetermined constant—predetermined on the basis of tolerable error and needed precision. On the other hand, the estimation of the standard deviation can be based on experience, the results of an exploratory or pilot survey, or other equivalent estimates.

When concerned with a mean an appropriate formula for estimating sample size is

$$n = \frac{\sigma^2 Z^2}{T^2} \tag{3.9}$$

where

$$Z = \frac{\overline{X} - \mu}{\frac{\hat{\sigma}}{\sqrt{n}}}, \quad T = \overline{X} - \mu$$

and

$n$ = sample size
$\hat{\sigma}$ = estimated standard deviation of the population
$Z$ = number of standard deviations for the desired precision or level of confidence
$T$ = allowable tolerance of variation

Consider the extra reserve plan as an example. Suppose a bank wants to estimate the average amount of money borrowed by depositors for a ninety-day period during the past year. The bank wants the tolerable variation *(T)* not to exceed $100. The level of confidence is a probability of .99, which corresponds to a standard deviation equivalent of $Z = 2.58$ (see Table 2 of the Appendix). Finally, the standard deviation of the population ($\hat{\sigma}$) is estimated to be $500. Putting these values into equation (3.9), we get:

$$n = \frac{(500 \cdot 2.58)^2}{(100)^2} = 166$$

Thus, a random sample of 166 depositors would yield a mean of which we can say that the chances were 99 to 1 that it would not deviate more than $100 from other means calculated from similar samples.

If the resulting sample size represents a significant proportion of the population, say 5 percent or more, the finite population multiplier is required and the sample size must be recalculated using the following formula:

$$n = \frac{N(\hat{\sigma}^2 Z^2)}{NT^2 + \hat{\sigma}^2 Z^2} \qquad (3.10)$$

where $N$ is the size of the population.

If the concern of the survey is estimating a proportion, the procedure for determining sample size is similar. In this situation the following information is needed:

1. An estimate of the proportions that will be found
2. The necessary or desired precision
3. The allowable tolerance of variation

To determine the sample size, the formula to use is:

$$n = \frac{Z^2(pq)}{T^2} \qquad (3.11)$$

where

$$Z = \frac{p - \pi}{\hat{\sigma}_p}, \ T = p - \pi$$

and

$p$ = estimated proportion of interest
$q = 1 - p$

Once again, if the resulting $n$ is 5 percent or more of the population size, the finite population multiplier is required, and the sample size can be computed from

$$n = \frac{NZ^2(pq)}{NT^2 + Z^2(pq)} \qquad (3.12)$$

The above discussion has been concerned with probability samples drawn by the process of simple random sampling. Space limitation does not allow us to discuss the process for other types of probability samples. In general, however, what is required is the use of the standard error formulas. Many of the references listed at the end of this chapter treat the subject.

For nonprobability samples, the approach is not as well determined. The best that can be said is that the investigator must use his judgment and experience in determining the sample size. By the very nature of the samples, desired precision cannot be predetermined, since sampling error cannot be measured in the first place, although it can be estimated. The technique to be discussed in Chapter 4 will be useful in determining sample size for nonprobability samples.

## Special Types of Sample Design

Earlier in this chapter we discussed alternative sampling techniques that lead to differing sample designs. Our subsequent discussion of probability samples, particularly concerning measuring the standard error and determining sample size, was in the context of simple random sampling. However, as shown in Table 3-1, there are many modifications that can be introduced ino the sampling process, and each leads to a specialized sample design. Of particular interest to investigators concerned wtih surveys related to marketing problems are such techniques as stratified sampling, area sampling, systematic sampling, multistage sampling, and fixed versus sequential sampling. Obviously, these are not all inclusive of the modifications that can be made; they are representative, however.

As would be expected, the measurement of standard error, and thus determination of sample size, tends to become more complex as we introduce modifications into the simple random sampling process. Of necessity, our discussion of these so-called specialized techniques must be incomplete. Our purpose is to present selected examples so that the reader will gain an appreciation of the complexities and problems facing the investigator wanting to use any of these techniques.[17]

### STRATIFIED SAMPLING

*Stratification* is a means to improve sample design by making use of information about the population. Stratified simple random sampling involves dividing the population into relatively homogeneous groups called strata and then selecting simple random samples from each of the strata. The population can be divided into groups on the basis of any criterion, provided the division results in strata that are relatively homogeneous. Commonly used stratification criteria are such characteristics as age, in-

17. For a more definitive discussion of these techniques the reader is referred to such standard works as Kish, *op. cit;* Yates, *op. cit.;* and M. H. Hansen, W. N. Hurwitz, and W. G. Madow, *Sample Survey Methods and Theory,* vol. 1 (New York: John Wiley & Sons, Inc., 1953).

come, level of education completed, stage in life cycle, sex, occupation, or any other criterion relevant to the research problem at hand. Of course, each element in the population must be placed in one and only one stratum.

Determination of the right number and type of stratifications is one of the most difficult problems in survey research. This depends upon the type and purpose of the sample as well as the number of different possible stratifications that will give the same minimum error of estimation.

The design advantage of stratified over simple random sampling is derived from the effect of homogeneity on variance. With stratification, the total variance is divided into two components—the variance *within* strata and the variance *between* strata. If everything is as it should be, the greater homoegeneity within strata results in a major part of the total variance between strata. Since the formulas for calculating the standard errors of means, proportions, and totals—which must be modified from those used in simple random sampling—exclude variance between strata, the sizes of the resultant standard errors are decreased. Thus, in general, stratification leads to reductions in standard error.

Stratified sampling consists of a general type, which is really disproportionate stratified sampling, and two special types, proportionate stratified sampling and optimum allocation.

*General Stratified Sampling.* The process of stratified sampling consists of taking random samples of size $n$ from each of $m$ strata. Given that a population of size $N$ is divided into $m$ strata and that random samples are drawn from each of the strata, an unbiased estimate of the population mean $(\overline{X})$ can be calculated from:

$$\overline{X}_s = \sum_{i=1}^{n_i} W_i \overline{X}_i \tag{3.13}$$

where

$$W_i = \frac{N_i}{N}, \quad \sum_{i=1}^{m} N_i = N, \quad \sum_{i=1}^{m} W_i = 1$$

and

$$N_i = \text{size of } i\text{th stratum}$$
$$\overline{X}_i = \text{mean of } i\text{th stratum.}$$

The standard error of the mean is:

$$\sigma_{\overline{X},s} = \sqrt{\sum_{i=1}^{m} W_i^2 \frac{\sigma_i^2}{n_i}} \tag{3.14}$$

where

$\sigma_i^2$ is the variance of the *i*th stratum

$n_i$ is the sample size of the *i*th stratum.

Since population variances usually are not known, $\hat{\sigma}_i^2$ must be used as an estimator of $\sigma_i^2$. Similarly, the standard error of a proportion is

$$\sigma_{p,s} = \sqrt{\sum_{i=1}^{m} W_i^2 \frac{\pi_i(1 - \pi_i)}{n_i}} \tag{3.15}$$

A simplified example will illustrate the use of the formula for the standard error of the mean. Assume that a bank is interested in estimating the mean amount of money borrowed by depositors for a ninety-day period during the past year. Depositors can be categorized on the basis of occupation into four groups. The total number of depositors is 20,000, broken down as follows:

|            | $N_i$              | $W_i$ |
| ---------- | ------------------ | ----- |
| Group I    | 10,000 depositors  | 0.50  |
| Group II   | 5,000 depositors   | 0.25  |
| Group III  | 3,000 depositors   | 0.15  |
| Group IV   | 2,000 depositors   | 0.10  |

The investigator has selected a sample of 200 depositors from Group I, 125 depositors from Group II, 100 depositors from Group III, and 75 depositors from Group IV. The sample means and standard deviations are

$$\overline{X}_{\text{I}} = \$130.20 \qquad s_{\text{I}} = \$42.00$$
$$\overline{X}_{\text{II}} = \$118.75 \qquad s_{\text{II}} = \$26.25$$
$$\overline{X}_{\text{III}} = \$125.40 \qquad s_{\text{III}} = \$60.30$$
$$\overline{X}_{\text{IV}} = \$\ 98.10 \qquad s_{\text{IV}} = \$35.50$$

The point estimate of the mean of the population from Formula 3.13 is

$$\overline{X}_s = 0.5(130.20) + 0.25(118.75) + 0.15(125.40) + 0.1(98.10)$$
$$= \$123.41$$

The investigator desires to construct a 95 percent confidence interval around $\overline{X}_s$. To do this, he must first compute the standard error of the mean. Since the various sample sizes are less than 5 percent of the corre-

sponding populations, the finite multiplier is not necessary, and formula (3.14) can be used:[18]

$$\hat{\sigma}_{\overline{X},s} = [\frac{1}{199}(0.5)^2(42.00)^2 + \frac{1}{124}(0.25)^2(26.25)^2 + \frac{1}{99}(0.15)^2(60.30)^2$$

$$+ \frac{1}{74}(0.1)^2(35.50)^2]^{1/2} = \$1.89$$

The confidence interval is

$$\overline{X}_s \pm 1.96\,\hat{\sigma}_{\overline{X},s} = \$123.41 \pm \$3.70$$

*Disproportionate Stratified Sampling.* In this type of stratified sampling, the within-strata sampling fractions vary among the strata. That is, the proportion of the elements of the $i$th stratum selected for the $i$th sample will not be the same as the proportion representing the $j$th or $k$th strata.

Although disproportionate stratified sampling is essentially the same as the general type, there are simplifications that can be made in the standard error calculations if it is known in advance that the sample was selected on a disproportionate basis. In more general terms, Formula 3.14 should always be used unless the sample was selected on a proportionate or disproportionate basis.

In disproportionate stratified sampling, both relative size of each stratum and wtihin-stratum variance is taken into account. Thus, the rule for sample allocation is

$$n_i = \frac{W_i\sigma_i n}{\sum\limits_{i=1}^{m} W_i\sigma_i} \qquad (3.16)$$

The formula for the standard error of the mean of a disproportionate stratified sample becomes

$$\sigma_{\overline{X},s} = \sqrt{\frac{\left(\sum\limits_{i=1}^{m} W_i\sigma_i\right)^2}{\sum\limits_{i=1}^{k} n_i}} \qquad (3.17)$$

18. It will be noted that we correct the sample variance $s_i^2$ to serve as estimators $\hat{\sigma}_i^2$ of the group variances $\sigma_i^2$ by using the multiplier, $n/n-1$. Since $n$ appears in both the numerator and denominator, it cancels out.

As usual, $\hat{\sigma}_i$ will have to be used as the estimator of $\sigma_i$.

Continuing the example of the bank survey, we now assume that $\sigma_i = s_i$ for $i = 1, 2, 3, 4$. With this assumption, we can determine the allocation of the total sample of 500 by applying Formula 3.16

$$n_1 = \frac{0.5(42.00)(500)}{0.5(42.00) + 0.25(26.25) + 0.15(60.30) + 0.1(35.50)} \simeq 261$$

$$n_2 = \frac{0.25(26.25)(500)}{0.5(42.00) + 0.25(26.25) + 0.15(60.30) + 0.1(35.50)} \simeq 82$$

$$n_3 = \frac{0.15(60.30)(500)}{0.5(42.00) + 0.25(26.25) + 0.15(60.30) + 0.1(35.50)} \simeq 113$$

$$n_4 = \frac{0.10(35.50)(500)}{0.5(42.00) + 0.25(26.25) + 0.15(60.30) + 0.1(35.50)} \simeq 44$$

We can now find, given the above assumptions, the standard error of the mean by use of Formula 3.17.

$$\sigma_{\bar{X},s} = \sqrt{\frac{[0.5(42.00) + 0.25(26.25) + 0.15(60.30) + 0.1(35.50)]^2}{500}} = \$1.796$$

When the cost of selecting sample members from one stratum is not necessarily the same as that from another stratum, Formula 3.16 must be modified. This modification gives the following allocation rule:

$$n_i = \frac{W_i \sigma_i n / C_i}{\sum\limits_{i=1}^{m} (W_i \sigma_i / C_i)} \tag{3.18}$$

where $C_i$ is the cost of selecting an individual from the $i$th stratum.

*Proportionate Stratified Sampling.* In contrast to disportionate sampling, in proportionate stratified sampling the same sampling fraction is used throughout all population strata. This means that the sample strata sizes bear the same ratio to the total sample size as do the population strata sizes to the total population size, or

$$\frac{n_i}{n} = \frac{N_i}{N}$$

In this type of stratified sampling, only the size of the stratum is used as the guide for determining allocation of the total sample. Thus,

$$n_i = \frac{W_i n}{\sum\limits_{i=1}^{m} W_i} \qquad (3.19)$$

The standard error of the mean for a proportionate stratified sample is

$$\sigma_{\bar{X},s} = \sqrt{\frac{\sum\limits_{i=1}^{m} W_i \hat{\sigma}_i^2}{\sum\limits_{i=1}^{m} n_i}} \qquad (3.20)$$

Once again, $\hat{\sigma}_i^2$ is used to estimate $\sigma_i^2$.

If the survey of bank depositors were to be based on a proportionate stratified sample, the allocation of the total sample of 500 depositors is quite simple:

$$n_1 = 0.5 \ (500) = 250$$

$$n_2 = 0.25(500) = 125$$

$$n_3 = 0.15(500) = 75$$

$$n_4 = 0.10(500) = 50$$

In addition, if we assume original data as being collected from the above sample, the standard error of the mean can be calculated from Formula 3.20, noting that we use

$$\frac{n_i}{n_i - 1} s_i^2$$

as the measure of $\hat{\sigma}_i^2$.

$$\sigma_{\bar{X},s} = \left\{ \left[ 0.5 \ \frac{250}{249} \left(42.00\right)^2 + 0.25 \left(\frac{125}{124}\right) \left(26.25\right)^2 \right. \right.$$
$$\left. \left. + 0.15 \left(\frac{75}{74}\right) \left(60.30\right)^2 + 0.1 \left(\frac{50}{49}\right) \left(35.50\right)^2 \right] \middle/ 500 \right\}^{1/2} = \$1.87$$

If the cost of selecting members varies among strata, the allocation rule of Formula 3.18 must be modified in a way similar to that shown for disproportionate sampling.

## CLUSTER SAMPLING

There are times when the investigator chooses to select primary sampling units larger than the individual or family. That is, he elects to sample clusters of elements. In cluster sampling, it is the clusters of individuals or families that are selected at random, or even systematically, rather than the individual elements. After the clusters are selected, either all or a sample of the members of a cluster are sampled. For example, in the extra reserve plan situation, a bank with branches in many cities may decide to make cities the primary sampling unit, and thus begin its sampling process by drawing a random sample of cities. The bank could then draw a random sample of depositors in each of the selected cities. This is a type of *multistage* sample, in which the random sampling process is applied to two or more stages. On the other hand, a bank with no branches might decide to cluster its depositors according to first letter of last name. In this case the investigator first draws a sample of the letters of the alphabet. Then, either all, or a sample of, depositors whose last names begins with each of the selected letters can be included in the final sample. There is a risk of bias entering, particularly concerning the over- or underrepresentation of ethnic groups, when using this particular method.

Our first hypothetical situation discussed in the preceding paragraph is an example of *area sampling*. Area sampling is a type of cluster sampling in which the primary sampling is of geographical areas, for example, cities, counties, census tracts, city blocks, etc. Once the primary areas are randomly selected, all subsequent sampling is restricted to the areas chosen in the first stage. Of course, if the sample is multistage, then the necessary substages within the primary unit are also chosen randomly.

The primary advantage of cluster sampling over simple random sampling lies in cost benefits rather than greater reliability. By concentrating the investigation in areas, the cost of the sampling operation is reduced, which may lead to greater reliability of the estimates per dollar expended. Although the formulas for the standard error, etc., relevant to cluster samples are beyond the scope of this book, we should point out, for example, that in an area multistage sample in which the sampling units are cities, census tracts, and city blocks the total sampling variance is the sum of three individual sampling variances: (1) in random selection of cities; (2) in random selection of census tracts; and (3) in random selection of city blocks. Consequently, estimation of standard error becomes somewhat complex.

## *Summary*

In this chapter our concern has been with sampling of human populations. Our approach primarily has been traditional, particularly when discussing the planning of samples and determination of sample size. In developing the theory of sampling, we have concentrated on probability sampling and, more specifically, simple random sampling. The chapter does point out that there are modifications that can be made to the simple random process that lead to more specialized types of sampling. Our justification for concentrating on the basic process of simple random sampling is that all modifications build on the conceptual and mathematical foundation of this basic sampling process.

Although the discussion of nonprobability sampling has been limited, this does not mean that it is unimportant. On the contrary, there are times when a nonprobability sample is more desirable than a probability one, especially when time and cost considerations limit the investigator or when only a rough estimate is needed. Chapter 4 discusses some of the problems present in both probability and nonprobability samples.

The methods discussed in this chapter concerning determining sample size are those used in basic research, in which the attempt is made to eliminate all nonsampling error and estimate or measure sampling error. In practice, we recognize that nonsampling errors cannot be fully eliminated. In decisional research designs where investigator judgments are allowed, estimates of nonsampling errors in design can be used to choose from alternative designs.

## SELECTED BIBLIOGRAPHY

Enis, Ben M. and Charles L. Broome. *Marketing Decisions: A Bayesian Approach.* Scranton: Intext Educational Publishers, 1971. A relatively short book providing a concise treatment of the fundamentals of Bayesian analysis, with particular application to the field of marketing. Chapters 5 and 6 are pertinent to the subject of sampling.

Ferber, Robert. *Market Research.* New York: McGraw-Hill Book Company, Inc., 1949. A classic book in marketing research, which emphasizes traditional statistical techniques. Seven chapters are devoted to sampling theory.

Green, Paul E. and Donald S. Tull. *Research for Marketing Decisions.* Englewood Cliffs: Prentice-Hall, Inc., second edition, 1970. A somewhat high-level book that describes the strategy and tactics of marketing research in the context of marketing decision making. One chapter is devoted to the traditional approach to sampling and one chapter to the Bayesian approach.

Kish, Leslie. *Survey Sampling.* New York: John Wiley & Sons, Inc., 1965. A book for students of the social sciences that emphasizes surveys of human populations. The book is oriented toward providing a working knowledge of practical sampling methods and their theoretical background.

Parten, Mildred. *Surveys, Polls, and Samples: Practical Procedures.* New York: Harper & Brothers, 1950. A traditional book dealing with the major aspects of survey research and the use of samples.

Yates, Frank. *Sampling Methods for Censuses and Surveys.* London: Charles Griffin and Co., Ltd., third edition, 1971. A comprehensive nonmathematical book on sampling. Both theory and practical application are treated.

## QUESTIONS AND PROBLEMS

3.1. The founder of a well-known consulting firm specializing in consumer research once stated that the way he would select a sample of housewives to obtain information to be used for redesigning a line of refrigerators would be to "start talking to housewives I happen to know, ask them to refer me to others they know, and keep talking to additional ones until I found one *who really knows how a refrigerator should be designed.*"

    a. What kind of a sampling plan has he described?

    b. What are its advantages? Disadvantages?

    c. What general method or methods of inquiry is/are implied in his statement?

*3.2. Intercontinental Air is considering adding an "excursion plan" on its New York–Paris–Rome flights. All passengers who travel on this plan must buy a round trip fare and fly on a space-available basis. The regular round-trip fare will be reduced 20 percent for those who travel under the new plan.

Before deciding whether or not to implement the plan, management decides to conduct an in-flight survey of passengers now traveling under the existing fares. Among the informational items they would like to know is the mean number of flights taken per year and the proportion originating in New York. They will determine this on the same survey.

They estimate the standard deviation of the number of flights per year at $\hat{\sigma} = 2.0$. They decide they need a 95.4 percent level of confidence and can safely allow a difference of sample mean and population mean of $\pm .10$ flight.

They estimate the proportion originating in New York at .10. They require that the sample proportion be within $\pm .02$ of the population proportion. They would like a confidence level of 95.4 percent for the proportion estimate also.

What sample size should they take if it is to be a simple random sample and the traditional method of determining sample size is used?

*3.3. Suppose simple random samples have been used in the following studies of Morning Fresh coffee just concluded by the marketing research department:

    a. This study was made to estimate the proportion of households which used Morning Fresh coffee during the past week. The following information is from the study:

Sample size $= 100$

Sample proportion of households using Morning Fresh brand $= 20$ percent

What is the interval estimate of the proportion of households using Morning Fresh coffee in the past week, assuming a confidence level of 95.4 percent is desired? How do you interpret this estimate?

    b. This study was made to estimate the mean amount of Morning Fresh coffee purchased per user during the past week. The following information is from the study:

Sample size $= 100$

Sample standard deviation $= .4$ pounds

Sample mean $= .25$ pounds

*The section following Chapter 9 provides the answers to those problems that are marked with an asterisk in the chapter and in the succeeding ones.

What is the interval estimate of the mean amount of coffee purchased during the past week by the population of users from which the sample was drawn, assuming a confidence level of 95.4 percent is desired? How do you interpret this estimate?

*3.4. Suppose an organization that conducts polls for political candidates is asked by a candidate for national office to conduct two polls, one in a state that has an upcoming primary and the other in the country as a whole. The state has a population that is 1/50 that of the country. What size should the sample in the state be relative to that in the nationwide poll?

*3.5. The Internal Revenue Service plans to audit a sample of 1,000 individual tax returns to estimate mean amounts paid by persons in each of three income brackets. The income strata for which the average tax paid is to be determined are 0–$10,000; $10,001–$15,000; and $15,001–$20,000. They estimate the relative size and standard deviations in code stratum to be as follows:

| Stratum | $N_i/N$ | $\sigma_i$ |
|---|---|---|
| 0 - $10,000 | .40 | $200 |
| $10,001 - $15,000 | .40 | $400 |
| $15,001 - $20,000 | .20 | $800 |

a. What should the sample size in each stratum be?
b. What would the interval estimates be for the mean of each stratum if a 95.4 percent confidence level is used?

# 4

# *Nonsampling Errors and*

# *Survey Research Design*

In the last chapter we dealt at some length with the variable error resulting from the sampling process. A body of sampling theory was introduced which allows inferences to be drawn about the probability of the sample statistic falling within some given distance from an assumed value of the population parameter.

If this were the best of all possible worlds for researchers, this would either be the only source of error in sample surveys or else other errors would be just as susceptible to systematic treatment. In the second-best world that survey researchers inhabit, such is not the case. Measurement error is always present, and other nonsampling error components—surrogate information, frame, selection, and nonresponse errors—are usually present as well. There has been no accepted body of theory that may be used to predict either the direction or magnitude of these errors.

In this chapter we first discuss the nonsampling errors and then consider each of the strategies for dealing with them. There are three strategies from which we may choose to deal with nonsampling errors. One may (1) *ignore,* (2) *estimate,* or (3) attempt to *measure* them. Our primary concern is with the effects of each of the strategies on research design. As a part of the estimation strategy, a method of combining the judgmentally determined probability distributions of the nonsampling error components with the sampling distribution to arrive at a total error probability distribution is discussed. The use of this distribution in choosing among alternative research designs is described.

## Nonsampling Errors

Measurements obtained from sample surveys are subject to both sampling and nonsampling errors. In considering nonsampling errors and their effects on survey design, you should keep clearly in mind the restricted sense in which the term *sampling error* was used in the last chapter. Sampling error refers only to the variable error resulting from the chance specification of population elements according to the sampling plan.

Nonsampling errors are diverse in origin. They may be usefully classified, however, as arising from the following sources:

1. Surrogate information error. Noncorrespondence of sought to required information
2. Measurement error. Noncorrespondence of achieved to sought information
3. Frame error. Noncorrespondence of sought to required sample
4. Selection error. Noncorrespondence of selected to sought sample
5. Nonresponse error. Noncorrespondence of achieved to selected sample

### NONCORRESPONDENCE OF SOUGHT TO REQUIRED INFORMATION—SURROGATE INFORMATION ERROR

In many problem situations in survey research it is necessary to obtain information that is a surrogate for that which we really require. The necessity to accept substitute information arises from either the inability or unwillingness of respondents to provide the information we need.

Decisionally oriented behavioral research is always concerned with prediction of behavior. While prediction is not necessarily limited to the future—espionage agents attempt to predict both the past and current behavior of individuals, for example—it is the future that is the principal concern for most decisional survey research projects. Further, it is usually nonverbal behavior that is of interest.

This limits most survey research projects to using proxy information. One cannot observe future behavior, so one must use a surrogate. Typically, one or more of several different kinds of information is obtained which is believed to be useful in predicting behavior. One may obtain information on past behavior because it is believed that there is sufficient stability in the underlying behavior pattern to give it reasonably high predictive validity. One may ask about intended behavior as a means of prediction. Or one may obtain information about attitudes, level of knowledge, or socioeconomic characteristics of the respondent in the belief that they individually or collectively have a high degree of association with future behavior.

In the example concerning the extra reserve plan, the information assumed to be desired is the total amount of money borrowed by depositors last year in small loans. This is information on past behavior. This proxy information was decided upon, presumably, because it was believed that it would be the most reliable indication of amounts depositors would borrow in the future. In a problem situation of this kind, questioning respondents concerning how much they would make use of the plan if it were available is not likely to yield reliable information. Information on intended behavior is often of limited value. Respondents are generally very poor predictors of their own behavior in "What would you do if . . ." situations posed to them. Similarly, information on attitudes, level of knowledge concerning loan sources and costs, and socio-economic characteristics are also likely to have a relatively low association with actual amounts borrowed.

It is apparent that the information on the amount borrowed last year can, at best, provide only a potential amount of borrowing through the plan. An estimate will have to be made of the share of that potential that the bank would obtain. There is thus a substantial margin for error as a result of using the surrogate variable "mean amount borrowed by depositors last year in small loans" for the variable of interest "mean amount that depositors would borrow per year in small loans through the extra reserve plan."

## NONCORRESPONDENCE OF ACHIEVED TO SOUGHT INFORMATION—MEASUREMENT ERROR

Measurement error potentially can arise in any stage of the sample survey, from the development of the instrument through the analysis of the findings. Figure 4–1 depicts the stages at which errors in eliciting information may arise in interviewing respondents.

In the transmittal stage there may be errors due to faulty wording of questions or preparations of nonverbal materials, to interviewer effects of the way he asks the question of the respondent, or the way in which the respondent interprets the question. In the response phase, errors may occur because the respondent gives incorrect information, the interviewer interprets it incorrectly, or there are errors in recording it. In the analysis stage, errors of incorrect editing and coding and descriptive summarization and inference can contribute substantially to measurement error.

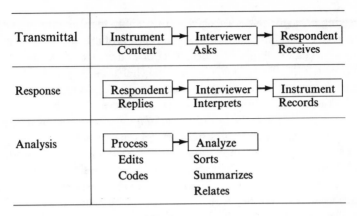

| Transmittal | Instrument → | Interviewer → | Respondent |
|---|---|---|---|
| | Content | Asks | Receives |
| Response | Respondent → | Interviewer → | Instrument |
| | Replies | Interprets | Records |
| Analysis | Process → | Analyze | |
| | Edits | Sorts | |
| | Codes | Summarizes | |
| | | Relates | |

FIGURE 4–1    Potential sources of measurement error in sample surveys

Validation studies have shown measurement error to range from being negligible to so large as to make the data useless or, even worse, misleading. A survey of 900 respondents in a single community was conducted in which data on a number of respondent characteristics were obtained.[1] It was possible to check a number of these characteristics against objective records. The resulting errors ranged from 2 to 40 percent. These errors resulted even though experienced interviewers were used. The evidence concerning the range of measurement errors with regard to financial transactions is even more dramatic. Maynes did a study of reported loans by members of a federal credit union which showed almost no inaccuracy in reporting.[2] Lansing and Blood found that automobile loans are underreported and that the rate of underreporting is greatest among high-income respondents.[3] Ferber reported validation studies on car and cash loans which showed errors of from 3.5 to 59.0 percent. The largest source of error was in nonreporting of loans by respondents.[4] One might, therefore, reasonably expect measurement errors of some magnitude in a study such as the hypothetical one for the extra reserve project.

The sources of measurement errors are dealt with in more detail in later chapters.

1. H. Parry and Helen Crossley, "Validity of Responses to Survey Questions," *Public Opinion Quarterly,* vol. 14.

2. E. Scott Maynes, "Minimizing Response Errors in Financial Data," *Journal of the American Statistical Association,* vol. 63, no. 321 (March, 1968), pp. 214–227.

3. J. B. Lansing and D. M. Blood, *The Changing Travel Market* (Ann Arbor: Survey Research Center, 1964), Monograph No. 38.

4. Robert Ferber, *The Reliability of Consumer Reports on Financial Assets and Debts* (Urbana: University of Illinois, 1966), pp. 56–64.

## NONCORRESPONDENCE OF SOUGHT TO REQUIRED SAMPLE—FRAME ERROR

A *sampling frame* is a means of accounting for all elements in the population. A listing of elements is a frame for a simple random sample, as in a map for an area sample.

The potential for frame error exists unless a perfect frame is available. A perfect frame identifies each element once, but only once. Perfect frames are seldom available for the sampling of human populations. Even the sampling of a population as well enumerated as the student body of a university or the work force of a sizable company is likely to reveal imperfections in listings. The recording of persons entering and leaving the population is likely not to be completely up to date. The sampling of people in cities, counties, or other governmental units involves far more serious frame problems.

The telephone book is a commonly used frame that introduces error. The findings of one study conducted indicates that only 90 percent of the subscribers to telephone service in the city studied (Cincinnati) were listed at the beginning of the directory year. The proportion declined to 82 percent by the end of the directory year.[5] The persons not listed at the beginning of the year are typically those who have chosen to have an unlisted number. This is likely to result in a bias with respect to income and education. There is an underrepresentation of listing of the geographically mobile, increasing the nonlisted subscribers as the year progresses.

These biases in the listing are in addition to the more obvious and important ones resulting from lack of representation of nonsubscribers. In 1965, for example, slightly more than 80 percent of the households in the United States had a telephone "available."[6] Since availability is defined as a telephone where one can be called and does not necessarily mean that a member of the household is listed in the telephone book, accessibility to households through telephone book listings was something less than 80 percent. Compared to the population as a whole, households with no availability to a telephone typically had lower incomes, the age of the head of the household was lower, and the head was more likely to be a single person.

Other frames have serious deficiencies as well. The enumeration of housing units by block by census tracts is a reasonably good frame as soon as it becomes available after each decennial census. It deteriorates between censuses, however, and may be a poor frame in a rapidly growing or

5. Sanford L. Cooper, "Random Sampling by Telephone—An Improved Method," *Journal of Marketing Research,* vol. 1 (November, 1964), pp. 45–8.
6. "Characteristics of Households with Telephones—March, 1965," *Current Population Reports,* U.S. Bureau of the Census, Series P-20, no. 146, (December 27, 1965).

declining area by the time the next census is approaching. Maps also become dated. City directories, if prepared with care, may be good frames shortly after publication, but likewise deteriorate over time.

In the extra reserve example, frame error will be minimal. One will be surveying a listing of depositors which should be complete. The only source of potential error that might be of concern is the difference in the depositor population now and at the time the plan would be placed in effect.

## NONCORRESPONDENCE OF SELECTED TO
## SOUGHT SAMPLE—SELECTION ERROR

*Selection error* arises from improper selection of respondents in a nonprobability sample. There is a natural tendency for investigators to select those respondents who are the most accessible and agreeable whenever there is latitude to do so. Convenience samples, almost by definition, are often comprised of friends and associates who bear some degree of resemblance in characteristics to those of the desired population. Quota samples typically have representatives in each cell who are the most easily reached, are better dressed, have better kept homes, and have more pleasant personalities. Judgment samples are comprised of the same types of people.

As we have already seen, the major reason for taking probability samples is to eliminate selection error.

## NONCORRESPONDENCE OF ACHIEVED TO SELECTED
## SAMPLE—NONRESPONSE ERROR

*Noncontact.* Errors arise in virtually every survey from the inability to reach the respondent. The inacessibility of some respondents is because they are not at home (NAH) on the initial call and call-backs. Others have moved or are away from home for the period of the survey. Kish reports one instance of a respondent who was drunk before he reached home every night of the survey period and was, thus, considered to be noncontactable.[7]

Not-at-home respondents are typically younger with no small children. There is a much higher proportion of working wives than among those households with someone at home. People who have moved or are away for the survey period have a higher geographic mobility than the average of the population. Thus, errors from noncontact of respondents can be anticipated in most surveys. In the four studies reported by Ferber on debt and cash loans, noncontacts ranged from zero to more than 20 percent of the sample.[8]

7. Leslie Kish, *op. cit.,* p. 534.
8. Robert Ferber, *op. cit.,* p. 59.

*Refusals.* Refusals may be by item or for the entire questionnaire. Income, religion, sex, and politics are topics which may elicit item refusals. Some respondents refuse to participate at all because of time requirements, a past experience in which an "interviewer" attempted to sell them a set of encyclopedias, their own ill health or other reasons.

A kind of refusal that is specific to the method is the nonresponse to a mail questionnaire. Nonresponse to mail questionnaires sometimes runs as high as 90 percent of the initial mailing even after several successive mailings.

In the studies reported by Ferber, refusals to provide information on money borrowed ranged from zero to only about 8 percent.[9]

# Strategies for Dealing with Nonsampling Errors

The usual confidence interval constructed around a sample value rests on the implicit assumptions that (1) sampling error is the only variable error and (2) there are no systematic errors. We know from the sampling theory introduced in the last chapter that we can reduce sampling error by either switching to a more efficient design and/or increasing sample size.

There are basically three strategies we can use to deal with nonsampling errors that we cannot control. We can (1) ignore, (2) estimate and/or (3) measure them. A discussion of these strategies follows.

### STRATEGY 1—IGNORE NONSAMPLING ERRORS

There can be little question but that this strategy is the most widely practiced of the three. Confirmation of this statement can be provided by picking up any professional journal in which empirical behavioral studies are published. If a nonprobability sample was taken, there will usually be a statement such as "if the sample taken had been a simple random one and the same values obtained the . . ." before the hypothesis is tested and the confidence interval constructed. If a random sample is taken, the usual procedure is to go ahead and test the hypothesis or construct the interval without explicitly assuming away systematic errors or other variable errors.

This may be condemned as an imprecise way to go about drawing inferences, but it is not necessarily a poor strategy in terms of results. We may examine the effects of such an assumption on inferences involving confidence intervals by calculating the change in confidence level that results from given amounts of nonsampling variable error or systematic error.

9. *Ibid.*

Total error includes sampling error and all other errors. If the variable errors in a design are independent, we may sum their variances to obtain the total variable error variance. Similarly, we may take the algebraic sum of the systematic errors to obtain a measure of the bias of the design. The expression for total error variance, also known as the *mean squared* error, is

$$(\text{Total Error})^2 = (\text{Variable Error})^2 + (\text{Systematic Error})^2$$

If $k_1$ is the nonsampling variable error measured as some multiple of the standard error of the sampling distribution, and for the moment it is assumed that there is variable nonsampling error but no systematic error, the total standard error becomes

$$\sigma_{\overline{xt}}^2 = \sigma_{\overline{x}}^2 + k_1{}^2 \sigma_{\overline{x}}^2 = (1 + k_1{}^2)\sigma_{\overline{x}}^2 \tag{4.1}$$

That is, total error variance is equal to the sum of the sampling and variable nonsampling variances.

The square root of the total error variance is the total standard error or

$$\sigma_{\overline{xt}} = \sqrt{1 + k_1{}^2}\; \sigma_{\overline{x}} \tag{4.2}$$

The total standard error can be used to calculate how the presence of $k_1\,\sigma_{\overline{x}}$ variable error affects the probability of a symmetrical confidence interval including the true population mean. We shall use a 95 percent confidence level for the example. The results for various values of $k_1$ are given in Column 2 of Table 4-1.

As indicated in the table, there is no serious deterioration of confidence level until $k_1$ reaches .25. At that point, a confidence level believed to be .950 has eroded only to .943. Beyond that, the confidence level begins to fall more sharply. Even so, at the point where the nonsampling error has become as large as the sampling error ($k_1 = 1.00$) the confidence level that is .950 with respect to sample error along is still .834 with both errors. This indicates that the confidence level is relatively insensitive to sizeable amounts of nonsampling variable error.

The effect of systematic error on the confidence level can be determined by making one change in the above procedure. We will continue to express the amount of error as a multiple of the standard deviation, but the confidence interval will be constructed around the biased estimate of the mean instead of an unbiased one. Letting $k_2$ represent the amount of systematic error as a multiple of the standard error, and assuming no nonsampling variable error, the values in Column 3 of Table 4-1 may be derived.[10]

10. This part of the table is taken from Robert Ferber, *op. cit.*, who reports that it is adapted from W. G. Cochran, *Sampling Techniques* (New York: John Wiley & Sons, 1963), p. 13.

TABLE 4–1    Effects of nonsampling variable error and systematic error on 95 percent confidence level

|  | Effect on Confidence Level of | |
|---|---|---|
| $k_i$*<br>(1) | Variable error<br>(2) | Systematic error<br>(3) |
| 0 | .950 | .950 |
| .10 | .948 | .949 |
| .25 | .943 | .941 |
| .50 | .920 | .921 |
| .75 | .883 | .883 |
| 1.00 | .834 | .830 |
| 2.00 | .618 | .484 |
| 3.00 | .465 | .149 |
| 4.00 | .365 | .021 |
| 5.00 | .300 | .001 |

*$i$ = 1 or 2

Again, we note a surprising degree of insensitivity of confidence level to systematic error. A rule of thumb of ignoring systematic errors up to one-fourth of sampling error ($k_2 = .25$) seems reasonable, if no nonsampling variable errors are believed to be present. If systematic and variable errors are *jointly* present, prudence dictates a rule of thumb that neither should exceed one-tenth of the sampling error.

It should be noted that we have dealt with the nonsampling errors as relative in amount to sampling error. As sample size increases, sampling error falls. Thus, nonsampling errors become more important as sample size increases insofar as their distorting effects on hypothesis tests and confidence intervals are concerned.

While adopting the strategy of ignoring the nonsampling errors in surveys may be sound, it should be done deliberately and explicitly. The reader of the report of the investigation should be advised that it has been done only after considering the probable size of the errors and the effects they will have. This relieves the reader of the need for estimating errors, a task that he is likely to be less well prepared to perform than the investigator.

## STRATEGY 2—ESTIMATION OF NONSAMPLING ERRORS

The exhortation just given to the investigator to ignore the nonsampling errors only after he has judged them to be of a tolerable size suggests that estimation of a kind is a necessary element of that strategy. The estimation procedure suggested here is a more formal one than required for the decisi    of whether or not to ignore the errors, however. It will also produce estimates that may be used in the decision concerning the survey design.

*Form of the Estimates.*[11] Suppose we let *r* represent the recorded sample value and *t* the true value. The *accuracy* of the estimate may then be expressed as the ratio

$$\frac{r}{t}.$$

For a particular sample this ratio will reflect the combined effects of the sample and all other variable and systematic errors present.

Estimation of the errors in the process generating *r* will allow us to draw inferences about the value of *r/t.* The sampling distribution in classical statistics is a conditional probability distribution of *p (r/t)* which includes only sampling error. An analogous distribution for our purposes is the conditional probability distribution

$$p\left(\frac{r}{t}\,\middle|\,t\right)$$

and one which includes both sampling and nonsampling errors.

For many research projects the value of *r/t* will be independent of *t.* The nonreporting of loans by respondents appears to be independent of size of the loan, for example. There also does not seem to be any relationship between size of the loan and amount of response error. [12] When such independence exists it is not necessary to condition by *t*, and the distribution used can be ρ *(r/t).*

We may then make estimates for each of the nonsampling error components using this distribution when *r/t* is independent of *t.* It will be a *prior* distribution in the Bayesian sense, as it will be subjectively determined. The amount of estimated systematic error will be shown as the difference of the expectation of this distribution and *t.* Both the variable errors in the generation process and the uncertainty of the estimate are reflected in the variance of the estimate.

We can describe the prior distribution of each nonsampling error component precisely if we are willing to assume that it is normal and specify the mean and the variance of it. In most instances the assumption of normality does no great violence to reality. A log-normal distribution may be used when the prior is skewed to the right.[13]

---

11. This section draws heavily from Rex V. Brown, *Research and the Credibility of Estimates* (Boston: Harvard University, 1969), and Charles Mayer, "Assessing the Accuracy of Marketing Research," *Journal of Marketing Research,* vol. 3 (August, 1970), pp. 285–91.
    12. See Ferber, *op. cit.*
    13. See Rex V. Brown, *op. cit.,* Appendix II B.

It is convenient to express variance in *rel-variance* units. Rel-variance is the variance divided by the mean squared or

$$rv = \frac{\sigma^2}{\mu^2} \qquad (4.3)$$

It may be more familiar as the square of the coefficient of variation.

The rel-variance is most easily estimated by use of the credible interval of the investigator. It will be recalled that a credible interval was defined in Chapter 2 as the subjective confidence interval for some designated level of confidence. A 95 percent confidence level ($\pm$ two standard errors approximately) is one with which it is seemingly easy for most investigators to work, although any confidence level may be used.

The rel-variance is estimated for a 95 percent confidence level by taking one-fourth of the credible interval, dividing it by the expectation of the error component distribution, and squaring. For the measurement error, for example, the formula is

$$rv = \left( \frac{CI}{4(m/t)} \right)^2 \qquad (4.4)$$

*Model for Combining Estimates.* We may obtain the distribution of $r/t$ by estimating the expected value and rel-variance of each of the error components and then combining them. The model for combining the expectations is

$$\left( \frac{r}{t} \right) = \left( \frac{m}{t} \right) \times \left( \frac{f}{m} \right) \times \left( \frac{s}{f} \right) \times \left( \frac{a}{s} \right) \times \left( \frac{r}{a} \right) \qquad (4.5)$$

where

> $r$ is the value recorded from the sample
> $t$ is the population value
> $m$ is the value that would result if a census were taken using this measurement technique
> $f$ is the value that would result if every element in the sampling frame were measured using this measurement technique
> $s$ is the expectation of the sampling distribution of the *selected* sample values and
> $a$ is the expectation of the sampling distrubution of *achieved* sample values

It follows that

> $1.0 - m/t$ is the noncorrespondence of achieved to sought information—the measurement error
> $1.0 - f/m$ is the noncorrespondence of sought to required sample —the frame error

1.0 − $s/f$ is the noncorrespondence of selected to sought sample —the selection error

1.0 − $a/s$ is the noncorrespondence of achieved to selected sample —the nonresponse error and

1.0 − $r/a$ is the random sampling error

The above model could be expanded to allow for surrogate information error. However, surrogate information error results from the process of *application* of the estimate of $t$ rather than the *estimation* of $t$. It is best to deal with it separately.

The formula for combining rel-variances is[14]

$$rv = \prod_{i=1}^{n} (1 + rv_i) - 1.$$

However, a satisfactory approximation is obtained from a simple addition of the rel-variances of the error components. In most instances the correction term is so small as to be negligible.

We may summarize the error estimating procedures as follows:

1. Determine which error components are to be included
2. For each nonsampling error component, estimate
    a. the mean of the ratio of the actual to the error-free measurement, and
    b. the credible interval
3. Calculate the resulting rel-variances
    a. If a *random* sample, calculate the standard error and the rel-variance of the sampling distribution
    b. If a *purposive* sample, estimate the credible interval of the sampling error and calculate the rel-variance of the sampling error
4. Combine the estimates of the means of the error component distribution by multiplying
5. Combine the estimates of the rel-variances of the error component distributions by adding

An example will illustrate the applications of this procedure.

*An Example of Error Estimation.* Suppose that personal interviews are to be taken of 250 depositors to obtain information for the extra reserve plan decision. A 10 percent noncontact refusal rate is anticipated, giving a usable sample of 225 depositors. The sampling frame is to be a list of present depositors of the bank.

The estimation of nonsampling errors can be made either before or after the survey is run. Estimation before conducting the survey permits using the estimates in the choice of the research design as well as for

14. Rex V. Brown, *op. cit.*, p. 132.

adjustment of the actual survey results when completed. Estimation after the survey allows the experience gained during the survey to be incorporated in the estimates. Estimates made after the survey are solely for the adjustment of the results.

In the example used it will be assumed that the estimation occurs before the survey is run.

1. *Determination of error components to be included.* Reflection suggests that *measurement, nonresponse,* and *random sampling* errors are present. There is no *selection error,* since a random sampling process is being used. If one assumed either that the present depositors are the population of interest or are fully representative of the depositor population after the extra reserve plan is initiated, no *frame error* is present. This assumption seems valid.

2. *Estimation of the mean of the ratio of actual to error-free measurement, credible intervals and calculation of rel-variances.* The *measurement errors* found in the validation studies reported by Ferber ranged, as stated earlier, from 3.5 to 59.0 percent. The principal error source was the non-reporting of debts by respondents. However, the investigators in one of the studies experimented with the technique of handing the respondent one envelope with the part of the questionnaire concerning outstanding loans and amounts enclosed. The respondent was asked to complete the questionnaire and mail it. For the respondents for whom this technique was used, measurement error was reduced to only about one-fifth of that for those respondents for whom it was not used. For those respondents who reported loans, the response error ranged from underreporting of 8 percent to overreporting of 10 percent with a mean of almost zero.

Assuming that these experiences provide a reasonable guide for measurement error estimation in the extra-reserve study and that the envelope technique will be used, the mean of the measurement error distribution is assessed as .75. The .95 percent credible interval is judged as .75 $\pm$ .40. The resulting rel-variance is $[.40/4 \times .75]^2 = .0177$.

Concerning the *nonresponse error,* both the validation studies reported by Ferber and those by Broida[15] indicate noncontacted and refusing respondents each had somewhat larger debts than those who responded. The amount of underestimation of the mean debt which resulted was approximately 2 percent for each. The investigator assesses the mean of the noncontact and the refusal distributions as .98 and the credible interval of each as .98 $\pm$ .02. The rel-variance for each is calculated as .0001.

3. *Calculation of the standard error and the rel-variance of the sam-*

15. Arther L. Broida, "Consumer Surveys as a Source of Information for Social Accounting—the Problems," *Studies in Income and Wealth,* vol. 26, National Bureau of Economic Research.

*pling distribution.* Since an unbiased estimate of the population mean is provided by a simple random sample, the expectation of the sampling distribution is 1.0.

It will be recalled that the mean and standard deviations of the population have been estimated earlier as $\hat{\mu} = \$125$ and $\hat{\sigma}_{\bar{x}} = \$175$. The estimated standard error of the mean is then

$$\hat{\sigma}_{\bar{x}} = \frac{\hat{\sigma}_x}{\sqrt{n}} = \frac{\$175}{\sqrt{225}} = \$11.67$$

and the coefficient of variation of the sampling distribution is

$$CV = \frac{\hat{\sigma}_{\bar{x}}}{\hat{\mu}} = \frac{\$11.67}{\$125} = \$.094$$

An additional source of random error other than that introduced by the process of sampling elements is possible and appears to be present in this situation. This is the variability in responses that would occur if the interviews were replicated a large number of times with the same respondents. The factor to allow for this source of variability is assessed at 1.2. Multiplying the coefficient of variation by 1.2 and squaring gives a rel-variance of sampling of .0127.

4. *Combination of the estimates of the means of the error component distribution.* The estimates are assembled in Table 5. The mean of the combined distribution, .72, is obtained as the product of the means of the individual distributions.

5. *Estimation of the rel-variance of the combined distribution.* The rel-variance of the combined distribution .0307, is also shown in Table 4-2. It was obtained by summing the individual component distribution rel-variances.

The correction term is shown for information only; it was obtained from Equation 4.6, subtracting the value obtained from summing the rel-variances from it. One logically either uses the sum of the rel-variances and ignores the correction term or uses the above formula.

The result of the error estimation is to emerge with a probability distribution, $p(\overline{X}/\mu)$, which permits us to allow for all the systematic and variable errors of the survey. Our best estimate of the population mean will be $\mu = 1.00/.72 \ \overline{X}$ (since $\overline{X}/\mu = .72/1.00$). Further, we can assert with a 95 percent level of confidence that the true population mean will lie between $\bar{\mu} - (1.96(.1725))$ and $\bar{\mu} + (1.96(.1725))$, since the coefficient of variation is

$$\sqrt{.0307} = .1725.$$

TABLE 4–2   Extra reserve plan—assessment of errors of projected personal interview survey

| Error source | Mean | Credible interval limits | Rel-variance |
|---|---|---|---|
| Measurement | .75 | .55 - .95 | .0177 |
| Frame | 1.00 | 1.00 - 1.00 | - |
| Selection | 1.00 | 1.00 - 1.00 | - |
| Noncontact | .98 | .96 - 1.00 | .0001 |
| Refusal | .98 | .96 - 1.00 | .0001 |
| Random sampling | 1.00 | not applicable | .0127 |
| Correction term | | | .0001 |
| Combined assessments | .72 | .47 - .97* | .0307 |

*The limits are derived from the values of the combined mean and combined rel-variance.

## STRATEGY 3—ERROR MEASUREMENT

It should be noted in Table 4-2 that the error from the measurement component is estimated to be larger than the random sampling error. It is obviously uneconomic to spend substantial sums of money to reduce the variable error from sampling if the equally large variable and systematic errors from other sources can be reduced or measured less expensively. By reducing the sample size of the personal interview study from 225 to 144 completed questionnaires, for example, sampling rel-variance is increased from .0127 to .0196. If the average variable cost per completed questionnaire is equal to $c$ over this range, an amount equal to $(225–144)\,c$ is saved. If this amount can be used to reduce the rel-variance from one or more other sources by more than the increase in the sampling rel-variance, net reduction in total rel-variance is realized.

The principle involved here is the equating of marginal products. The reduction in rel-variance at the margin should be the same for sampling, measurement, frame, and each of the other error components. While an exact equating of rel-variance reductions is a goal that can only be approximated at best, it is a principle that should be considered in the design of every project.

*Measuring Measurement Error.* Measurement error was defined earlier as $1.0 - m/t$, where $m$ is the value that would result if a census were taken using this measurement technique and $t$ is the true value.

Several procedures are useful for estimating measurement error. An estimate of the error may be obtained by obtaining data from a subsample of respondents through carefully conducted verification call-backs. Special procedures can be devised for these respondents—the best interviewers assigned for the call-backs, observation used whenever possible, corroboration from neighbors sought, etc. The "error" of the initial measurement for the subsample of respondents can be determined and applied to the sample as a whole. The rationale for using this procedure on only a follow-up subsample rather than the entire sample of respondents initially is an economic one.

A close variation of this procedure is to include alternate means of measuring the same value in the survey design. This in effect involves setting up an experiment within the survey to determine the effect of different measurement methods on resulting recorded values. In instances where the recorded values show wide variations, one may, of course, not be able to determine the true value. However, sensitivity analysis may indicate that if the measured values at each extreme were the true value that the same decision would be made. In this case it will have been determined that the measurement error is within tolerable limits and so there is no need to know the true value.

One may use other variables in the survey as experimental treatments as well. Measured values by interviewer should be recorded, and a comparison made among interviewers. If respondents have been assigned to interviewers on a reasonably random basis, significant variations in average value between interviewers is suggestive that *interviewer effects* are likely to be present. Verification call-backs may be indicated or adjustment may be made to correct for interviewer biasing effects, if there is other evidence they are present.

Alternate wording for questions to avoid *order bias* and positioning of question to avoid *position bias* are potential treatments which should be considered in preparing questionnaires. If the question is asked, "Which kind of gasoline do you prefer, leaded or non-leaded?" it is probable that substantially different responses will be received than if the question were ended with the reverse order of alternatives, for example, "non-leaded or leaded?" It is not clear whether the referent of "better" is the respondent's car or the air he breathes. It is almost certain that a significantly different set of responses would be received if several questions to be asked on air pollution were asked before this question than if they were asked after it.

Asking the question in both alternate forms or in alternate positions in the questionnaire to subsamples of respondents is a way of determining these differential effects. Two or more questionnaires may be necessary for this purpose. The investigator may be more interested in canceling errors than in measuring them; in the ordering of alternatives in questions, for example, neither question form will necessarily give the "true" value.

*Frame Error.* It is the exceptional survey research project for which a perfect frame is available. In the extra reserve project, a reasonably close approximation to a perfect frame is provided by the listing of present depositors for either a personal interview or mail questionnaire design. The frame for a telephone survey would be considerably less than perfect, however. In many survey research projects, the best listing of population elements that is available is the telephone book.

Frame errors consist of both over- and underrepresentation of various strata of the population in the sample. So long as one can identify respondents by the variables that are used for stratification, the strata proportions in the populations are known, and the assumption is made that the sample elements included in the underrepresented stratum are representative of all elements in the stratum, errors can be measured and adjustment made for them.

Sometimes such assumptions are not justified. People in households with telephones may differ significantly from those without telephones with respect to the characteristic of interest, even though life cycle stage, income, occupation, education and other demographic variables are the same. In such cases frame error can be measured only by taking a sample of those population elements that are underrepresented by the frame.

*Selection Error.* Potential selection error for nonprobability sampling plans is indicated when the strata proportions in the sample are different than those in the sampling plan. The procedure for measuring selection error is the same as that for frame error.

*Noncontact Error.* While a complete measurement of noncontact error is not possible, information for estimating it more accurately can usually be obtained. Noncontact can be the result of inability to reach the respondent for reason of his having moved out of the area, his being temporarily out of the area (vacation, business, etc.), illness (physical or mental), language barrier, or illiteracy. It can also result from inaccessibility (lighthouse keeper, forest ranger); storms or floods may make the respondents in some survey areas inaccessible for the entire period.

Clearly, some of these sample respondents not contacted for the above reasons can be reached with the expenditure of extra time and effort. Movers can be called, and illiterate respondents can be interviewed personally. Floods subside and storms abate, people return from vacations and recover from illnesses. The number of noncontacts, therefore, can be reduced. A hard core will remain, however. Those that remain may well be substantially different in the characteristics of interest than those contacted after special effort. Unless external sources of data are available (the credit report in the extra reserve project is an example), they must remain in the noncontact category. One must be careful about extrapolating the results from surveying the respondents who were originally noncontacts but who were reached with special effort to the remaining hard core noncontacts.

*Nonresponse Error.* Nonresponse errors resulting from refusals are similar to noncontact errors with respect to difficulty of measurement. Respondents may refuse to give information they are able to give because they believe that to comply would be a violation of privacy, time pressures, lack of rapport with interviewer, lack of motivation, or other reasons. In addition to being unwilling to give information, respondents are sometimes *unable* to provide the information for which they are asked.

The approach to measuring the errors resulting from refusals is identical to that for noncontacts. Some respondents will succumb to extra effort, and external data may be available for others.

A discussion of the measurement of the validity and the reliability of measurements is given in the next chapter. These measurements are closely allied to the ones just discussed.

## Error Ratio Analysis

One of the important reasons for the estimation of nonsampling errors is for the selection of a research design. The two criteria of major importance in selecting one design from among contending designs are (1) the amount of total error believed to be present and (2) cost. In error ratio analysis, we have an effective means of dealing with the total error criterion.

Suppose we recast the example we have been using into a design choice situation. To do this we may suppose that the researcher has narrowed the alternative designs for the survey research project in the extra reserve plan to a personal interview, mail survey, and telephone survey. Further, suppose that he is operating from a fixed research budget and wishes to choose the best of the three within this budgetary constraint.

We have already described the personal interview alternative. The mail survey option will involve an initial mailing of 1,500 questionnaires to a simple random sample of depositors. Four follow-up mailings will be made. A final return of 60 percent is expected which will result in 900 usuable questionnaires. The telephone survey will consist of selecting 875 depositor households by simple random sample and calling them. An 80 percent interview completion rate is expected resulting in 700 completed interviews.

Assessments of the errors in the mail and telephone survey design are made by the same procedure as was used for the personal interview designs.

We may assume that the results of his assessments are as shown in Table 4-3. (Table 4-2 has been reproduced as part of Table 4-3 for convenience.)

The data in Table 4-3 indicate that the mail survey design should be chosen. All three designs are estimated to cost the same, so that cost is not a factor in the decision. The total error criterion can be reduced to a consideration of rel-variance only as corrections are made for the systematic errors. Since the rel-variance of the mail survey is the smallest by a substantial margin, it should be chosen.

TABLE 4–3   Extra reserve plan—assessment of errors of mail, telephone, and personal interview surveys

| Error source | Mean | Credible interval limits | Rel-variance |
|---|---|---|---|
| *Mail Survey* | | | |
| Measurement | .90 | .75 - 1.05 | .0068 |
| Frame | 1.00 | 1.00 - 1.00 | - |
| Selection | 1.00 | 1.00 - 1.00 | - |
| Noncontact | 1.00 | .90 - 1.10 | .0025 |
| Refusal | .95 | .85 - 1.05 | .0031 |
| Random sampling | 1.00 | not applicable | .0026 |
| Combined assessments | .86 | .67 - 1.05 | .0150 |
| *Telephone Survey* | | | |
| Measurement | .70 | .45 - .95 | .0319 |
| Frame | 1.00 | .80 - 1.20 | .0100 |
| Selection | 1.00 | 1.00 - 1.00 | - |
| Noncontact | .98 | .95 - 1.01 | .0002 |
| Refusal | .97 | .94 - 1.00 | .0002 |
| Random sampling | 1.00 | not applicable | .0045 |
| Combined assessments | .67 | .38 - .96 | .0473 |
| *Personal Interviews* | | | |
| Measurement | .75 | .55 - .95 | .0177 |
| Frame | 1.00 | 1.00 - 1.00 | - |
| Selection | 1.00 | 1.00 - 1.00 | - |
| Noncontact | .98 | .96 - 1.00 | .0001 |
| Refusal | .98 | .96 - 1.00 | .0001 |
| Random sampling | 1.00 | not applicable | .0127 |
| Combined assessments | .72 | .47 - .97 | .0307 |

## Summary

In this chapter, our concern has been with nonsampling errors and their effects on sample survey measurements. That these errors are a proper subject for concern in survey design was demonstrated in the chapter; even individually they may be substantially larger than sampling error.

We begin with an identification and description of the principal sampling errors. Errors arising from surrogate information, measurement, the sampling frame, selection, and nonresponse were discussed at some length.

The proposal has been made that a validation study should be included as a part of virtually every behavioral science survey.[16] This proposal argues for the near universal adoption of a strategy of measuring nonsampling errors. Two additional strategies were presented in this chapter; ignoring and estimating nonsampling errors were discussed as well as measuring them. It is our contention that the choice among these strategies should be governed by a consideration of the value of the information provided versus the cost of obtaining it in each instance.

Nonsampling errors and their effects on design have received far less attention in the sampling literature than they deserve. The reason for this has largely been the lack of a theoretical framework which would permit systematic treatment. The development of procedures for assessing and combining subjective probability distributions for the nonsampling error components permits the joint and formal consideration of nonsampling and sampling errors in designing the sample survey project.

### SELECTED BIBLIOGRAPHY

Brown, Rex V. *Research and the Credibility of Estimates.* Boston: Harvard University, 1969. The pioneering work in error ratio analysis.

Ferber, Robert. *The Reliability of Consumer Reports on Financial Assets and Debts.* Urbana: University of Illinois, 1966. The report of a series of carefully done investigations of error in the reporting of household financial data.

Kish, Leslie. *Survey Sampling.* New York: John Wiley & Son, 1964, especially Chapter 13. An authoritative book, in which theoretical requirements and practical constraints are presented. The statistical treatment is non-Bayesian.

Madow, W. G. "On Some Aspects of Response Error Measurements," *Proceedings of the Social Statistics Section of the American Statistical Association.* Washington: American Statistical Association, 1965, pp. 102–192. An excellent review article on the measurement of response error.

Mayer, Charles. "Assessing the Accuracy of Marketing Research," *Journal of Marketing Research,* vol. 7 (August, 1970). A tightly written article which presents and applies error ratio analysis.

16. W. G. Madow, "On Some Aspects of Response Error Measurement," *Proceedings of the Social Statistics Section of the American Statistical Association* (Washington: American Statistical Association, 1965), pp. 102–192.

## QUESTIONS AND PROBLEMS

4.1. Discuss the extent of the surrogate information error present in each of the following research situations:

| Information Required | Information Sought |
|---|---|
| a. Consumer purchases of medium priced table wines during the next 12 months | Consumer purchase intentions over the next 12 months |
| b. Purchases of ten-speed bicycles during the next 12 months | Actual purchases during the last 12 months |

4.2. An experiment was once conducted in which three matched samples of respondents were asked one of the following three questions:

1. Do you think anything should be done to make it easier to pay doctor or hospital bills? (82 percent replied "Yes")
2. Do you think anything could be done to make it easier to pay doctor or hospital bills? (77 percent replied "Yes")
3. Do you think anything might be done to make it easier to pay doctor or hospital bills? (63 percent replied "Yes")

These questions are identical except for the use of the words *should, could* and *might.*

Is this an example of measurement error? Explain.

4.3. Suppose you are conducting a telephone survey to determine the proportion of retailers that carry a certain product. Further suppose the critical proportion for an action being considered is 25 percent. Assume that you obtain the following results:

| | |
|---|---|
| Sample size | 500 |
| Number carrying | 90 |
| Number not carrying | 360 |
| Number not responding | 50 |

What alternatives does the researcher have with regard to this situation? Which one would you recommend he choose?

4.4. The formula for the measurement error rel-variance for a 95 percent confidence level is

$$rv = \left( \frac{CI}{4(m/t)} \right)^2$$

Derive this formula.

*4.5. Assume that the measurement rel-variance in the mail survey example (Table 6) could be reduced to .0035 by a series of personal interviews. To do so, however, would require a reallocation of expenditure that would result in an initial mailing sample size of about 1,040 instead of 1,500. The number of usable returns would correspondingly be reduced from 900 to about 625.

a. What would the new total rel-variance be for the mail survey?

b. Would this reallocation of resources be a reasonable one? Explain.

4.6. Explain what you understand by the statement: "The major design principle for survey research projects is the equaling of marginal reduction in rel-variance among error components. The reduction in rel-variance at the margin should be the same for sampling, measurement, frame, and each of the other error components."

# 5

# *Measurement and Scaling*

One of the major kinds of nonsampling errors discussed in Chapter 4 is measurement error. The overall quality of a survey research project depends not only upon the appropriateness and adequacy of the research design and sampling techniques used but also on the measurement procedures used. Measurement can proceed only after defining the variable or variables to be studied. In other words, the investigator must first know *what* he must measure before tackling the problem of *how* to measure it.

In this chapter, we are concerned with both constructing a measuring instrument, or scale, and using it, although the emphasis is on development rather than use. How various measuring instruments can be used is discussed in Chapter 6. Even though we separate our discussion, the instrument or scale and the means of implementing its use are directly related. Moreover, the subject of measurement is also related to questionnaire construction (a subject discussed in Chapter 7). A questionnaire is in itself a measurement instrument that uses different types of more specific measuring devices or scales.

We begin our discussion by looking at the concept of measurement and the major types of measurement scales. Next we discuss the major causes of variation in measurement scores. Finally, validity and reliability of measurement are covered in some detail.

## Concept of Measurement

We shall view measurement as it pertains to properties or characteristics of objects and not to the objects themselves. In general, we can think of measurement as "the assignment of numbers to objects to represent amounts or degrees of a property possessed by all of the objects."[1] More narrowly, we define measurement in survey research as the assignment of numbers indicative of quantity to properties or characteristics or behavior of people.

If one is to be able to represent a characteristic or property or behavioral act by numbers, there must exist a one-to-one correspondence between the number system used and the relations between various quantities (degrees) of that which is being measured. Three important characteristics or features of the real number series itself are as follows:

1. *Order.* Numbers are ordered
2. *Distance.* Differences between numbers are ordered
3. *Origin.* The series has a unique origin which is indicated by the number zero

In measurement, then, numbers are assigned to objects (people) in such a way that the relations between the numbers reflect the relations between the objects (people) with respect to the characteristic involved.[2] The end result is establishment of a scale of measurement, which allows the investigator to make comparisons of amounts and changes in the property being measured.

Measurement can be distinguished on the basis of level, according to the characteristics of order, distance, and origin. Measurement occurs at different levels according to the number of these characteristics possessed by the numbers. This leads to different types of scales.

Before proceeding further, a note of caution is in order. The process of assigning numbers to properties does not eliminate the qualitative nature of the property. The result of quantification is that greater precision and reliability is achieved in measuring the *qualities* which are considered important. In addition, it should be recognized that all measurement is to some extent indirect. For instance, as we pointed out in Chapter 4, surrogate information often is utilized in survey research, and such information is a source of error.

## Scales of Measurement

In our everyday lives, we tend to think about measurement in the sense of well-defined scales having a natural zero point and constant unit

1. Warren S. Torgerson, *Theory and Methods of Scaling* (New York: John Wiley & Sons, Inc., 1958), p. 19.
2. *Ibid.,* p. 15.

of measurement. At one time or another, we have found it helpful or necessary to use measuring instruments such as yardsticks, gasoline gauges, and weighing scales to determine such things as heights, volume, and weights.

There are various types of scales which are based on the underlying assumptions regarding the correspondence of numbers to the properties of objects and the meaningfulness of performing mathematical operations on these numbers. One classification of scales that is useful to investigators engaged in survey research is that proposed by Stevens: *nominal, ordinal, interval,* and *ratio.*[3] The relationship among these four types of scales —with respect to empirical operations, mathematical group structure, and allowable statistical treatment—is presented in Table 5–1.

The types of scales are listed in ascending order of "power" in that the "stronger" scales presuppose the ability to perform the empirical and mathematical operations of the "weaker" ones. As such, the columns are cumulative; to an empirical operation, a mathematical transformation, and

TABLE 5–1   Types of measurement scales

| Scale | Basic empirical operations | Mathematical group structure | Permissible statistics (invariantive) |
|---|---|---|---|
| Nominal | Determination of equality | *Permutation group* $Y = f(X)$ $f(X)$ means any one-to-one correspondence | Number of cases Mode Contingency correlations (Chi-square, Fisher's exact test) |
| Ordinal | Determination of greater or less | *Isotonic group* $Y = f(X)$ $f(X)$ means any increasing monotonic transformation | Median Percentiles Rank-order correlation Sign test Run test |
| Interval | Determination of equality of intervals or differences | *General linear group* $Y = a + bX$ | Arithmetic mean Standard deviation Average deviation Product-moment correlation Correlation ratio $t$-test; $F$-test |
| Ratio | Determination of equality of ratios | *Similarity group* $Y = aX$ $a > 0$ | Coefficient of variation Geometric mean Harmonic mean |

Sources: Adapted from Stevens, "On the Theory of Scales of Measurement," p. 678; and, S. S. Stevens, "Measurement, Statistics, and the Schemapiric View" in Dennis P. Forcese and Stephen Richer, eds., *Stages of Social Research: Contemporary Perspectives* (Englewood Cliffs: Prentice-Hall, Inc., 1970), p. 80.

3. S. S. Stevens, "On the Theory of Scales of Measurement," *Science,* vol. 103, no. 2684 (June 7, 1946), pp. 677–680.

the types of statistical operations indicated as appropriate to a particular type of scale, must be added all those listed above it or them.

## NOMINAL SCALE

The lowest level of measurement is classification measurement, which consists simply of classifying objects, events, individuals, etc., into categories. Each category is given a name or assigned a number; the numbers are used only as labels or type numbers. Nothing else is inferred, that is, there is no empirical relation among the numbered categories. Hence, the classification scheme is referred to as a *nominal scale.*

The basic requirement for constructing a nominal scale is that the investigator be able to distinguish at least two categories, which are mutually exclusive and collectively exhaustive with respect to the property or characteristic under study. Each object or individual must be able to be placed into one and only one category. For example, in survey research the investigator often is interested in knowing the breakdown of his population or sample according to such nominal variables as sex, nationality, religion, marital status, and so forth. These and other similar variables can usually be the basis of a nominal scale in that individuals can be assigned relatively easily to only one category, and everyone can be assigned to some category. Similarly, in the extra reserve plan example used throughout this book, a bank would be able to classify its depositors according to whether or not money was borrowed during the past year. The simplest scale would have two categories—"borrowed money" and "did not borrow money."

The empirical operation followed in assigning objects or inividuals to categories is simply that a specific object belongs in a specific category, or it does not. Consequently, there must be criteria specified for placing objects in one or another category. The end result of this operation is the determination of so-called equivalence classes of objects. All members of a given class are equal with respect to a specified property.

Although the use of numbers as names for groups is a definite example of assigning numbers according to a rule, a nominal scale is qualitatively different from the other three types of scales. Nominal scales are both discrete and qualitative. Since any numbers that are assigned to categories making up a nominal scale serve only as tags or labels (in the same ways as words or letters), any arithmetic operations performed other than counting have no meaning whatsoever. One can find the modal category of the scale, because it involves a count of the number of items in that category. There is no mean for the category, however, as there is no quantitative difference between items in it. Thus, numbers are not assigned to represent amounts or degrees of a property. Also, classification or categorization does not necessarily imply the existence of a continuum. Although nominal scaling is not scaling in the same sense as the other types, it is a very useful related concept.

Due to its limitations concerning statistical treatment, a nominal scale is characteristic of exploratory research where the emphasis is on uncovering relationships rather than on specifying the form of relationship, or where the objective is to look at the pattern of relationship among two or more characteristics of the individual. In this type of survey research, we often are interested in determining the number of people possessing certain amounts of a characteristic, specifying the most numerous class, or using contingency methods to test hypotheses about distributions of objects among the classes comprising a nominal scale.

## ORDINAL SCALE

Categorization of objects or individuals is usually a relatively easy task. More difficult is the ordering of classes or individuals according to relevant criteria. The task of ordering, or ranking, results in an ordinal scale, which defines the relative position of objects or individuals according to some property. There is no determination of distance between positions on the scale. The investigator is limited, therefore, to determination of "greater than," "equal to," or "less than." For any given individual from the set of individuals being measured, one cannot say how much more or less of a property this individual possesses than any other individual.

In the extra reserve plan situation, an investigator may ask a sample of depositors to express their preferences concerning various forms of borrowing. Suppose that credit cards are the most preferred, followed by installment purchase and then a direct loan. These data form an ordinal scale.

A key characteristic of an ordinal scale is the property of transitivity (that is, if $X > Y$, and $Y > Z$, then $X > Z$). If this does not hold for all objects or individuals, then a true ordinal scale does not exist, although it is possible for ties to exist. If borrowing for purchases by using a credit card is preferred to using an installment purchase plan and using installment buying is preferred to a monetary loan, then using credit cards must be preferred to a monetary loan if the relationship is transitive. If such is not the case, we might suspect that more than one dimension is involved and a unique ordering on a single dimension is not truly possible.[4]

The kinds of statistical procedures that can be used with ordinal

4. This type of situation brings up the distinction between scales that are *unidimensional* and those that are *multidimensional*. Our discussion so far has been concerned with the former, although much of what we have said is also applicable to the latter. Multidimensional scaling involves techniques for combining positions on the number of dimensions involved into a single score to represent the amount of a property, which can then be scaled. We will discuss multidimensional scaling later in this chapter.

measures are outlined in Table 5-1. Over the years, many techniques have been developed especially for use with no higher level of measurement than ordinal measurement. These are called *nonparametric statistics*. In addition to the rather limited types of statistics that can be applied "legitimately" to data that allow only rank ordering, we find that means and standard deviations often are used. While it may be useful to run such analyses, it should always be kept in mind that when one does so he is assuming that the data are from a scale that measures distances (interval or ratio scale) rather than only order.

## INTERVAL SCALE

The interval scale has all the characteristics of the ordinal scale, and, in addition, the units of measure—or intervals between successive positions—are equal. This type of scale is of a form that is truly "quantitative," in the ordinary and usual meaning of the word. Almost all the usual statistical measures are applicable to interval measurement, unless a measure implies knowing what the true zero point is.

With an equal interval scale one cannot make assertions about the ratios of a property possessed by one object as compared to another. We can say, however, how much more one set of differences in amounts is compared to another set of differences. This means that while a score of 90 is not necessarily twice that of 45, the difference between 90 and 50 is four times the difference between 45 and 35. Thus, differences between amounts on an interval scale can be treated as ratios.

The reason for the above "limitation" is that the origin or zero point is not natural but is arbitrarily determined. This is evidenced by the fact that the scale form is invariant when a constant is added—that is, the set of numbers associated with an interval scale is determined to within a linear transformation of the form $Y = bX + a$. The centigrade and fahrenheit temperature scales are widely used interval scales, and the relationship between them $(F = 32 + 9/5C)$ illustrates the linear transformation property of interval scales.

Interval scales, or attempts at creating such scales, are found often in behavioral research. This is particularly true for measurement of attitudes and certain psychological characteristics such as intelligence and learning. A measure of the degree of "friendliness" of a bank from $-5$ ("very unfriendly") to $+5$ ("very friendly") is designed to be an interval scale measurement.

To sum up, the interval scale possesses the characteristics of order and distance of the number system. The investigator has freedom, however, to assign two numbers arbitrarily: the unit of measure and the origin.

## RATIO SCALE

In essence a ratio scale is an interval scale with natural origin (that is, "true" zero point). Thus, the ratio scale is the only type possessing all characteristics of the number system. Such a scale is possible only when there exist empirical operations for determining all four relations: equality, rank-order, equality of intervals, and equality of ratios. Once a ratio scale has been established, its values can be transformed only by multiplying each value by a constant. Thus, on a ratio scale, a score of 90 is twice that of 45.

Ratio scales are found more commonly in the physical sciences than in the social sciences. Measures of weight, length, time intervals, area, velocity, etc., all conform to ratio scales. In the social sciences, we do find properties of concern that can be ratio scaled: money, age, years of education, etc. However, successful ratio scaling of behavioral attributes is rare.

If one were asked to choose between data that were nominal, ordinal, interval, or ratio scaled, and there were no differences in cost, one would always choose ratio scaled data. The logic behind this choice is that it is always better to be in a position to do more than is necessary in measurement than not be able to do enough. For decisional research purposes, however, the added value associated with developing and using a ratio scale may not be worth the added cost that would be incurred. Even if basic research is involved, ratio scales, while definitely desirable, are not absolutely necessary, because most of what has to be done in behavioral measurement can be done with equal-interval scales or equal-appearing interval scales.[5] The most serious limitation is the lack of an equal interval. Moreover, there are certain properties, characteristics, and behavior of people that are just not ratio scalable.

## OTHER TYPES OF SCALES

Clyde H. Coombs expands on Stevens' four categories of scale types by adding two additional types.[6] Between nominal and ordinal scales lies the *partially ordered* scale. This type of scale exists when the members of a class (in the nominal scale sense) are more of something than the members of another class and it is meaningful to signify that the relation "greater than" holds, in some respect. If the relation holds between some pairs of

5. Fred N. Kerlinger, *Foundations of Behavioral Research* (New York: Holt, Rinehart and Winston, Inc., 1964), p. 426.

6. See Clyde H. Coombs, "Theory and Methods of Social Measurement," in Leon Festinger and Daniel Katz, eds. *Research Methods in the Behavioral Sciences* (New York: Holt, Rinehart and Winston, 1953), pp. 471–535.

equivalence classes from a nominal scale, the result is a partially ordered scale.

Between the ordinal and interval scale, Coombs places the *ordered metric* scale, which is characterized by a simple ordering of the objects on a scale and by at least a partial ordering on the magnitudes of the distances between adjacent objects.[7] The ordered metric scale is one in which for any triplet of cases $a > b > c$, and that for at least some intervals between classes, say the intervals $\overline{ab}$, $\overline{bc}$ ... $\overline{ij}$ ... $\overline{kl}$, either $\overline{ij} > \overline{kl}$ or $\overline{kl} > \overline{ij}$ Coombs uses as an example the scaling of authority in the military, according to rank. If an ordered metric scale exists, one must be able to say that the difference in authority between, say, a corporal and a sergeant is either greater than, less than, or equal to the difference in authority between, say, a private and a corporal. Thus, differences between adjacent objects can be ordered, but comparisons of differences cannot be expressed as numerical ratios.

## Sources of Variation in Measurement

Variations in a set of measurements compiled from any measuring instrument arises from a variety of specific sources or factors. These sources may affect both the characteristic or property of concern as well as the measurement process itself. In evaluating the results of any measurement, a major problem arises in attempting to distinguish the portion of the variation among individual scores that can be considered as representing true differences in that which is being measured from the portion of variation that represents error in measurement. Although there are many possible sources that can cause variations in scores, they can be categorized as shown in Table 5–2. The sources indicated are, of course, potential sources; for any given survey, not all necessarily will be operative.

In the first place, variation within a set of measurements can represent only true differences in the characteristic being measured. This, of course, is the ideal situation. For instance, a bank wanting to measure attitudes toward establishing an extra reserve plan would like to feel confident that differences in measurements concerning the plan represent the individuals' differences in this attitude, and that none of the differences are a reflection of chance variations or other attitudes, such as the individuals' attitudes toward the bank itself.

Obviously, the ideal situation seldom, if ever, arises. Often, measurements are affected by characteristics of individual respondents such as intelligence, education level achieved, and personality attibutes. Therefore, the results of a survey will reflect not only differences among individuals in the characteristic of interest but also differences in other characteristics of

7. *Ibid.*, pp. 477–481.

TABLE 5–2 Possible sources of variation in measurement scores

---

I. *True differences in the characteristic or property being measured.*

II. *Other relatively stable characteristics of individuals which affect scores*: e.g., intelligence, extent of education, information processed.

III. *Transient personal factors*: e.g., health, fatigue, motivation, emotional strain.

IV. *Situational factors*: e.g., rapport established, distractions that arise.

V. *Variations in administration of measuring instrument*: e.g., interviewers.

VI. *Sampling of items included in instrument.*

VII. *Lack of clarity of measuring instrument*: e.g., ambiguity, complexity, interpretation.

VIII. *Mechanical factors*: e.g., lack of space to record response, appearance of instrument.

IX. *Factors in the analysis*: e.g., scoring, tabulation, statistical compilation.

X. *Variation not otherwise accounted for (chance)*: e.g., guessing an answer.

---

Source: Adapted from C. Selltiz, et al., *Research Methods in Social Relations* (New York: Holt, Rinehart and Winston, Inc., Rev. Ed., 1959), pp. 149-154, and Robert L. Thorndike, *Personnel Selection: Test and Measurement Techniques* (New York: John Wiley & Sons, Inc., 1949), p. 73.

the individuals. Unfortunately, this type of situation cannot be controlled easily, unless the investigator knows all the relevant characteristics of the members of the population such that control can be introduced through the sampling process.

Differences in measurement scores also may arise when personal factors such as health, mood, state of fatigue, etc., vary among the respondents. These transient personal characteristics of people do not necessarily affect different measurement instruments in the same way. Closely related to these personal factors is the setting in which measurement occurs. For instance, if measurement is to be limited to a sample of married women, individual responses may vary depending upon whether the husband is present. Not only is this source of variation potentially present in a cross-sectional survey, but it is often an even greater danger in longitudinal studies. In any event, the danger lies in the investigator not knowing that this source of variation is operative.

Other sources of variation in measurement scores come from the instrument inself. In the first place, any measuring instrument includes only a sample of items relevant to the characteristic or property of concern. Thus, if we attempt to analyze variations in a characteristic, for example, an attitude, that was measured by different instruments, we must recognize that the measures are not entirely comparable. Obviously, the effect of this source decreases as the number of relevant items included in an instrument increases.

Another source of variation in responses is the clarity of the measuring instrument itself. Ambiguity and complexity resulting from choice of words or context may mean that respondents have to interpret meaning. People tend to interpret statements differently and will respond accordingly.

The more mechanical aspects of measurement also can have an effect on measurement. These arise from both the construction of the instrument and the recording and analysis of responses. One must be extremely careful in performing tasks such as scoring, tabulation, and statistical manipulation if errors are to be prevented.

Finally, there may be some variation that is not otherwise accounted for. This may arise because respondents simply guess at answers. Consequently, responses are a result of chance.

The above discussion shows that there are many influences on a measurement other than the characteristic of concern—that is, there are many sources of error. What we have presented can be called *measurement error*, which, it will be recalled from Chapter 4, is only one major source of error. Measurement error has a constant (systematic) dimension as well as a random (variable) dimension. These two subtypes of measurement error affect the validity and reliability of measurement, to which we now turn.

## Validity and Reliability of Measurement

In the last chapter the total error was defined as $1 - r/t$, where $r$ represents the value recorded from the sample and $t$ the true value. If one wants to measure total error one has to take one of three possible approaches. He may (1) try to measure each error component and obtain an algebraic sum of all errors, (2) he may obtain a measure of $t$, or (3) he may measure the variation in $r$ that results from one or more forms of replication of the measure.

The first of these approaches was used in the last chapter. It is a relatively recent development. Consideration of approaches (2) and (3) and how they can be performed have gone on as long as formalized research projects have been conducted, however. The attempt to measure $t$ and compare it to $r$ is concerned with the *validity* of the measurement. The measure of the variability in $r$ is the *reliability* of the measurement. The literature on each is extensive.

If a measurement is valid, then reliability is of little or no concern, since replication is not a matter of the utmost concern in decisional research. If a measurement is reliable, however, there is still concern about validity. Reliability does not guarantee that the results are correct—that is, that the instrument truly measures what the investigator wants to measure.

## VALIDITY

A scale or a measuring instrument is said to possess *validity* to the extent to which differences in measured values reflect true differences in the characteristic or property being measured. To measure validity, therefore, one must compare $m$ with $t$.

Most of the literature has dealt with the different types of validity rather than how it can be measured. *Content validity* has been designed as the representativeness of the content of a measuring instrument. It deals with validity essentially from the standpoint of the closeness of the surrogate or surrogates being measured to the actual characteristic or property that we want to measure. *Construct validity* is concerned with knowing more than just that a measuring instrument works. It is involved with the factors that lie behind the measurement scores obtained; with what factors or characteristics (that is *constructs*) account for, or explain, the variance in measurement scores.

Both of these types of validity are important to decisional research, as they are to basic research. Of more direct concern in decision research, however, is *pragmatic validity*. Here the interest centers in being able to distinguish (1) among individuals who will differ in the future and (2) among individuals who differ in their present status. The adequacy of a measuring instrument to accomplish the former is called its *predictive* validity, while the adequacy for accomplishing the latter is *concurrent* validity. In general, these two types of validity are basically the same, differing only in the time dimension. For both, the approach to validation is pragmatic in that validity is usually associated with practical problems and outcomes. The decision maker is interested simply in whether the measuring instrument works, so that he can make better decisions than he would be able to without using it.[8]

Predictive validity is of course of greater interest to the decision maker than is concurrent validity; the outcome of his decision will take place at some time in the future. At best, however, we can usually measure only concurrent validity. The value of $t$ for some future period involves a forecast which is in itself subject to error. It is conceivable, however, that the predictive validity of a measurement instrument may be determined through repeated usage.

*Measurement of Content Validity.* The content of a measurement instrument concerns the substance, matter, and topics included as they relate to the characteristic that is being measured. Since any measuring

8. There is a direct relation between content and pragmatic validity: the higher the content validity, the greater the probability that there is pragmatic validity, other things being equal.

instrument represents a sample of the possible items that could have been included, content validation is concerned with how representative the scale or instrument is of the universe of the content of the property or characteristic being measured. For example, a bank that is contemplating initiating an extra reserve plan might be interested in estimating need for such a plan by attempting to measure need of individuals for borrowing money. If the measurement instrument includes items concerned with annual income, age, size of family, education level achieved, occupation, number of times money borrowed during some previous time period, home ownership, etc., the level of content validity of the instrument depends upon how representative these surrogates are of need for borrowing money.

By its very nature, content validation is basically judgmental. The two most commonly used methods of validation involve the use of logical reasoning and personal judgments of groups of experts in the field. Logical validation, which is difficult to apply, refers simply to a type of theoretical, intuitive, or common-sense analysis. This type of validation is derived from the careful definition of the continuum of a scale and the selection of items to be scaled. Thus, in an extreme case, the investigator reasons that everything that is included is done so because it is "obvious" that it should be that way. Because things often do not turn out to be as obvious as believed, it is wise not to rely on logical validation alone.

Another approach to determining content validity involves the use of a group of people considered to be experts in the general field of interest to the investigator. These experts constitute a *jury* of expert opinion, and validity is based upon their judgments.

Closely related to the jury of expert opinion approach to content validation is a method involving "known groups." With this approach, validation comes from the known attitudes and other characteristics of antithetical groups, and not from specific expertise. For instance, if a scale were being constructed to measure attitudes toward a brand of a product, the questions could be tested by administering it to a group known to be regular buyers of the product, which presupposes a favorable attitude. The results would be compared to those from a group of former buyers or other nonbuyers who presumably have a negative attitude. If the scale did not discriminate between the two groups, then its validity with respect to measuring attitude is highly questionable. There is the danger in using this method that there might exist other differences between relevant groups besides their known behavior, which might account for the differences in measurement.

*Measurement of Concurrent Validity.* The suggestion that we determine $t$ and compare it to $r$ to measure the validity of the survey data seems an obvious paradox. If $t$ were available why would the survey have been necessary in the first place? If we could measure *t* why would we have been content to settle for *r* in the survey?

The proposal that we measure *t* is not as devoid of logic as this reasoning suggests, however. There are three general ways of obtaining such measurements, all of which may be logically, as well as economically justifiable in given situations. These are:

1. *Surrogate measure of* t. Two types of surrogate measures are available. The first is the use of variables or attributes as validation measures which are not central to the study but whose population values are known. The *Census of Population* will have published data on the age, educational level, home ownership, and many other characteristics of the area or areas from which a sample of consumers is drawn. Similarly, there are registers of voters, car ownership, ownership of driver's license, and possession of telephone that can be checked to determine the extent of error in the recorded values of those characteristics.

The logic of the use of this kind of surrogate validation measure is simple and obvious. If reported average age, educational level, and home ownership for the sample corresponds closely to known values for the population, one may have somewhat more confidence in the validity of the central measures of interest in the study.

The second type of surrogate measure consists of a characteristic that is a substitute for the central measure or measures of interest. An example is afforded by the extra reserve plan survey. The population value of mean amout of money borrowed by depositors last year may not be known, but it is a simple and inexpensive procedure to check the amounts reported as being borrowed against the actual loans of the bank to respondents. A reasonably good approximation of the degree of nonreporting and under- and overreporting can be obtained on all loans by this method.

2. *Measurement of* t *for a subsample.* It may also be that the true value could be obtained, but it is too expensive to do so for all respondents. The survey has thus been used as a somewhat less accurate but considerably less expensive way of obtaining confirmation. In this circumstance it is often feasible to obtain true values for a small subsample of respondents and to determine measurement error for them. The results for the subsample can then be extended to the survey sample as a whole.

The extra reserve plan project can be used to illustrate this situation as well. A complete credit check on each respondent would provide a close approximation to the true value of loans and credit sales to each respondent over the past year. However, such a check would be considerably more expensive than surveying the respondents. A credit check for a subsample of respondents might well be economically feasible, however.

3. *Use of a corroborative design.* A corroborative design, as the name

implies, involves multiple measurements using different methods.[9] At least two and preferably three measurements of the same value are made. The hope is that there will be reasonable agreement of results among all methods. If so, the indication of valid data is obtained. If not, and especially if there is not close agreement among two of the three or more measurements, invalidity of the data is indicated.

In the extra reserve study, for example, one might use telephone calls and personal interviews in addition to the mail survey.

## RELIABILITY

In addition to validity, the investigator must be concerned with the reliability of his measuring instrument or scale. A measurement device is reliable when it will consistently produce about the same results when applied to the same sample or to different samples of the same size drawn from the same population. Reliability indicates the precision of measurement scores, or how accurately such scores will be reproduced with repeated measurements. The extent to which the same results will appear from independent and comparable repeated measurements of the same thing is affected by the variable or random errors that are present. The less such errors are present, the higher the reliability. It should be obvious that the reliability of a measurement device should be known in advance rather than after it has been used. Only in this way can the investigator take the necessary action, subject to cost and other resource considerations, to increase the chance of achieving significant and meaningful results. Often, however, the reliability test must be built into the application.

*Methods of Measuring Reliability.* In general, measurement of the variability in $r$, the reliability of the recorded value, may be obtained by one of three methods. These are: (1) test-retest or the repetition of the same measure; (2) alternative measurement forms or giving another form of the measure deemed to be equivalent, and (3) split-half or dividing a measurement instrument into at least two equivalent parts. We briefly examine each of these.

1. *Test-retest.* This method of estimating reliability involves administering the measurement instrument twice to the same group and comparing the results. While any of the usual statistical techniques suitable for the purpose of comparison may be used, some form of correlation often is used. Before reliability can be assumed there must be a high level of association between the two sets of measurement.

9. This approach is strongly recommended in Eugene J. Webb et. al., *Unobtrusive Measures: Nonreactive Research in the Social Sciences* (Chicago: Rand-McNally and Company, 1966), Chapter 1.

There is inherent in this method a potential source of trouble, namely that the first measurement may have an effect on the second one. This may arise (1) because remeasurement may affect transient factors such that the second situation is not really equivalent to the first or (2) because an individual remembers what his response was on the first measurement. The second situation can be corrected for by lengthening the time interval between measurements. The first situation is not handled so easily. Moreover, there is even the possibility that the first measure caused a change in the characteristic being measured; this can happen particularly with measures of such things as attitude, interest, conviction, etc.

Fortunately, this effect can be measured rather easily through a relatively simple experimental arrangement of randomly dividing the original population, or sample (adjusted upwards in size), into halves and utilizing a control group approach. The experimental group would be given both measurements while the control group receives only the second one:

|                    | First Measurement | Second Measurement |
|--------------------|-------------------|--------------------|
| Experimental group | $E_1$             | $E_2$              |
| Control group      |                   | $C_2$              |

Thus, in testing the reliability of an attitude measure, if the difference between $E_2$ and $E_1$ is significantly greater than that between $C_2$ and $E_1$, there is evidence that the first measurement has affected responses to the second measurement. If this be the case, then the meaning of the reliabiliity coefficient is in doubt.

Subject to this inherent problem, the test-retest method is a way to measure stability of response. However, the method cannot evaluate equivalence of response obtained by different ways of measuring the same thing.

2. *Alternative measurement forms.* This approach attempts to overcome the shortcomings of the test-retest method by administering successively to the same sample alternate equivalent forms of the measure. Equivalent forms can be thought of as instruments built in the same way to accomplish the same thing but consisting of different samples of items in the defined area of interest. The same types and structures of questions should be included on each form, but the specific questions should differ. In applying the forms of the measurement device they may be given one after the other or after a specified time interval depending upon the investigator's interest in stability over time. Reliability is estimated by correlating the results of the two "equivalent" forms.

This approach does not necessarily solve the problem of the first measure affecting responses to the second one. If the two forms are highly correlated to measure the same thing, then it may be likely that the individual being exposed to both will see the relationship. In fact, any time two or more measures are applied to an individual such a risk exists, the extent depending upon the time interval between measures.

This method is not that much better than the test-retest method. In general, the third method may very well be superior to the first two since it does not require an individual to be measured twice.

3. *Split-half.* This approach to measuring reliability of a measurement instrument is really a modification of the alternate-form approach. The procedure we will explain concerns only scoring, not the administration of the instrument. One application oí the instrument is sufficient to obtain the measure, and it is given at a single sitting with a single time limit.

To apply the split-half method, the investigator randomly divides the measurement instrument into two halves. These halves are treated as if they were alternate forms of the instrument. Random division can be done in any practical way. The most common and easiest way is to separate the instrument by using the odd-numbered items for one half and the even-numbered items for the other. Of course, if the items were listed in a systematic way, such a procedure may not be appropriate, and use of a table of random numbers or similar technique may be necessary.

Each of the two sets of items is treated as a separate instrument form and scored as such. The two sets of scores are correlated and this is considered to be the estimate of the measure of reliability—in this case, an equivalence coefficient. It should be noted, however, that this correlation is between two half-length measurements, which is not directly applicable to the full-length test. To correct for the situation that a full length scale will be more reliable than would either half, the Spearman-Brown formula is applied.

$$r_n = \frac{nr}{1 + (n - 1)r} \tag{5.1}$$

where

  $r_n$ is estimated reliability of the entire instrument,
  $r$ is the correlation between the half-length measurements,
  $n$ is the ratio of the number of items in the changed instrument to the number in the original.

Equation 5.1 is a general expression of relationship between length of instrument and reliability. When the length is doubled, as in the split-half method, the formula becomes:

$$r_n = \frac{2r}{1 + r} \tag{5.2}$$

Thus if the correlation between the two forms in a split-half test is .50, the estimated reliability of the entire instrument is

$$r_n = \frac{2(0.50)}{1 + 0.50} = \frac{1.0}{1.5} = .67$$

One obvious condition is that each half-scale must contain enough items to be reliable itself. This is often considered to be eight to ten items, which means that the entire scale should consist of at least sixteen to twenty items.

*Comparison of Methods.* A summary comparison of the alternative methods for estimating reliability is presented in Table 5–3. Shown are four factors, or sources of variation, that may make a single measurement score an inaccurate indication of any individual's usual performance. It should be noted that the procedure using alternate forms with a time interval between is the only one that allows all sources of variation to have their effects.

TABLE 5–3   Sources of variation represented in different procedures for estimating reliability

| Source of Variation | Experimental Procedure for Estimating Reliability | | | | |
|---|---|---|---|---|---|
| | Immediate retest, same test | Retest after interval, same test | Parallel test form without time interval | Parallel test form with time interval | Odd-even halves of single test |
| *How much the score can be expected to fluctuate owing to:* | | | | | |
| Variations arising within the measurement procedure itself | X | X | X | X | X |
| Changes in the individual from day to day | | X | | X | |
| Changes in the specific sample of tasks | | | X | X | X |
| Change in the individual's speed of work | X | X | X | X | |

*Source:* R. Thorndike and E. Hagen, *Measurement and Evaluation in Psychology and Education* (New York: John Wiley and Sons, Inc., Third Edition, 1969), p. 182.

Another approach to measuring reliability utilizes estimation of variances.[10] Any set of measures has a total variance (that is, a total obtained variance) which consists of a "true" variance and an error variance. It is the error variance that is of concern, for we define reliability through error: the relationship between the two is inverse. Thus, from a practical and operational point of view, a measure's reliability can be estimated if its error variance can be estimated. Reliability can be defined as the proportion of the "true" variance to the total obtained variance of the data obtained from a measurement instrument, or

$$r_{tt} = \frac{V_t - V_e}{V_t} \qquad\qquad (5.3)$$

where $r_{tt}$ is the coefficient of reliability, $V_e$ is the error variance, and $V_t$ is the total variance. If the measuring instrument is split into subsamples, such as a split-half, applying Equation 5.3 gives results approximately the same as the Spearman-Brown correction.

We show how this approach works by presenting a hypothetical example. Suppose we have obtained data using two different instruments. Each instrument consists of four items administered to six individuals. The items are six-point scales, relevant to determining attitude toward an extra reserve plan. To estimate variance we use a two-way analysis of variance. The summary ANOVA table is shown in Table 5–4, and serves as the basis of the following calculations using Equation 5.3:

Test I
$$r_{tt} = \frac{V_{ind} - V_e}{V_{ind}} = \frac{9.06 - .96}{9.06} = .89$$

Test II
$$r_{tt} = \frac{5.12 - 2.27}{5.12} = .56$$

Test I is an example of high reliability, while Test II exemplifies low reliability. It will be noted that Equation 5.3 has been rewritten to take into account that the variance due to items has been removed from the total variance. Our interest is in the individual variances. Actually, the total variance of Equation 5.3 is an index of differences between individuals. Thus, we write $V_{ind}$, instead of $V_t$, to mean the variance resulting from individual differences.

10. Our discussion is based upon material contained in Kerlinger, *op. cit.*, pp. 432–443.

TABLE 5–4   Hypothetical analysis of variance for computation of coefficient of reliability

*Test I* ANOVA

| Source | Degrees of freedom | Sum of squares | Mean square | F |
|---|---|---|---|---|
| Items | 3 | 7.20 | 2.40 | 2.50 |
| Individuals | 5 | 45.30 | 9.06 | 9.44 |
| Residual | 15 | 14.40 | .96 | |
| TOTAL | 23 | 66.90 | | |

*Test II* ANOVA

| Source | Degrees of freedom | Sum of squares | Mean square | F |
|---|---|---|---|---|
| Items | 3 | 7.20 | 2.40 | 1.06 |
| Individuals | 5 | 25.60 | 5.12 | 2.26 |
| Residual | 15 | 34.10 | 2.27 | |
| TOTAL | 23 | 66.90 | | |

*Level of Reliability.* It should be obvious by now that, other things equal, the more reliable a measuring instrument or procedure, the better off we will be. A question that often plagues us is: What is a satisfactory level of reliability or what is the minimum level that is acceptable? There is no simple definitive answer to this question. Much depends upon the investigator's or decision maker's purpose in measurement and on the approach used to estimate reliability. In trying to arrive at what constitutes satisfactory reliability, the investigator must at all times remember that reliability can affect (1) validity, (2) the ability to show relationships between variables, and (3) the making of precise distinctions among individuals and among groups.[11]

There are clearly many ways to improve reliability. Added care at each stage of the survey will serve to improve both validity and reliability. One suggestion for improving reliability may not be so obvious, however, and is thus worth making. That is to increase the sample of items included. Make the instrument longer, by adding items of equal kind and quality, and the larger item sampling will itself tend to reduce variability. When observation is involved, this means increasing the number of observers and/or the number of occasions on which each person is observed.

11. See Selltiz et. al., *Research Methods in Social Relations* (New York: Holt, Rinehart and Winston, Inc., revised edition 1959), pp. 178–182.

## *Summary*

The primary emphasis of this chapter has been on the concept of measurement and on developing measuring instruments. We have defined measurement in survey research as the "assignment of numbers indicative of quantity to properties or characteristics or behavior of people." At all times it must be remembered that measurement of any type is justified in a decision context to the extent that it enables decision makers to understand and/or predict the behavior of people who may be affected by, or who may affect, the person or organization making the measurement.

The major scales of measurement—nominal, ordinal, interval, and ratio—were discussed, as were the various sources of variation in measurement. In addition to true differences in that which is being measured, other potential sources of variation were specified. These other sources can be viewed as causing measurement error, although not every one will necessarily be operative in a project. Validity and reliability of measurement are of constant concern to all investigators. We discussed how validation can be performed depending upon whether the interest is in content or pragmatic validity. In addition we presented the major ways in which reliability can be estimated. The reader must recognize that validity and reliability of measurement and measuring instruments is distinct from that associated with the sampling process.

### SELECTED BIBLIOGRAPHY

Kerlinger, Fred n. *Foundations of Behavioral Research.* New York: Holt, Rinehart and Winston, Inc., 1964. A comprehensive book on scientific research methodology for the behavioral sciences. The subject of measurement, particularly the reliability and validity of measuring instruments, is given rather extensive coverage.

Selltiz, Claire, et al. *Research Methods in Social Relations.* New York: Holt, Rinehart and Winston, Inc., revised edition, 1959. An excellent book on research method in the social sciences. One chapter is devoted to a discussion of some general problems of measurement.

Stevens, S. S. "Measurement, Statistics, and the Schemapiric View," *Science,* vol. 161 (1968), pp. 849–856. Some recent thoughts on measurement by this leading scholar.

Stevens, S. S. "Oh the Theory of Scales of Measurement," *Science,* vol. 103, no. 2684 (June 7, 1946), pp. 677–680. A classic paper by one of the pioneer scholars in the field of measurement and scaling.

Thorndike, Robert L. and Elizabeth Hagen. *Measurement and Evaluation in Psychology and Education.* New York: John Wiley & Sons, Inc., third edition, 1969. A somewhat pragmatic, rather than theoretic, view of measurement in psychology and education. Some of the general techniques discussed are finding increased use in marketing research.

Torgerson, Warren S. *Theory and Methods of Scaling.* New York: John Wiley & Sons, Inc., 1958. A theoretical treatment of measurement and scaling.

## QUESTIONS AND PROBLEMS

5.1. The number series 1, 2, 3, 4, 5, and 1, 8, 14, 23, 39 could each be used equally well to denote the rank order assigned to a set of five objects. Explain why it is not permissible to calculate such statistics as the arithmetic mean or the standard deviation from such a series.

5.2. Categorize each of the following measurements by the type of scale it represents:

a. A determination of whether a respondent has used instant coffee within the past four weeks

b. A determination of the number of ounces of instant coffee a using respondent has bought within the past 4 weeks

c. A determination of preference among instant coffee brands A, B, and C

d. The range of summer temperatures in which respondents drink iced coffee

5.3. What is the highest scale implicit in the rel-variance calculation described in Chapter 4? Explain.

5.4. Suppose that properly gathered and tabulated data show the same results over many replications. Are the results valid? Are they reliable? Explain.

5.5. A measurement of the reliability of data can be made in several ways. Describe three commonly used procedures.

5.6. The proposal has been made that a validation study should be included as a part of every survey research project. Do you agree? Explain.

5.7. It has been asserted that for decisional research purposes the investigator is interested in predictive validity to the exclusion of reliability or any other kind of validity. Do you agree? Explain.

# Scaling Techniques

# and Models

In the last chapter we established the fact that some sort of scale was necessarily involved every time a measurement was made. We discussed the four commonly used types of scales—the nominal, ordinal, interval, and ratio scales—as well as two less well-known ones, the partially ordered and the ordered-metric scales. It will be recalled that these scales reflect different levels of measurement, according to the number of characteristics of the real number series (order, distance, origin) possessed by a scale type.

In this chapter we continue our discussion of how scales are developed. In addition, we discuss how some of the more common scaling techniques and models can be used. We begin with a discussion of the methods of obtaining data. We then consider unidimensional scales and the recent developments in multidimensional scaling.

Our discussion will reflect certain observations concerning the role of scaling in decisional research. First, at the present state of understanding we can only occasionally use interval data. Second, even if we get interval data we often end up treating it as ordinal data anyway, since the decision situation model is not sufficiently quantified in most situations to allow us to know the functional relationships between outcome and actionable and environmental variables. Third, scales at the nominal level of measurement are used widely in decisional research. Finally, ratio scales are seldom used, except for such variables as age, education, money, etc. Often, even these variables are treated at a nominal level of measurement.

These observations do not mean that we are complacent concerning the measurement situation. There is work being done to develop better decision models. When we get them we will need better data, in the sense of greater accuracy and higher level of measurement.

## Methods of Obtaining Data

There are many different ways in which data can be obtained, each of which reflects the task to be performed by the respondent. Because of space limitations we cannot discuss all of the procedures, nor can we discuss in depth those that are mentioned. We do include, however, those procedures most commonly used by survey researchers tackling marketing-oriented problems.

### PAIRED COMPARISIONS

The method of paired comparisons is a commonly used method for obtaining data that leads to a rank ordering of stimuli. The resulting scale is an ordinal one, although the method can be used with other models, such as Thurstone's Law of Comparative Judgment, to arrive at an interval scale.

To use the paired comparison approach, each stimulus is paired with each other stimulus, and the respondent is asked to indicate which one of the pair he prefers, or which one appears to have more of the attribute or characteristic to be scaled. The total number of possible pairs is $n(n-1)/2$. If a meaningful ranking of stimuli is to be achieved, a large number of comparisons of each pair must be made. Although the usual way in which this method is implemented is to have many respondents judge each pair once, relevant data can also be obtained by having a single respondent judge each pair many times or have a group of respondents judge each pair more than once. Which of these approaches should be used depends upon the purpose of the study, the extent of differences between individuals, and the nature of the stimuli. For instance, when the investigator's objective is to arrive at an average scale value for a population, which is often the case in marketing research, a properly drawn sample of respondents each judging each pair will provide the necessary data, if consistency can be assumed. On the other hand, if respondents' judgments are not consistent (that is, if they prefer $A$ to $B$ on one trial but $B$ to $A$ on another), then there exists an underlying preference probability distribution. In this situation, replicated judgments are needed.[1]

1. See Morris J. Gottlieb, *A Modern Marketing Approach in Measuring Consumer Preference* (New York: Audits and Surveys, Inc.), Modern Marketing Series Number 4.

The method of paired comparisons is used often in marketing research to scale products with respect to such attributes as quality, flavor, brightness, overall preference, etc. The resulting scale is ordinal of the form $A > B > C$. One problem that may arise is that a respondent's judgments are not transitive. That is, he may prefer $A$ to $B$ and $B$ to $C$, but also $C$ to $A$. One major reason for this situation is that each pair may not be judged on the same dimension. Also, some judgments may be undimensional while others are really multidimensional. Given that the scale will be used to predict behavior, such as product purchasing, one way out of this dilemma is to have the respondent rank order all the products at once, without considering pairs. Although this approach will not remove the dimensionality differences among respondents, it does presumably force each respondent to use the same dimension or dimensions in his ranking.

It would appear from the above discussion that the paired-comparison approach is more suited to controlled experimental research than to nonexperimental research. On a de facto basis, this is probably true. However, on normative grounds there is nothing inherent in the approach that would preclude its use in nonexperimental survey research.

## RANKING

Direct ranking of stimuli is a most useful technique where a scale of measurement is not easily constructed, but where some ordering with respect to a prescribed attribute is desired. In the simplest form, the task of the respondent is to present the set of stimuli in what he feels is the proper rank order, from high to low. For example, a group of respondents may be asked simply to rank order five products in terms of overall quality or durability. Or the task for the respondent may be to rank a group of products according to the importance they have for him. The resulting ranking may be on the basis of the absolute number of preferences or on the basis of mean values obtained from a frequency distribution of preference.

## METHOD OF CHOICES

This method provides a procedure for indirectly arriving at paired-comparison proportions of the form $p(B > A)$. Each respondent is presented with a set of $n$ stimuli and is asked to indicate which one appears greatest or largest on, or has the most of, the attribute or characteristic being studied. The resulting data are the frequency with which each stimulus was the first choice. For any two stimuli, $X$ and $Y$, the sum of the two frequencies gives the total number of observations in which we know the result of comparing the two stimuli. The proportion of times that $X$ appeared greater than $Y$ is given by

$$p(X>Y) = \frac{f(X)}{f(X) + f(Y)} \qquad (6.1)$$

where

$f(X)$ is the number of times $X$ was first choice,

$f(Y)$ is the number of times $Y$ was first choice.

For example, if stimulus $X$ was the first choice of 10 respondents and stimulus $Y$ the favored choice of 15 respondents,

$$p(X>Y) = \frac{10}{10 + 15} = .40$$

Equation 6.1 can be applied to all pairs of the stimuli to arrive at a matrix of preference proportions.

This method has some deficiencies. In the first place, full use is not made of the ranked data that may be available—only top rankings are considered. Second, each proportion is based on different subsets of respondents. In addition, the number of observations upon which each proportion is based will differ. Third, those stimuli that never receive a first choice cannot be scaled. Finally, this method does not provide for appropriate goodness-of-fit tests.[2]

## RATING

As a method of obtaining data, rating involves having a respondent place that which is being rated (that is, a person, object, or concept) along a continuum, or in one of an ordered set of categories. The point or category is then assigned a number so as to facilitate arriving at a scale value. Obviously, there are many different types of rating scales and different ways in which rating is used in other scaling models. Rating is also possible with differing degrees of distinctions that can be made, Rating, then, is a way of registering differences in degrees by direct placement on a scale. The resulting scale is generally ordinal, particularly when the scaling model is one of direct rating. There are instances, however, as we discuss shortly, where rating models may be used to arrive at what is treated as an interval scale or "equal-appearing" interval scale. For instance, the semantic differential utilizes the method of rating.

2. Warren Torgerson, *Theory and Methods of Scaling* (New York: John Wiley & Sons, Inc., 1958), p. 194.

## SORTING

The method of sorting requires that the respondent be able to take a set of stimuli amd separate them in a meaningful way, according to a prescribed continuum. For instance, if the stimuli are statements pertaining to some object, such as a bank, the respondent might be asked to divide the stimuli into a certain number of piles. These piles may simply be ordered, or the respondent may be asked to create piles that have subjectively equal intervals between them. The resulting scales will be ordinal and (hopefully) interval, respectively.

## *Unidimensional Scaling Techniques*

A unidimensional scale measures one and only one variable. It will be recalled that in measurement the investigator often is interested in making distinctions of degree as well as of kind. The nature of such distinctions of degree has a profound influence on the manner in which data are collected.

Two broad types of techniques for determining differences in degree can be specified. For the first type, a respondent makes a judgment about some characteristic (attribute) of a person, object, state, or event and places him or it on a scale defined in terms of the characteristic. This involves the use of *rating scales,* which are constructed so as to indicate various degrees of the characteristic. The second broad type of technique involves the use of a measuring instrument that has been constructed such that the score of the responses from a respondent places him on a scale. The various techniques of this type, which have been used most often to measure attitudes, can be called *indirect placement scales.*

Both of these broad types of scales have the same purpose: to assign individuals to numerical scale positions, with respect to a characteristic, so as to allow differences of degree to be specified. In general, only the ordering of positions can be determined, resulting in no more than ordinal measurement. However, certain techniques do lend themselves to treatment as if they were based on interval measurement.

## NUMBER OF SCALE POSITIONS.

In considering the alternative types of unidimensional scales, the question of how many scale positions or categories should there be must be answered for most of them. There are two aspects to this question:

1. Should there be many or few positions? This is a matter of number per se

2. Should an odd or even number be used? This involves one way of looking at the question of forced-choice versus nonforced-choice

As far as *absolute number* per se is concerned, if the number of positions is too many, respondents may be forced to make finer distinctions than they, in fact, do or are capable of doing. Yet, if too few positions are used, the scale may be of little value in determining the degree of attitude. For example, Guest studied the question of using two-position versus four-position scales. He concluded that the so-called multiple-choice option is better than the dichotomous one in that it is more flexible and provides more information. Respondents may not want to make an all-or-none response concerning an issue; they may feel more comfortable with multiple alternatives; or when presented with an all-or-nothing situation, respondents may give a qualified answer, which leaves it up to the interviewer or investigator to infer what the response really means. Moreover, if all that is needed is dichotomous responses, these can be derived in the scoring phase.[3]

## ODD VERSUS EVEN NUMBER

With an odd number of positions, the respondent has available a midpoint for neutral responses, while with an even number he has to make a choice in one direction or the other. Proponents of the even number scale argue that people really do have an attitude, and that they should be forced to indicate it. Yet, forcing a choice often leads to nonresponse, and some provision must be made for recording responses of people who cannot or will not make a forced choice. Our discussion on this matter so far assumes a scale with an unfavorable and favorable dimension. One way to avoid the issue would be to construct the scale in degrees of one or the other direction. A major concern with the odd-numbered scale is what should be done with the neutral responses. In general, the investigators can use one of these methods: (1) equally divide the neutral responses, (2) divide the neutral responses into the preference categories in proportion to the obtained ratio of preferences, or according to some rule, and (3) drop the neutral responses from the analysis. A study conducted by Ross comparing the first two methods concluded that neither of the two allocation methods was superior in terms of validity. Ross, however, pointed out that the equally divided method is advantageous in that it is the easiest of the two in computation, and that in terms of Type I error, it always results in a more conservative test of the difference between the two preference categories.[4]

In addition to the definition of forced-choice presented above, we can

3. Lester Guest, "A Comparison of Two-Choice and Four-Choice Questions," *Journal of Advertising Research* (March, 1962), pp. 32–34.

4. Ivan Ross, "Handling the Neutral Vote in Product Testing," *Journal of Marketing Research*, vol. 6 (May, 1969), pp. 221–22.

view forced-choice in the context of forcing an attitude from a person who has no knowledge of the attitude object or considers the scale used to be irrelevant. A study by Hughes concludes that forced choice scales confound unawareness and indifferent attitudes.[5] The nonforced-choice scale exists when a respondent is given the opportunity to indicate "don't know," "no information," "not applicable," and so forth.

## RATING SCALES

A rating scale is a measuring instrument that requires the person doing the rating or observing to assign the person or object being rated directly to some point along a continuum or in one of an ordered set of categories. Each point and each category has a numerical value attached to it. There are many types of rating scales that can be used, differing in the fineness of the distinction they allow and in the procedures involved in the actual process of rating.

In constructing a new rating scale, or in choosing from among the types commonly used, three related elements must be taken into account: (1) the person (that is, "judges") who will be doing the rating; (2) the person, object, or phenomena to be rated; and (3) the continuum along which the rating takes place. In addition, decisional-oriented measurement would require that selection of a rating scale involve the following two criteria:[6]

1. Which rating scale best predicts behavior?
2. Which scale is the most sensitive—that is, which has the chance of detecting real changes in attitude, if that is all that is required or possible?

## Types of Rating Scales

For convenience we adopt the classification of rating scales used by Selltiz et al.: graphic, itemized, and comparative.[7]

## GRAPHIC

A *graphic* rating scale is one in which lines or bars are used in conjunction with descriptive phrases. There are many varieties of graphic

5. G. David Hughes, "Some Confounding Effects of Forced-Choice Sales," *Journal of Marketing Research,* vol. 6 (May, 1969), pp. 223–226.

6. Jack Abrams, "An Evaluation of Alternative Rating Devices in Consumer Research," *Journal of Marketing Research,* vol. 3 (May, 1966), p. 189.

7. C. Selltiz, et al., *Research Methods in Social Relations* (New York: Holt, Rhinehart and Winston, Inc., revised edition, 1959), pp. 345–356.

scales: vertical segmented lines, continuous lines, unmarked lines, horizontal lines marked to create equal intervals, etc. The line runs from one extreme of a characteristic to the other. Regardless of the type, a respondent indicates his rating by placing a mark at the appropriate place on the line. An example of a graphic scale for the characteristic "importance" would be:

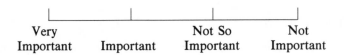

|          |          | Not So    | Not       |
| Very     |          | Important | Important |
| Important| Important|           |           |

In addition, numerical values may be indicated at points along the line. In the purest form of graphic rating scale, points along the line are intended to serve as a guide to the respondent in locating his rating, rather than to provide distinct categories.

Perhaps the greatest advantage of this type of scale is that it is easy to use and understand. In addition, it fixes a continuum in the mind of the rater, and, in certain forms, suggests an interval scale. Yet, for effective use, "end statements so extreme that they are unlikely to be used should be avoided; descriptive statements should be placed to correspond as closely as possible with numerical points on the scale; etc."[8]

## ITEMIZED

These rating scales are also referred to as *category* scales or *numerical* scales. This type of scale presents the rater with several categories, and he is to indicate the one that best fits the behavior or characteristic of what is being rated. An example of such a scale is:

1. Please mark an "X" in the appropriate space to indicate the *importance* you attach to each of the following in choosing a retail store to patronize.

|                        | Very Important | Fairly Important | Neutral | Not So Important | Not Important |
|------------------------|----------------|------------------|---------|------------------|---------------|
| Cleanliness of Store   |                |                  |         |                  |               |
| Location               |                |                  |         |                  |               |

8. *Ibid.*, p. 346.

Another version of the itemized rating scale simply lists the alternative after the question:

> In general, what has been the reaction of people to your new service? (Check one.)
> _____Very great interest and use
> _____Substantial interest and use
> _____Moderate interest and use
> _____Disinterest and little use

The numerical version of this type of scale might result from either of the above types by placing numbers with each of the categories. Another way in which numerical scales can be constructed is to ask respondents to rate objects according to some characteristic on a scale of, say, 1 to 10, with the number 10 signifying the most favorable (or most unfavorable) position.[9] Obviously, any range of numbers can be used. For example, a bank might use this type of scale in the following way:

> Please indicate the importance to you of having your bank provide each of the listed services by writing a number between 1 and 5, with the number 5 being "Very Important" and the number 1 being "Not Important."
> _____Paying checks that overdraw an account
> _____Buying and selling foreign currencies
> _____Providing an automatic "extra reserve" plan
> _____Opening checking accounts for juveniles
> _____Christmas Club accounts

The itemized scale can have any number of categories, or scale positions. When constructing this type of scale, the investigator must be concerened with potential problems arising from semantic interpretation, particularly ambiguity in meaning. The more clearly and unidimensionally defined the categories, the more reliable the ratings will be.

## COMPARATIVE

Ratings on a *comparative* scale clearly imply relative judgments between positions. The positions on the scale are *expressly* defined in terms of a given population or in terms of people of known characteristics. For example, one approach to this kind of scale would be as follows:

> Listed below are four possible factors that influence the success of a business firm. Assume that you have 100 points to allocate among the

9. In addition, a pure numerical rating is often used in other scaling models, for example, the Stapel scale to be discussed in the next section.

four, so as to indicate the relative extent to which each has contributed
to your company's success.

_____Pricing policies
_____Promotion
_____Product R & D
_____Marketing research

Moreover, some of the versions of it are so closely related to rank ordering,
they are perhaps more properly classified as ranking scales. Although involving essentially an ordinal level of measurement, the comparative rating
scale may, as the example illustrates, exhibit properties of interval measurement.


## EVALUATION OF RATING SCALES

We can briefly summarize the strengths and weaknesses of rating
scales for decisional research in more or less absolute terms. Concerning
strengths, the following become apparent:

1. Both intensity of opinion and the opinion itself can be measured
2. Rating scales can be completed and analyzed quickly
3. There is flexibility in the way it can be administered; mail, telephone, and personal interview all can be used

There are significant drawbacks and potential drawbacks, however. In
the first place, all responses receive equal weights. There is no consideration
given to differences in intensity of feelings for a choice. Second, depending
upon the wording used, the meaning to respondents may not be unidimensional. Third, unless otherwise provided for as suggested earlier, respondents may be forced to make a choice whether or not they have one. Fourth,
there is a risk that a "halo effect" or "carryover effect" may arise. This
systematic error occurs when more than one characteristic is to be rated,
and then respondents carry over a generalized impression of the person or
object from one rating to the next. Fifth, some respondents have a tendency
to overestimate the desirable features of subjects they like. This is known
as the *generosity error.* The converse of this, of course, is when the desirable
features of things disliked are underestimated or the undesirable features
rated overly harsh. Finally, the most important problem in the use of rating
scales seems to be related to their validity. There is little evidence of validation, and this seems to be a result of the lack of meaningful external criteria
against which ratings can be judged. Despite these limitations, rating scales
are presently, and will continue to be, widely used in decisional research.

# *Indirect Placement Scales*

In contrast to the "direct placement" characteristic of rating scales is the "indirect" approach to scaling. Indirect placement scales differ in the way in which they are constructed, how response is obtained, and the basis for interpreting scores. All have one thing in common, however. A person is placed on a scale by the score of his responses. That is, the investigator's interest is in the total score or subscores assigned to each person from the combination of his responses to various items, and not in the individual items or questions themselves.

Based upon method of construction and method of scoring, we can specify three major types of indirect placement scales: (1) differential; (2) summated; and (3) cumulative. All three types utilize a number of items, statements, or questions related to that which is being measured, which is usually attitudes. Respondents are asked for their opinions about these items, usually in some form of agreement or disagreement. There are times, however, when such scales are used as separate individual items.

## DIFFERENTIAL SCALES

When using a differential scale, it is assumed that a respondent will agree with only a subset, say one or two, of the items presented him concerning an object, concept, person, etc. The items agreed with correspond to his position on the dimension being measured, while the items disagreed with are on either side of those selected. This means that the respondent localizes his position.

Each of the items or statements used to construct a differential scale has attached to it a score (that is, a position on the scale) determined by outside judges. Judgments of scale position can be made by one of the following methods: paired-comparisons, equal-appearing intervals, or successive intervals. The most commonly used method is equal-appearing intervals, and it is this approach that we discuss in the framework of the model developed by L.L. Thurstone.

The Thurstone differential scale attempts to develop an interval scale through the method of equal-appearing intervals. Both respondents *and* attitudes can be scaled by this model. To develop this type of scale, the following procedure is involved:

1. The attitude to be measured is specified.
2. A large number (100–150) of statements related to the specified attitude is collected. These represent a wide variety of opinions, covering as much as possible all gradations from one end of the scale to the other

3. The statements are presented to a group of judges (as many as 300) who are asked to sort independently each one into one of eleven piles, ranging from opinions most strongly positive (favorable) to those most strongly negative (that is, least favorable), with regard to the specified attitude. The sixth pile is the "neutral" point

4. The scale value for each statement is computed as the *median* position (pile) to which it is assigned by the judges. In some instances, the *mean* is used instead of the median

5. A final selection of statements is made for actual use that constitute as closely as possible an evenly gradated series of scale values. This final list, consisting usually of 20 to 30 statements, includes statements whose dispersion across judges is relatively small

6. The final list of statements is put into questionnaire form (with scale values ommitted), the order determined by a random process. Respondents are asked to indicate only those that they are in agreement with, or a specified number with which they are in most agreement

7. The respondent's score—that is, his scale value—is calculated as the mean (or median) of the scale values of the statements with which he agrees

To illustrate how this technique can be used to scale people, we turn again to our example of the extra reserve plan proposed by a bank. The bank has prepared 125 statements related to consumer attitudes toward borrowing money. These statements are presented to a group of judges who sort them into eleven piles that have been labeled 1, 2, 3 . . . 11, from "most favorable" to "least favorable." A scale value (weighted mean) is calculated for each statement using the procedure discussed above. For simplicity, we assume that the following items represent statements used in the final questionaire:

1. A bank is a good place to borrow money (4.0)
2. Credit is bad for the American economy (10.2)
3. A person's standard of living cannot increase without his being able to borrow money (2.3)
4. Lending institutions should be cautious in loaning money (2.3)
5. Credit cards are a nuisance (8.6)
6. The procedure for borrowing money should be as simple as possible (1.7)
7. Credit encourages people to buy products they do not really need (9.7)
8. Lending institutions are progressive (3.1)

The number following each statement is the scale value, and, of course, is not included on the questionaire.

Assume that a respondent was presented with the above list of statements and was asked to select only the two statements with which he was in most agreement. If he chose items 3 and 6, his score would be

$$\frac{2.3 + 1.7}{2} = 2.0$$

Another respondent may have chosen items 2 and 7. In this case, the respondent's score would be

$$\frac{10.2 + 9.7}{2} = 9.45$$

By using this procedure, respondents could be rank-ordered according to score values.

Certain questions and objections can be raised about this technique. The first question concerns whether the resulting scale really is an interval scale. This leads some investigators to use medians rather than means as scores. Whether the Thurstone approach leads to an interval scale or not, it is possible to generate at least a useful ordinal scale. Second, the same scale value for two respondents may really represent two different attitudinal patterns. This is a result of using scale values with different dispersions. For instance, a respondent selecting items 1 and 4 would have a score of 5.2, while a respondent selecting items 5 and 6 would have a score of 5.15. Third, the attitudes of the original judges may influence the scale values of items, even though judges are supposed to ignore their own feelings about a statement. Fourth, the usefulness of Thurstone scaling in longitudinal studies has been questioned. The concern here, of course, is whether changes in attitude can be detected. In a field experiment, Hughes concluded that the nine-item scale he used lacked the sensitivity to detect attitude changes under field conditions. Of course, Hughes did not ignore the possibility that a larger item scale could have sufficient sensitivity.[10] Finally, for decisional research purposes this type of scaling may not be practical. The process involved can be quite time consuming, and the decision maker may not be able to delay making his decision.

## SUMMATED SCALES

A summated scale is a set of attitude items to which the respondent is asked to react. All items have an aproximately equal attitude scale value in that no attempt is made to find items that are distributed equally over the whole range of the scale. Instead, the items used are apparently either

10. G. David Hughes, "Selecting Scales to Measure Attitude Change," *Journal of Marketing Research,* vol. 4 (February, 1967), pp. 85–87.

"favorable" or "unfavorable." Respondents are asked to agree or disagree with the statements, and are able to indicate degrees of agreement or disagreement. Each response category is assigned a numerical score indicating its favorableness or unfavorableness. Agreement with a favorable item and disagreement with an unfavorable item are both interpreted as a favorable (or positive) attitude. The scores of the individual's responses to each item are summed algebraically to yield his attitude score, which is taken to represent his position on a favorable (or agreement-disagreement) scale of attitude toward the object, person, concept, etc. of concern. The end result of summated scaling is that respondents only are scaled, and in an ordinal manner.

The type of summated scale used most often is patterned after the one devised by Likert.[11] In this so-called Likert-type scale, the respondent can indicate degrees of agreement with each item, according to the following types of categories: strongly agree; agree; undecided (or "neither agree nor disagree"); disagree; strongly disagree. Usually, five categories are used; more or fewer categories could be used, however.

The procedure used to construct a Likert-type summated scale for measuring a specific attitude is summarized as follows:

1. A number of items (statements) believed to be relevant to the attitude being measured are collected and classified either "favorable" or "unfavorable." Items that appear to be neutral are omitted

2. A pretest is conducted in which a group of respondents, representative of the final sample to be used, indicate their opinions of each item according to one of the response categories presented

3. Each response is given a numerical score (for example, $+2$, $+1$, $0$, $-1$, $-2$), based on a series of integers in arithmetic sequence. Scores are assigned in such a way that the direction of attitude (favorable to unfavorable) is consistent over all items. For example if a $+2$ is assigned to "strongly agree" for favorable items, the same score is assigned to "strongly disagree" for unfavorable items

4. Each respondent's total score is obtained by adding his item scores

5. The items to be included in the final test are determined by analyzing the results of the pretest. Items selected are those that seem to discriminate best between respondents with high and low scores[12]

6. The final test is administered to the group of respondents of interest, and is scored the same as in the pretest

11. Rensis Likert, "A Technique for the Measurement of Attitudes," *Archives Psychology*, no. 140 (1932).
12. William J. Goode and Paul K. Hatt, *Methods in Social Research* (New York: McGraw-Hill Book Company, 1952), pp. 270–276.

The end result of the Likert-type scale is that the measurements have only ordinal properties on an intersubject basis, although a (presumed) interval scale measurement is obtained for each individual subject.

To illustrate the use of this scale, suppose the eight items used by the bank for a differential scale were put into Likert-scale form. The following presentation of item 3 illustrates how they would appear:

3. A person's standard of living cannot increase without his being able to borrow money.

| Strongly Agree | Agree | Undecided | Disagree | Strongly Disagree |
|:---:|:---:|:---:|:---:|:---:|
| $(+2)$ | $(+1)$ | $(0)$ | $(-1)$ | $(-2)$ |

Each respondent would be asked to put a circle around, or underscore, the category that most closely fits his feeling about the statement. The numbers under each category are the scores assigned and do not appear on the questionaire. The scores shown above would apply to items 1, 3, and 8 since, by assumption, they are classified as "favorable" statements. For items 2, 5, 6, and 7, the order of the scores would be reversed, since we classify them as unfavorable. Item 4 would not be included, since it is a neutral item.

Suppose a respondent evaluated the seven items as follows:

| Item | Response | Score |
|:---:|:---:|:---:|
| 1 | Strongly agree | $+2$ |
| 2 | Strongly disagree | $+2$ |
| 3 | Agree | $+1$ |
| 5 | Undecided | $0$ |
| 6 | Strongly agree | $+2$ |
| 7 | Disagree | $+1$ |
| 8 | Agree | $+1$ |

This subject's total score would be 9. Meanwhile, another respondent might provide the following responses to the seven items:

| Item | Response | Score |
|:---:|:---:|:---:|
| 1 | Strongly agree | $+2$ |
| 2 | Disagree | $+1$ |
| 3 | Disagree | $-1$ |
| 5 | Agree | $+1$ |
| 6 | Agree | $+1$ |
| 7 | Strongly agree | $-2$ |
| 8 | Undecided | $0$ |

His score would be 2. Comparison of the two respondents indicates that the second would have a less favorable attitude toward borrowing money than does the first respondent.

The Likert-type scale seems to have certain advantages over the Thurstone differential scale. First, the procedure is such that it is simpler to construct. Second, the Likert-scale provides for expression of intensity of feeling. Third, this scale appears to be more reliable. The Likert scale is not without its drawbacks, however. Like the Thurstone scale, the Likert-type may provide total scores whose meaning is not clear, since many patterns of response to the items may result in the same score. Also, the Likert-type scale provides a score only for respondents.

A serious question that we have ignored so far concerns determining the optimum number of response categories. Although five are usually used, is there anything magic in this number? Obviously, too few categories leads to loss of much of the respondents' powers of discrimination, while too many may go beyond the respondent's ability to discriminate. Jacoby and Matell looked at this question by conducting an experiment utilizing eighteen different category sizes, ranging from a 2–point to a 19–point format.[13] They concluded that both reliability and validity are independent of the number of scale points used for Likert-type items. Their conclusions, however, seem to be concerned with the question of collapsing the response categories for scoring after the data have been obtained from an instrument with some degree of intensity.

## CUMULATIVE SCALES

Like the preceding two types of attitude scales, cumulative scales are constructed of a set of items with which the respondent indicates agreement or disagreement. If a cumulative scale exists, the items included are unidimensional. This means that they are related to each other such that (in the ideal case) a respondent who responds favorably to item 2 also responds favorably to item 1; one who responds favorably to item 4 also responds favorably to items 1, 2, and 3, etc. This scale is based on the cumulative relation between items and the total scores of individuals. An individual's score is calculated by counting the number of items answered favorably. This score places him on a scale of favorable-unfavorable attitude based on the relationship among the items. The basic idea is that if individuals can be ranked along a unidimensional continuum, then if A is more favorably inclined than B, he should endorse all the items the B does plus at least one other item. There is a *pattern* of item responses that is related to total score.

13. Jacob Jacoby and Michael S. Matell, "Three-Point Likert Scales are Good Enough," *Journal of Marketing Research* vol. 3 (November, 1971), pp. 495–500.

If the scale is truly cumulative, when we know a person's total score we can predict his pattern.

In addition, if we know responses to "harder" items we can predict the responses to the easier items. For instance, if we gave a respondent three mathematical problems to solve, each of differing difficulty, if he correctly answered the most difficult one he is likely to answer the other two correctly. On the other hand, a respondent who incorrectly solves the most difficult problem, but correctly solves the next most difficult one most likely will answer the least difficult one correctly. In a similar manner, people can be asked attitudinal-oriented questions, and if the patterns of responses arrange themselves similarly to the mathematical problem situation, then the questions are unidimensional. Consequently, people can be *ranked* on the basis of their scale responses. The resulting scale is ordinal.

One of the best-known approaches to cumulative scaling is *scalogram analysis,* developed by Louis Guttman.[14] The technique is designed to determine whether the items used to measure an attitude form a unidimensional scale. That is, if we know a person's rank order on a set of questions can we predict his response to each question in some area of content? Both items and people can be scaled. A so-called universe of content is unidimensional, using the Guttman approach, if it yields a perfect or almost perfect cumulative scale. Unfortunately, scalogram analysis is useful ex post, and does not help in selecting items that are likely to form a cumulative scale.

To illustrate this approach we will present a highly simplified example.[15] Assume our interest is in obtaining a measurement of the ability of an advertisement to stimulate a consumer to some kind of action. We select four items representing actions that might occur, and transform these actions into questions that call for a yes-no answer:

1. Would you go out of your way to look at this product in a store?
2. Would you stop to look at this ad in a magazine?
3. Would you buy this product after reading this ad?
4. Would you want to show the ad to a friend or a neighbor?

We present this set of questions to a group of respondents, whose task is to indicate "yes" or "no" to each one. Their responses indicate the relative difficulty of answering "yes." Assume the ranking of difficulty from most to least is items 3, 1, 4, 2. To determine whether the questions form a cumulative scale we look at whether a pattern exists such that a respondent

14. See L. Guttman, "Measuring the True-State of Opinion," in R. Ferber and H. Wales, eds., *Motivation and Market Behavior* (Homewood, Ill.: Richard D. Irwin, Inc., 1958), pp. 293–315.

15. Adapted from Manuel N. Manfield, "The Guttman Scale," in Gerald Albaum and M. Venkatesan, eds., *Scientific Marketing Research* (New York: The Free Press, 1971), pp. 167–178.

who answers "yes" to a difficult question also answers "yes" to the less difficult ones. If a scale exists, then a respondent can be classified into one of five types of respondents depending upon his response pattern. Table 6–1 shows the response patterns for an ideal cumulative scale. The responses shown could easily be those of just five respondents. In practice this perfect pattern will not exist. According to Guttman, we can have a cumulative scale if no more than 10 percent of the answers vary from this geometric pattern.[16]

So far we have discussed only the content component of Guttman scales. There are, however, other components, such as *intensity* and *location of origin*. Discussion of these are beyond the scope of this book. The reader is referred to Guttman (see footnote 14), Torgerson (see footnote 2) and Manfield (see footnote 15) for more details of scalogram analysis.

## SEMANTIC DIFFERENTIAL

The semantic differential, developed by Osgood and his associates, is a measurement and scaling technique that can be used rather easily and usefully in decisional survey research.[17] The technique has been used in too many ways, and for too many purposes, for us to list them all. Some of the major uses have been to compare company "images" and brands, determine attitudinal characteristics of consumers, and analyze the effectiveness of promotional activities.

The semantic differential is a technique for measuring the psychological meaning of things—usually concepts or objects or people—to individuals or groups of people. Thus, one object can be presented to a group of

TABLE 6–1    Patterns for ideal scale model

| Type of respondent | "Yes" answers | | | | "No" answers | | | | Scale score |
|---|---|---|---|---|---|---|---|---|---|
| | 3 | 1 | 4 | 2 | 3 | 1 | 4 | 2 | |
| 1 | X | X | X | X | | | | | (4) |
| 2 | | X | X | X | X | | | | (3) |
| 3 | | | X | X | X | X | | | (2) |
| 4 | | | | X | X | X | X | | (1) |
| 5 | | | | | X | X | X | X | (0) |

16. *Ibid.*, p. 171.
17. Charles E. Osgood, George J. Suci, and Percy H. Tannenbaum, *The Measurement of Meaning* (Urbana: University of Illinois Press, 1957).

people, or the individuals could be asked to rate more than one object. The semantic differential consists of a series or set of descriptive (adjectives or phrases) polar-opposite rating scales, each assumed to be an equal-interval ordinal scale. The scale can have any number of positions, although usually it is an odd-numbered position scale, generally seven-point.

Respondents are asked to describe the concept or object under investigation according to the set of scales, using the method of rating. Thus the technique enables an investigator to examine both the content and intensity of peoples' attitudes. Through the use of factor analysis, the set of scales can be reduced to a smaller set of "factors" which are then defined as components of attitude that can be measured by the semantic differential:

1. An individual's *evaluation* of that which is being rated, corresponding to the favorable-unfavorable continuum of more traditional attitude scales
2. His perception of the *potency* or power of the concept or object
3. Perception of the *activity* of that which is being rated

To score the semantic differential, weights or values are assigned to each interval on a scale and these are usually transformed into individual or group mean scores and presented as "profile."[18] In addition, investigators often are concerned with the distance in semantic space between two concepts or objects. This distance $(D_{ij})$ is used as the measure of closeness in meaning for the individual or group making judgments about concepts or objects, and is computed from

$$D_{ij} = \Sigma d_{ij}^2 \qquad (6.5)$$

where $D_{ij}$ is the linear distance in semantic space between two concepts, and $d_{ij}$ is the algebraic differences between the coordinates $i$ and $j$ on the same dimension or factor (for example, evaluative). Unfortunately, the distribution of $D$ is not known; it is felt, however, that it is probably not normal. This may signify that perhaps the best we can do is make some subjective of impressionistic and descriptive appraisals.

The essence of the semantic differential, in terms of both construction of the instrument and resulting profiles is shown in Figure 6–1. We assume that this set of sixteen scales was administered to a group of respondents whom we asked to rate the following concepts: "trading stamps" and "retail advertising." Certain characteristics can be noted:

1. The scales in Figure 6–1 are arranged such that all the "positive"

18. The semantic differential data can also be analyzed by summing values over the set of scales (see William D. Barclay, "The Semantic Differential as an Index of Brand Attitude," *Journal of Advertising Research*, vol. 4, no. 1 (March, 1964), pp. 30–33).

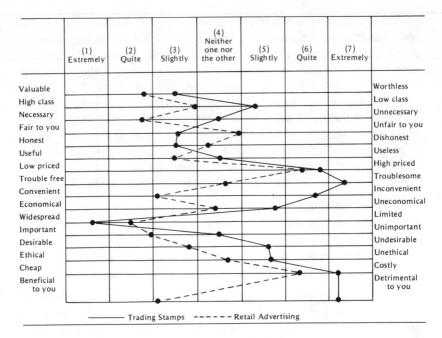

|  | (1) Extremely | (2) Quite | (3) Slightly | (4) Neither one nor the other | (5) Slightly | (6) Quite | (7) Extremely |  |
|---|---|---|---|---|---|---|---|---|
| Valuable |  |  |  |  |  |  |  | Worthless |
| High class |  |  |  |  |  |  |  | Low class |
| Necessary |  |  |  |  |  |  |  | Unnecessary |
| Fair to you |  |  |  |  |  |  |  | Unfair to you |
| Honest |  |  |  |  |  |  |  | Dishonest |
| Useful |  |  |  |  |  |  |  | Useless |
| Low priced |  |  |  |  |  |  |  | High priced |
| Trouble free |  |  |  |  |  |  |  | Troublesome |
| Convenient |  |  |  |  |  |  |  | Inconvenient |
| Economical |  |  |  |  |  |  |  | Uneconomical |
| Widespread |  |  |  |  |  |  |  | Limited |
| Important |  |  |  |  |  |  |  | Unimportant |
| Desirable |  |  |  |  |  |  |  | Undesirable |
| Ethical |  |  |  |  |  |  |  | Unethical |
| Cheap |  |  |  |  |  |  |  | Costly |
| Beneficial to you |  |  |  |  |  |  |  | Detrimental to you |

———— Trading Stamps    – – – – – Retail Advertising

FIGURE 6–1    Scale format of semantic differential

descriptors are on the same side. In practice the investigator should reverse one-half of these, the ones reversed being determined by random process

2. The particular scales shown are evaluative. If the investigator wants to include other factors, then other bipolar sets would have to be used. For instance, a potency scale would be "heavy-light." If it were not possible to plan coverage of factors in advance, factor analysis would have to be applied to determine what factors exist. Often, labeling a factor is difficult

3. The degrees of intensity may or may not appear on the instrument. The same applies to the numbers used for scoring

4. The particular order in which the scales are presented should be determined by a random process. This is important, since the problem may arise concerning the order of presentation of concepts or objects, when two or more are used[19]

5. The profiles shown illustrate one use of the techniques. It is quite apparent that the hypothetical group of respondents view the two concepts differently. Values indicated for each scale are mean scores

19. See E. Laird Landon, Jr., "Order Bias, the Ideal Rating, and the Semantic Differential," *Journal of Marketing Research,* vol. 8, (August, 1971), pp. 375–378.

To administer the semantic differential, personal interview is generally used. The rationale is that it is first impressions (or immediate "feelings") that are relevant in measuring meaning. Respondents must complete the semantic differential as quickly and honestly as possible and not puzzle over or reflect on any particular scale or concept. The only way to ensure this is to be present when the test is being taken. Unpublished research by one of the authors of this book tends to refute this belief. This research indicates that under certain conditions, administration by mail yields reliable results compared to those obtained through personal contact.

A modification of the semantic differential is the Stapel scale.[20] The scale is an even-numbered nonverbal rating scale that is used in conjunction with single adjectives, rather than bipolar opposites, to rate an object, concept, person, etc. Figure 6–2 shows the format of this scale, although it is not necessary that the scale be ten-point. Both intensity and direction are measured at the same time. It cannot be assumed that the intervals are equal and that ratings for a respondent are additive.

## THURSTONE'S LAW OF COMPARATIVE JUDGMENT[21]

This model illustrates how data obtained from direct rank ordering, method of choices, and paired comparisons can be used in another type of scaling model. In its fundamental application, the law of comparative judgment allows us to develop an interval scale based on the judgments of a

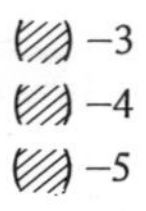

<br>

```
( ) +5
( ) +4
( ) +3
( ) +2
( ) +1
(//) −1
(//) −2
(//) −3
(//) −4
(//) −5
```

FIGURE 6–2   A Stapel scale

20. Irving Crespi, "Use of a Scaling Technique in Surveys," *Journal of Marketing,* vol. 25, no. 5 (July, 1961), pp. 69–72.

21. L.L. Thurstone, *The Measurement of Values* (Chicago: University of Chicago Press, 1959).

single respondent who compares a set of stimuli by the method of paired-comparisons (no equal judgments allowed).[22] The only stipulation is that the respondent compares each pair enough times to allow the determination of a proportion of which member is the greater or the more preferred for each pair of stimuli. On a practical level, however, this law leads to an interval scale based on the judgments of a group of respondents. This is the process most useful in decisional marketing research. Concerning the methods of obtaining data other than direct paired comparisons, all that is required is that paired comparisons be derivable from the data.[23] Thus, to apply the law we need data on comparative preference proportions.

The law states that in assigning scale positions to two stimuli, $A$ and $B$, the magnitude of the interval between them depends upon two factors:

1. The frequency which one stimulus is preferred to the other
2. The variability of judgments about $A$ and $B$, and the way in which the judgments about the two stimuli are related

To simplify the law, it is usually assumed that the variability in judgment about each stimulus is the same, and that the common factors present in making pairs of judgments always operate to the same extent.

The process by which people react differently to a set of stimuli, such as products, is called the *discriminal process*. Since a person's reactions to the same stimuli are not constant over time, we must consider the discriminal process that occurs most often, which is called the *modal discriminal process for a stimulus*. The scale differences between the discriminal processes of two stimuli involved in the same judgment is called the *discriminal difference*. These discriminal differences are assumed to be normally distributed.

The scale distance between the modal discriminal processes for any two stimuli is the distance which is assigned to the two on the psychological scale. Thus, the two stimuli are so allocated on the scale that the distance between them is equal to that between their modal discriminal processes. Unfortunately, discriminal processes cannot be measured directly. Rather, the investigator must infer scale values from comparative proportion data.

In its most complete form, the law of comparative judgment is stated as follows:

$$S_j - S_k = Z_{jk} \sqrt{\sigma_j^2 + \sigma_k^2 - 2\rho\sigma_j\sigma_k} \qquad (6.2)$$

where

$S_j$ and $S_k$ are the psychological scale values of the two compared stimuli ($S_j - S_k$, then is the scale difference)

22. *Ibid.*, p. 41.
23. For example, a method of getting paired comparisons from direct ranking is presented in Louis Cohen, "Use of Paired-Comparison Analysis to Increase Statistical Power of Ranked Data," *Journal of Marketing Research*, vol. 4, no. 3 (August, 1967), pp. 309–311.

$Z_{jk}$ = sigma value corresponding to the proportion of judgments $p(J < K)$

$\sigma_j, \sigma_k$ = discriminal dispersion of the stimuli

$\rho$ = coefficient of correlation between the discriminal deviations in the same judgment

To simplify matters, we can assume that the discriminal dispersions are equal $(\sigma_j = \sigma_k)$ and that the correlation between discriminal deviations of the judgment is zero $(\rho = 0)$. When we let $\sigma_j = \sigma_k = 1$, Equation 6.2 becomes

$$S_j - S_k = Z_{jk}\sqrt{2} \qquad (6.3)$$

To obtain individual scale values, we can apply a least squares solution when all of the elements in the comparative proportion matrix are present. An origin for the scale has not been specified. Since we are dealing with an interval scale, we can arbitrarily set this, and for convenience we set the origin at the mean of the estimated scale values. This procedure results in the following relationship for $S_j$

$$S_j = \frac{\sqrt{2}}{n} \sum_{k=1}^{n} Z_{jk} \qquad (6.4)$$

Equation 6.4 can be used to derive social values for all stimuli. It will be noted that the scale value for each stimulus is derived from the average unit normal deviate corresponding to the proportion of times stimulus *j* is preferred to other stimuli.[24]

To illustrate the application of this scaling procedure, assume that a group of 200 people were asked to compare three banks *(A, B, C)* in terms of "adequacy of services offered." Each person made three judgments on a paired-comparison basis. The observed preference proportions for each comparison are shown in Table 6–2. These data show, for instance,

TABLE 6–2  Observed proportions preferring bank j (top of table) to bank k (side of table)

|   | A | B | C |
|---|---|---|---|
| A | - | .63 | .58 |
| B | .37 | - | .21 |
| C | .42 | .79 | - |

24. There may be times when an observed proportion $(\hat{p}_{jk})$ will be 1.00 or 0.00. Such situations lead to an incomplete proportion matrix, and the analytical procedure leading to Equation 6.4 cannot be used, because Z values cannot be obtained. Other procedures must be used. (See Torgerson, *op. cit.*, pp. 173–179).

TABLE 6–3   Z-values corresponding to observed proportions

|   | A | B | C |
|---|------|------|------|
| A | 0.00 | 0.34 | 0.20 |
| B | -0.34 | 0.00 | -0.81 |
| C | -0.20 | 0.81 | 0.00 |
| Z | -0.54 | 1.15 | -0.61 |

that 63 percent of the respondents preferred bank B to bank A. Using these data, we prepare a matrix of corresponding $Z$-values, as shown in Table 6–3. The $Z$-values are obtained from a standard unit normal curve (Table 2 of Appendix) and correspond to a given proportion of the total area under the curve. If the observed proportion is less than 0.50, a negative sign is attached to the $Z$-value; if the proportion is greater than 0.50, the $Z$-value is positive. To obtain scale values for $A$, $B$, and $C$, we apply Equation 6.4 as shown below for $A$:

$$S_A = \frac{\sqrt{2}}{n} \sum_{k=1}^{3} Z_{Ak}$$

$$= \frac{\sqrt{2}}{3} \quad (-.54)$$

$$= -0.255$$

In a similar way we determine that
$$S_B = 0.542$$
$$S_C = -0.287$$

These scale values indicate the following preference order: $B > A > C$.

## Multidimensional Scaling

Up to this point, our discussion has been concerned with unidimensional scales in which stimuli or respondents are placed along a linear continuum. In multidimensional scaling models, the existence of an underlying multidimensional space is assumed. The stimuli in such models are represented by points in a space of several dimensions. Both stimuli and respondents can be scaled. The dimensions of this space represent attributes that are perceived to characterize the stimuli or respondents. We use the term *dimension* to specify each attribute by which respondents or stimuli, or both, can at least be ordered. Thus, dimension is synonomous with *attribute,* which is defined as a property of an object that is capable of further subdivision. Only in this way can we then talk about the quantity, or amount, of an attribute assignable to each stimulus or respondent.

Multidimensional scaling is characterized by respondent judgments concerning the degree of similarity of *pairs* of stimuli on a similarity or distance basis. The scale value assigned each stimulus pair may be either *metric,* that is, interval or ratio scaled, or *nonmetric,* that is, ordinally scaled. In either case, the scale value reflects the psychological similarity (or dissimilarity) of each stimulus pair. And this concept of psychological distance is central to the theory behind multidimensional scaling as a measurement technique.

According to Green and Carmone, multidimensional scaling can take three basic forms: (1) fully metric, (2) fully nonmetric, or (3) nonmetric.[25] The assumptions required, the input data form, and the output form for each of these are displayed in Table 6–4.

Because of the advantages inherent in a technique which utilizes ordinal input data but generates interval output, the *nonmetric* method is the most prominent and interesting in current social science research. Many

TABLE 6–4    Basic forms of multidimensional scaling

|  | Assumptions | Input | Output |
|---|---|---|---|
| Fully metric | Respondent can provide a rank order of all stimulus pairs and these ranks represent ratio scaled distances between the stimuli | Ratio scaled (metric) | Ratio scaled (metric) |
| Fully nonmetric | Respondent can provide a rank order of all stimulus pairs | Ordinal scaled (nonmetric) | Ordinal scaled on each dimension (nonmetric) |
| Nonmetric | Respondent can provide a rank order of all stimulus pairs | Ordinal scaled (nonmetric) | Interval scaled (metric) |

25. Paul E. Green and Frank J. Carmone, *Multidimensional Scaling and Related Techniques in Marketing Analysis* (Boston: Allyn and Bacon, 1971), pp. 32–37.

examples of applied nonmetric multidimensional scaling have been reported, in the marketing literature in particular.[26]

As an illustration of nonmetric scaling applied in marketing, consider the situation where a respondent judges the similarity of all possible pairs of six banks in a particular city. In this case, the respondent, who is a customer in the market, ranks each bank pair from most similar to least similar by assigning a rank of 1 to 15. Such a ranking is shown in Table 6–5.

From the table, it appears that the respondent perceives bank pair 1,2 to be the most similar and bank pair 1,6 to be the least similar. By using these ordinal input data in one of the many nonmetric scaling computer programs which are available, a multidimensional representation (configuration) of the data is derived.[27] Such a spatial configuration is shown in Figure 6–3.

Once again, the value of this technique is that the interpoint distances in the configuration are interval scaled. In addition, the distances between the various points are *monotone* with the imput similarity measures. By monotone, we mean that the configuration point distances have the same ranks as the input data. The objective of this type of scaling analysis is to find the "lowest dimensionality for which the monotonicity constraint is 'closely' met."[28] Each of the computer programs calculate a quantitative measure of this monotone "fit" for dimensionality of about 1 to 8.

TABLE 6–5    Ranking of similarity of pairs of banks

| Stimuli (banks) | 1 | 2 | 3 | 4 | 5 | 6 |
|---|---|---|---|---|---|---|
| 1 | - | 1 | 5 | 9 | 12 | 15 |
| 2 | | - | 4 | 8 | 11 | 14 |
| 3 | | | - | 7 | 10 | 13 |
| 4 | | | | - | 2 | 6 |
| 5 | | | | | - | 3 |
| 6 | | | | | | - |

26. For example, see Green and Carmone, pp. 11–14. Also, Ronald E. Turner, "Marketing Measures from Salesmen: A Multidimensional Scaling Approach," *Journal of Marketing Research*, vol. 7 (May, 1971), pp. 165–172. Also Joseph Fry and John D. Claxton, "Semantic Differential and Nonmetric Multidimensional Scaling Descriptions of Brand Images," *Journal of Marketing Research*, vol. 8 (May, 1971), p. 238. Or Lester A. Neidell, "The Use of Nonmetric Multidimensional Scaling in Marketing Analysis," *Journal of Marketing*, 33 (October, 1969), pp. 37–43.

27. For a brief discussion of many of the programs, see Green and Carmone, *op. cit.*, pp. 144–149.

28. Green and Carmone, p. 37.

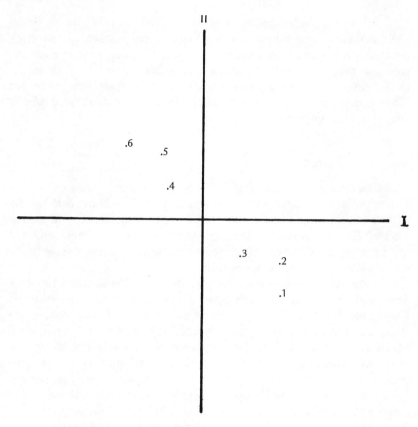

FIGURE 6–3   Multidimensional representation of six banks*

*Derived with the M-D-SCAL program. Stress = 0.0062

While this example demonstrates placement of stimuli only, it is possible to place respondents in the same multidimensional space. When both stimuli and respondents are included, the output is said to be a "joint space" configuration.

Nonmetric multidimensional scaling appears to be the most attractive in situations where we cannot reasonably assume that the respondent can make ratio-scaled judgments concerning various stimuli; or where the respondent may not desire to make ratio-scaled judgments. In either case, nonmetric scaling techniques allow for transition of ordinal input data into interval output data and hence, the value of the technique.

Further discussion of this exciting approach to scaling is not within the scope of our book; the reader will find excellent discussions in the sources listed at the end of this chapter by Torgerson, Green and Carmone, and Coombs.

In closing, the techniques of multidimensional scaling appear to be useful in market segmentation analysis, product life cycle analysis, advertising evaluation, vender evaluation, test marketing, and attitude measurement generally.[29] Certainly, other uses and applications will arise. However, further development will be limited by some of the problems and limitations inherent in the methods such as data availability, computational problems, and theoretical questions.

## *Summary*

The main focus of this chapter has been on various scaling techniques and methods. In classifying the alternatives available, we have been careful to distinguish scaling model from method of obtaining information used in models. Our discussion has been primarily in terms of unidimensional scaling, although at the end of the chapter we briefly discussed some of the characteristics of multidimensional scaling.

So far we have ignored a significant question. The question simply is how good are the various techniques of scaling at predicting behavior. Unfortunately, most of the research on methodological issues concerning scales seems to be concerned primarily with the reliability of the techniques and instruments used. Little has been devoted to validation, specifically pragmatic validity (concurrent and predictive validity). There are some indications, however. For instance, in a study related to trading stamps, Udell concluded that the Thurstone attitude indexes (from the differential scale) were predictive of the stamp-saving behavior of the respondents.[30] This was *concurrent validity*. Another study prediction of behavior dealt with testing four types of rating devices.[31] In this study, it was determined that the predictive accuracy of the rating devices varied in terms of predicting purchase behavior. Since the behavior was measured several months after attitudes were measured, this study looked at *predictive validity*. The limited nature of these two studies serves to reinforce the urgency of further research on the pragmatic validity of scaling devices.

### SELECTED BIBLIOGRAPHY

Coombs, C. H. *A Theory of Data.* New York: John Wiley and Sons, Inc., 1964. A book based upon the quadrant approach to describing both unidimensional and multidimensional scaling techniques.

29. These and other applications are discussed in Green and Carmone, *op. cit.,* pp. 14–19.
30. John G. Udell, "Can Attitude Measurement Predict Consumer Behavior?" *Journal of Marketing,* 29, no. 4 (October, 1965), pp. 46–50.
31. Abrams, *op. cit.,* pp. 189–193.

Edwards, Allen. *Techniques of Attitude Scale Construction.* New York: Appleton-Century-Crofts, 1957. An excellent book on constructing scales for measuring attitudes. Primary attention is devoted to "indirect placement" scales. Rating scales and multidimensional scaling are not covered.

Green, Paul E. and Frank J. Carmone. *Multidimensional Scaling and Related Techniques in Marketing Analysis.* Boston: Allyn and Bacon, Inc., 1970. The most comprehensive treatment of multidimensional scaling in marketing, by two of the pioneer scholars in this area.

Green, P. E. and D. S. Tull. *Research for Marketing Decisions.* Englewood Cliffs: Prentice-Hall, second edition, 1970. Two chapters in this book are devoted to scaling; one of them discusses multidimensional scaling of perception and preference only. Application to marketing is stressed.

Oppenheim, A. N. *Questionnaire Design and Attitude Measurement.* London: Heinemann Educational Books Ltd., 1966. An authoritative exposition of the subject presenting the viewpoint of research in the United Kingdom.

Osgood, Charles E. et al. *The Measurement of Meaning.* Urbana: University of Illinois Press. 1957. The pioneering book on the development of the semantic differential technique of scaling.

Torgerson, Warren. *Theory and Methods of Scaling.* New York: John Wiley and Sons, Inc., 1958. A theoretical treatment of unidimensional and multidimensional scaling.

## QUESTIONS AND PROBLEMS

6.1. Consider the applications of scale data in the situations listed below. For which ones are interval or ratio data required? For which ones are ordinal data sufficient? For which ones are nominal data adequate?

a. Measurement of price elasticity of demand for a new product

b. Determination of preference of three levels of sweetness for a new product

c. Measurement of change of attitude toward a political candidate as the campaign progresses

d. Measurement of proportion of voters who will vote for candidate X rather than candidate Y

e. Determination of which respondents have tried a particular brand of product

f. Measurement of which of three advertisements has the greatest readership

g. Measurement of which stores stock one or more brands of a product class

h. Measurement of the proportion of "triers" who make repeat purchases of a new product

6.2. Select the scaling technique you would reccomend to obtain the measurements required for the situations described in (a), (b), and (c) in 6.1 above. Explain why you chose each.

*6.3. A researcher obtains preference data from 21 purchasing agents with respect to suppliers A, B, and C of an individual product. The data are as follows:

Preferences for Supplier $j$ (Top of Table)
to Supplier $k$ (Side of Table)

|   | A | B | C |
|---|---|---|---|
| A | — | 14 | 13 |
| B | 7 | — | 9 |
| C | 8 | 12 | — |

Transform these data to an interval scale value for each of the suppliers using Thurstone's Law of Comparative Judgment.

6.4. List the attributes of each supplier you think may have been considered by the purchasing agents in arriving at the preferences given in the table in Problem 6.3. How would these attributes correspond to dimensions if these date were to be scaled using a fully nonmetric multidimensional scaling model?

6.5. Consider your answer with respect to the first part of question 6.4. How do the attributes you listed relate to your normative model of the marketing program of an industrial product supplier?

# 7

# Objectivist

# and Subjectivist

# Survey Research

When we wish to find out something from someone in the course of our everyday experiences we either ask or we observe or we do both. Survey research, whether objectivist or subjectivist in nature. uses these same basic techniques. Behavioral scientists have developed ingenious methods of asking questions and of observing behavior. The basic processes are the same as the ones each of us use informally in our ordinary concerns with other people's behavior, however.

In this chapter we first consider communication with respondents. Interpretive, reactive, and interviewer-induced errors in communication are examined. We then consider objectivist and subjectivist research methods. The chapter is concluded by a discussion of observation.

## Communication with Respondents

Our principal concern with the process of communication with respondents is in keeping measurement error to a minimum. We have already seen (Chapter 5) that measurement error may result from interpretive errors in asking the question, receiving the answer, or in aggregating and analyzing the results. Interpretive errors are unintended but nonetheless can be a major source of error in a survey.

Another source of response error in communication is reactive error from the respondent. The reaction of the respondent to the process of being questioned may result in serious error, even when the investigation is well designed and carefully conducted. It is apparent that reactive errors may be even more serious when the project is poorly designed or when respondents are not cooperative.

An additional source of response error is interviewer-induced error. Response to questions may be influenced by voice inflections, appearance, or mannerism, without either the interviewer or the respondent being aware that this is occurring.

## INTERPRETIVE ERRORS

There are a number of reasons why interpretive errors occur. They include (1) different underlying assumptions, (2) use of ambiguous construction, and (3) use of ambiguous words. Since these terms are also subject to misinterpretation, it is necessary to explain each of them.

*Different Underlying Assumptions.* When I say something to you, we may become involved in interpretive error because you hear me say something different than I heard myself say. This happens because the assumptions that you used to organize and relate my statement within the context of our conversation are different than the ones which I used in making it. The same problem, of course, exists with written statements.

An example will illustrate the point. Immediately below you will see a rectangle made of nine dots:

●   ●   ●

●   ●   ●

●   ●   ●

Suppose I ask you to try to connect all nine of the dots using only four straight lines. I also ask that you do not raise the pencil from the paper while drawing the four lines. Read this paragraph again and then try and work out an answer before you read on.

This is not an easy problem for most people to solve the first time they try it. It is difficult because they assume that the lines must not extend beyond the outside dots of the rectangle. If you were trying to solve the problem with this constraint you should now recognize that it was self-imposed—you read something different than was written in the problem instructions. Try solving the problem now if you were unsuccessful before. The solution is shown in Figure 7-1 on page 136.

*Ambiguous Construction.* Interpretive errors can also arise from the way sentences are phrased. Suppose you were asked the following question:

> Did you decide to have the air conditioner installed after the loan was approved?

with response categories of "yes," "no," and "don't remember." Any one of these responses is ambiguous because the question is ambiguous. It is not clear whether "yes" means "I decided *before* I got the loan approved to have the air conditioner installed *after* the loan was approved," or "I decided *after* I got the loan approved to have the air conditioner installed."

Questions which are phrased such that two questions are actually asked instead of one can obviously result in ambiguous interpretations. Consider the following example:

> Do you believe borrowing from personal finance companies is faster and more pleasant than borrowing from banks?
> Yes ___
> No ___
> No opinion ___

Any response will leave the questioner uncertain as to the relative degrees of "fastness" and "pleasantness" the respondent associates with the two types of institutions.

Ambiguity, then, arises from two sources: (1) the question itself, and (2) the answer to the question. There are three general forms of questions that can be constructed based upon the form of answer solicited:

1. *Free answer* or *open-end question.* No fixed responses are provided from which the respondent is to choose. The interviewer (or the respondent himself) records the answer to the question asked. An example:

> What do you think about banks not being open on Saturday?

2. *Dichotomous question.* Response categories for a positive, negative, and neutral response are provided. An example:

> Do you think banks should be open on Saturdays?
> Yes ___
> No ___
> No opinion ___

3. *Multiple choice question.* Several response categories are provided allowing the respondent to answer in terms of degree. An example:

> If banks were open on Saturday I would:
> a. do all my banking then ___
> b. do most of my banking then ___
> c. do some of my banking then ___
> d. not do any of my banking then ___

There is no one best form of question for obtaining all types of information. Looking only at the concern over ambiguity of the question or that of the answer, Table 7–1 shows how the relative probability of ambiguity varies among the three types of questions.

*Ambiguous Words.* The English language is unusually rich in words with multiple meanings. The word *interest,* for example, has more than fifty possible meanings including *payment, benefit, advantage, profit, concern, regard, weight, possession, claim, title, due,* and *attention.* A question such as

What interest do you have in the Heritage Bank?

provides an obvious opportunity for interpretive error.

*Vocabulary Level.* The use of a level of vocabulary that is too high for the respondents is a source of error that is easily avoidable. The median number of years of formal schooling of adults in the United States has risen rapidly and is now slightly over twelve. However, about 40 percent of the population have not gone beyond the tenth grade.[1] Vocabulary charts are available which serve as indicators of proper vocabulary levels. One widely known such aid is Fry's Readability Graph.[2] It indicates average number of syllables per 100 words and average number of sentences per 100 words by grade level. For a grade ten level of readability, for example, the number of syllables per 100 words should range between 148 and 152, and the number of sentences per 100 words between 4.2 and 4.3. Put differently, the average sentence in a questionnaire that is to be read should have no more than twenty-four words. The words used should average no more than one

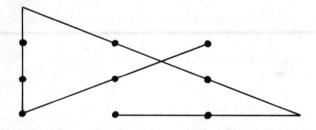

FIGURE 7–1    Solution to dot connection problem

1. U.S. Bureau of the Census, *Statistical Abstract of the United States, 1971,* 92nd edition, (Washington, D.C., 1971), p. 108.
2. Edward Fry, "A Readability Formula that Saves Time," *Journal of Reading,* vol.11, no. 7 (April, 1968) pp. 513–516; 575–578.

TABLE 7–1    Relative probability of ambiguity

|  | Ambiguity of | |
| --- | --- | --- |
| Type of question | Question | Answer |
| Free-answer | Lowest | Highest |
| Dichotomous | Average | Lowest |
| Multiple choice | Highest | Average |

Source: Adapted from Paul E. Green and Donald S. Tull, *Research for Marketing Decisions*, Second ed. (Englewood Cliffs: Prentice-Hall, Inc., 1970), p. 132.

and one-half syllables. For a sentence to be read to a respondent, these averages should be even lower.

## REACTIVE ERRORS

Reactive errors, as the name implies, arise from respondent reactions to the measurement process. Most people pose when they know that a picture is being taken of them; an analogous kind of change occurs when they know that the answers to the questions they are being asked are to be recorded.

Reactive errors take at least three different forms. There is a reaction to the awareness of being tested, of having been selected as a guinea pig. There is measurement process acting as a change agent. Persistent biases in response styles comprise the third kind of reactive error.

The value of identifying kinds of errors lies in improving the possibilities of either avoiding them, allowing for them in the analysis, or both. The errors are briefly described below, and a discussion of means of avoiding and allowing for them follows.

*Awareness of Being Tested.* This error source has been described as follows:

> The measurement process used in the experiment may itself offset the outcome. If people feel they are "guinea pigs" being experimented with, or if they feel they are being "tested" and must make a good impression, or if the method of data collection suggests responses or stimulates an interest the subject did not previously feel, the measuring process may distort the experimental results.[3]

3. Claire Selltiz et al., *Research Methods in Social Relations* (New York: Holt, Rinehart and Winston,1959), p. 97.

Typically, respondents react in ways which they preceive will present them favorably. There is a tendency to underreport liquor consumption and overreport pay levels[4] and to understate age and overstate registration and voting frequency,[5] for example. Reactions vary, however. Some respondents resent the intrusion on time and privacy and react by giving brief, brusk, "shoulder-shrugging" replies. Others appear to try to depersonalize the situation and gain a measure of anonymity by giving replies they believe an "average man" would give.[6]

*Measurement Induced Changes.* There is a central European folk tale about a grandfather who was asked if he slept with his long white beard under or outside of the covers. He replied that he did not himself know, but would look that night to find out. Night came and he went to bed; every time he was about to go to sleep he would wonder about the beard. Raising up to see where his beard was kept him awake all that night. This happened the next night and for so many succeeding nights that he eventually died from lack of sleep.

While the measurement process seldom results in changes with such dire consequences, it has been known at least as far back as Socrates that respondents tend to clarify views through the process of answering questions. The Socratic method is supported by the findings of Crespi that a significant shift away from "no opinion" answers results upon readministering the same questionnaire.[7]

Such changes can be helpful rather than detrimental. When used by a skillful interviewer in an unstructured situation, the respondent may be able to clarify opinions that were previously unclear. Questioning of this kind must be handled with great care, however. Schanck and Goodman demonstrated in what has become a classic study that leading questions will tend to change opinions of those who answer them, not only at the time of answering but subsequently as well.[8]

So long as we are only interested in the view of the respondent at the time a *single* interview is conducted, the changes induced by the measurement are not a problem. In continuous panel measurement situations this may become a serious problem, however. There is reason to believe that families change their purchasing behavior after they become members of a

4. Helen H. Lamale, *Methodology of the Survey of Consumer Expenditures in 1950* (Philadelphia: University of Pennsylvania, 1959).

5. Hugh J. Parry and Helen Crossley, "Validity of Responses to Survey Questions," *Public Opinion Quarterly*, vol. 14, no. 1 (Spring, 1950), pp. 61–80.

6. E. Scott Maynes, "The Anatomy of Response Errors: Consumer Saving," *The Journal of Marketing Research*, vol. 2, no. 4, (November, 1965) pp. 378–387.

7. L. P. Crespi, "The Interview Effect on Polling," *Public Opinion Quarterly*, vol. 12, no. 1, (Spring, 1948), pp. 99–111.

8. R. L. Schanck and C. Goodman, "Reactions to Propaganda on Both Sides of a Controversial Issue," *Public Opinion Quarterly*. vol. 3, no. 1, (Spring, 1939) pp. 107–112.

consumer panel. Fortunately, this measurement effect appears to wear off relatively quickly.[9]

*Response Styles.* There are a number of response styles, or patterns, that produce biases from the way questions are asked. There is a tendency for respondents to agree with a statement more readily than to disagree with its opposite.[10] A counterbiasing effect results in questionnaires in which the respondent learns after a few questions that a "yes" answer will result in his having to answer several additional questions, whereas a "no" answer produces no such penalty.

There is a bias favorable to alternatives dogmatically phrased in multiple choice questions; strongly worded statements are preferred to less decisive ones. An order bias exists which favors the first few and the last of a list of items. A sequence of questions of any length with similar possible responses ("Agree," "Disagree," "No Opinion"; for example) tend to be answered in patterns which to some extent are independent of the question order.

## INTERVIEWER-INDUCED ERROR

In an early study, Rice[11] examined the reports of interviews by a socialist and a prohibitionist interviewer and the self-reports of chronically unemployed respondents concerning the causes of the unemployment. He found that the reports of the socialist interviewer indicated that the "economic system" was the major cause while those of the teetotaler ascribed the major cause to "liquor." He also found that the self-report of the respondent was correlated with that of the interviewer who had interviewed him, thus indicating a "contagious interviewer bias."

Bias can arise from the age, religion, race, social class, and sex of the interviewer as well as the views he holds. In a study of behavior of adolescent girls, older interviewers obtained fewer indications of violations of adult norms than the younger interviewers.[12] In another study, black inter-

---

9. A. S. C. Ehrenburg, "A Study of Some Potential Biases in the Operation of a Consumer Panel," *Applied Statistics.* vol. 9, no. 1, (January, 1960), pp. 20–27.

10. R. F. Sletto, *A Construction of Personality Scales by the Criterion of Internal Consistency* (Hanover: Sociological Press, 1937).

11. S. A. Rice, "Contagious Bias in the Interview: A Methodological Note," *American Journal,* vol. 35, no. 4 (June, 1929), pp. 420–423.

An excellent review article with an extensive bibliography on interviewer bias is by Harper W. Boyd, Jr. and Ralph Westfall. "Interviewer Bias Revisited," *Journal of Marketing Research,* vol. 2 (February, 1965), pp. 58–63. Also see Harper W. Boyd, Jr. and Ralph Westfall, "Interviewer Bias Once More Revisited," *Journal of Marketing Research,* vol. 7 (May, 1970), pp. 249–253.

12. June Erlich and David Riesman, "Age and Authority in the Interview," *Public Opinions Quarterly,* vol. 25, no. 1, (January, 1961), pp. 39–56.

viewers obtained a significantly greater amount of information from black respondents on resentment toward discrimination than did white interviewers.[13] Interviewers from middle-class backgrounds tend to receive less radical economic and political views from respondents than do working-class interviewers. In this connection, it has been suggested that the reason for the persistent underestimation of the Democratic candidates' percentage of the vote in the thirties was the use of middle-class interviewers.[14] In yet another study it was found that male and female interviewers obtain fewer responses from members of their own sex than do interviewers of the opposite sex.[15]

## Conditions Leading to the Use of Objectivist versus Subjectivist Survey Methods

It will be recalled from Chapter 2 that the essential difference between an objectivist and a subjectivist design is in the degree to which investigator judgments are permitted in the information gathering and interpreting for hypothesis testing. When the data collection instrument is a questionnaire which permits the investigator little or no latitude in what is asked, the way in which it is asked, or how it is to be recorded, and when the data collected are interpreted literally, the method is *objectivist* in nature. When, to the contrary, the investigator is allowed to conduct an unstructured interview in which he phrases questions in a conversational context, probes and explores at his discretion, selects what he records, and examines the data for indirect meanings and explanations, a *subjectivist* method is being used.

In order to use an objectivist approach successfully at least three conditions must be met:

1. *The respondent and the interviewer must have a common understanding of the information that is desired.* If the respondent does not understand what is meant by such concepts as "social class" or "innovator" or "compound interest," he cannot answer questions about them

2. *The respondent must be able to formulate the information required.* The respondent must have had the experiences, formulated the intentions, known the facts, or developed the opinions/attitudes that are sought by the

---

13. Herbert Hyman et al., *Interviewing in Social Research* (Chicago: University of Chicago Press, 1954).

14. D. Katz, "Do Interviewers Bias Poll Results?" *Public Opinion Quarterly*, vol. 6, no. 2, (Summer, 1942), pp. 248–268.

15. M. Benney, D. Riesman and S. Stor, "Age and Sex in the Interview," *American Journal of Sociology*, vol. 62, no. 2 (September, 1956), pp. 143–52.

investigator. He must also remember them well enough to relate them within the accuracy required by the study

3. *The respondent must be willing to provide the information desired.* Respondents may be unwilling to provide information that they perceive as either an invasion of privacy or which will result in lowering of prestige

If, in the judgment of the investigator, all of these conditions are met an objectivist design will be the usual choice. Information which is free of the judgments of the investigators is always to be desired over that which is not, so long as content and costs are the same. This prescription applies to decisional as well as to basic research.

In cases where one or more of these conditions does not hold, however, it will be necessary to use a subjectivist design, if information is to be obtained at all. Indirect means of eliciting information may be required where the respondent does not understand the nature of the information required, has not fully formulated it, or is unwilling to provide it.

## *Objectivist Survey Research*

It is reasonable to suppose, along with Robert Merton, that all human activities have both a manifest and a latent content.[16] The manifest content is the sense data that an observer receives as a result of the act. In an interview situation, the manifest content is that which could be recorded by a motion picture camera and a tape recorder.

The latent content of the act is the motivation which prompts it. Such motivations may be either rational or emotional in nature. The books that are on the coffee table of a friend's house may be identified and recorded so that the authors and titles represented are not open to question; why they are there is not so easily established, however. Were they left there after an evening's reading? Are they there as conversation pieces? Are they there to create an image of scholarship or culture or modernity?

Objectivist survey research methods requires that only the manifest content of responses be recorded. If we were to conduct a survey concerning reading preferences, it would be necessary for us to accept the responses given at full value, unless there is reason to believe that deliberate misrepresentation is involved. The same requirement applies to a study of amounts borrowed, extent of credit card usage, or any other topic on which information is sought from respondents.

16. See Robert K. Merton, *Social Theory and Social Structure,* revised edition (London: The Free Press of Glencoe, 1957), Chapter 1, for a discussion of manifest and latent behavioral functions.

## MODES OF OBJECTIVIST SURVEYS

Objectivist surveys can be and are conducted by one or more of the same media we use for every day communication: we may interview people personally, use the telephone, or ask the questions via mail questionnaires.

*Personal interviews* have the advantage of providing the greatest degree of control over the question asking and responding process. The person or persons in the household who should be answering the questions— husband, wife, child, or a random selection, depending upon the situation— can more often be reached through personal interviews than by either of the other means.[17] Greater assurance can also be obtained that the respondent understands the question asked and the interviewer understands the response; interpretive errors are reduced.

The cost per completed personal interview is usually substantially higher than that for telephone or mail questionnaires, however. There is therefore normally a sacrifice of sample size in a fixed research budget whenever personal interviewing is used in preference to the other modes.

An advantage of *telephone interviewing* is the relative high first trial contact rate one obtains. Proper timing of calls will insure a large number of "at homes" and thus an opporutnity to begin interviews. The rapidity with which one can take a sample of several hundred telephone subscribers and call them makes for a short elapsed time for data collection. The low cost per completed interview has already been alluded to.

The telephone survey is restricted to relatively short questionnaires dealing with nonpersonal topics. Most respondents will not talk at any length on the telephone to a stranger and especially about matters they consider private. It is much too easy to hang up the receiver to expect otherwise. In addition to this problem, the biased nature of the telephone book as a sampling frame was discussed earlier (Chapter 4).

*Mail questionnaires* allow anonymity and respondent choice of time of answering questions. Private information is much more likely to be given on a mail questionnaire in which the respondent's name is not requested (or is optional) than by either of the other methods. They are relatively inexpensive as well.

---

17. In a study involving income, it appears that the type of occupation may influence whether the husband or wife should be the preferred respondent. Wives tend to underreport income for husbands in professional or sales occupations whose incomes tend to fluctuate. They are more reliable reporters of income in families in which the income is from a single source and which is a periodic pay check. See Paul W. Haberman and Jack Eliason, "Family Income Reported In Surveys: Husbands Versus Wives," *Journal of Marketing Research,* vol. 4 (May, 1967) pp. 191–194.

For a discussion of how one may overcome some of the problems of obtaining a random selection of respondents in households when using telephone surveys, see Verling C. Troldahl and Ray E. Carter Jr., "Random Selection of Respondents Within Households in Phone Surveys," *Journal of Marketing Research,* vol. 1 (May, 1964), pp. 71–76.

The difficulties with mail questionnaires are easily surmised. They require a considerable amount of elapsed time to conduct; the usual mailing pattern has been to wait for responses to the first mailing for three weeks before sending the second mailing.[18] Response rates vary widely from 10 to 70 percent on the first mailing, depending upon technique, subject, length of questionnaire, type of postage used, and sample, but second mailings are almost always worthwhile and third ones are usually sent out.[19] Four or five weeks is the normal planned minimum time for data collection if mail questionnaires are to be used. There is little control over who responds and little chance to reduce interpretive error once the questionnaire has been formulated. Probing or amplification of responses cannot be carried out on an individualized basis.

It is often useful to combine two or more of these modes of obtaining information in objectivist surveys. Sudman has described the benefits to be obtained through use of the telephone for advance screening of individuals and for interviewing distant respondents, both within the context of a study using personal interviews as the predominant means of collecting data.[20] Telephone interviews of nonrespondents are often used to supplement initial responses of either personal interviews or mail questionnaires. Payne has described a home product use test which is designed to consist of (1) personal placement of products, self-administered questionnaires, and return envelopes: (2) mail returns of the questionnaires: and (3) telephone follow-up interviews.[21] Other investigations have involved interviewing one household member personally and leaving questionnaires for self-administration and subsequent mailing by other household members.[22]

18. Cox presents evidence that the traditional pattern of mailings may be too long. Based on evidence from fifteen mail surveys, he concludes that mailings should be made at seven-day intervals. See William E. Cox, Jr., "Response Patterns to Mail Surveys," *Journal of Marketing Research,* vol. 3 (November, 1966), pp. 392–397.

19. A comprehensive study of the use of mail questionnaires is presented in C. Scott, "Research on Mail Surveys," *The Journal of the Royal Statistical Society,* Series A, vol. 124 (1961). Advance contact appears to be effective in increasing response rate in many cases. See James E. Stafford, "Influence of Preliminary Contact in Mail Returns," *Journal of Marketing Research,* vol.3 (November, 1966), pp. 410–411, and Neil M. Ford, "The Advance Letter in Mail Surveys," *Journal of Marketing research,* vol. 4 (May, 1967) pp. 202–204.

Monetary inducements are also productive in increasing response. See Thomas R. Wotruba, "Monetary Inducements and Mail Questionnaire Research." *Journal of Marketing Research,* vol. 3 (November, 1966) pp. 398–400.

There is some evidence to refute the widely held view that response rates are higher for short questionnaires than for long ones. See Scott, p. 167 and Dean J. Champion and Alan M. Sear, "Questionnaire Response Rate: A Methodological Analysis," *Social Forces,* vol. 47 (March, 1969), pp. 335–339.

20. Seymour Sudman, "New uses of Telephone Methods in Survey Research," *Journal of Marketing Research* 3 (May, 1966), pp. 163–167.

21. Seymour Sudman, Andrew Greeley, and Leonard Pinto, "The Effectiveness of Self-Administered Questionnaires," *Journal of Marketing Research,* vol. 2 (August, 1965), pp. 293–298.

22. Stanley L. Payne, "Combination Survey Methods," *Journal of Marketing Research,* vol. 1 (May, 1964), pp. 61–62.

Flexibility in the objectivist research design with respect to the mode of collecting information is important. With the exercise of some ingenuity, combinations of methods may permit better information at lower cost than the use of a single collection mode.

## DESIGN OF THE INSTRUMENT

Despite the long period of experience in formulating questionnaires and the visual devices that are sometimes used with them, there are still only a limited number of generalizations that can be offered to assist in the preparation of research instruments. We may speak of the types of information sought and suggest the ordering in which experience suggests they appear. We may also offer some general advice about the ordering of questions within the body of the questionnaire. We can urge that there be careful pretesting of instruments before use. Attempts to prescribe principles beyond these few lead to tenuous generalizations that are best left unstated.

*Types of Information.* Any questionnaire will consist of four types of information. These will be (1) basic information sought, (2) classification information, (3) respondent appraisal information, and (4) identification information sections. These sections will normally appear in the order listed.

The *basic information* desired from the survey of course refers to that information which is needed to solve the problem which prompted the survey to be taken. In the extra reserve example, it is the prediction of how much depositors would borrow through the use of overdrafts on their checking account up to some maximum amount. Suppose it is decided that the best predictor of this usage would be the amount of money borrowed last year in amounts less than the maximum allowable overdraft (say $500). This information becomes the basic information sought.

*Classification information* consists of data which can be used for segmenting the sample by the various characteristics and attributes of interest. Age, marital status, occupation, number of children and their ages, and ownership of housing unit are examples.

*Respondent appraisal information* is only available for personal and telephone interviews. It consists of the interviewer's evaluation of both the respondent's willingness and ability to provide information. Hesitancies, uncertainties, seeming contradictions, willingness to consult records or check answers, and just the general tone of the responses are recorded. This information is often invaluable in estimating direction and extent of response biases.

*Identification information* consists of information which identifies the respondent, the interviewer, the editor, and the associated times and place (when appropriate). One may or may not choose to ask for names of the respondent depending upon the degree of privacy of the information. However, one will want to know the address of the respondent, the name of the interviewer, the date and time of the interview, the name of the person who edited the questionnaire and the date it was edited.

This information is necessary for purposes of both accounting and control. Interviewers are often paid on a completed interview basis,[23] and editors sometimes are. It is obviously necessary to know who did what in order to determine amounts of payment in such situations. In addition, it is necessary for making call-backs to insure that an interview was actually conducted and of asking respondent (and interviewers) for clarification of vague or undecipherable answers. One also will want to review each interviewer's and editor's questionnaires to evaluate quality of performance.

*Ordering of Questions in Basic Information Section.* Experience suggests the following principles are generally valid for organizing and sequencing the questions concerned with the basic information sought.[24]

1. A "funnel sequence" should be used which results in ordering questions from the most general to the most specific
2. Questions should be sequenced to engage interest at the beginning, obtain the most difficult or threatening information in the middle, and obtain amplifying and ancillary information at the end of the basic information section
3. In general, a battery of questions is preferable to a single question, both for reasons of reliability and validity
4. Transitions between topic areas should be facilitated by "bridging" materials written into the questionnaire

It is clear that these generalizations may be superseded in some instances by considerations arising from specific interviewing objectives or population characteristics. They should be used in the absence of any such overriding consideration, however.

## AN EXAMPLE OF AN OBJECTIVIST QUESTIONNAIRE AND OTHER RESEARCH FORMS

The extra reserve case will be used again to provide the setting for an example.

---

23. See Seymour Sudman, "New Approaches to Control of Interviewing Costs," *Journal of Marketing Research,* vol. 3 (February, 1966) pp. 56–61 for a discussion of payment of interviewers.

24. These principles are adopted from a similar set given in Charles F. Cannell and Robert L. Kahn, "Interviewing," Chapter 15 in Gardner Lindzey and Elliot Aronson, eds., *The Handbook of Social Psychology,* second edition, vol. 2, *Research Methods* (Reading, Mass.: Addison-Wesley Publishing Co., 1968), pp. 570–571.

It will be assumed that the basic information of interest is the amount of money borrowed by each sample depositor household in the last twelve months. It is not as unnecessary as it might seem to state that one should always decide what basic information is required before starting to formulate the questionnaire. While this is obviously a sensible procedure, it is all too often ignored.

We will need to decide upon the mode of the survey. In this section we are dealing with objectivist surveys, but we will need to decide whether a particular survey should be by personal interview, telephone, or by mail, or by some combination of two or all three of these methods.

Inasmuch as the conduct of one's financial affairs is commonly viewed as a matter of some privacy, the use of the telephone as a means of collecting the basic information sought can be ruled out. The experiment by Ferber suggests that a personal interview to collect classification information and to give the respondent a self-administered questionnaire to be sealed in an envelope for mailing appears to give substantially better results than direct personal interviews for obtaining information on loans.[25] We shall assume that a telephone call is made initially to arrange an appointment for the interviewer.

An early decision must be made concerning whether or not the bank is to be identified as the sponsor of the study. The usual procedure is to avoid commercial sponsor identification in surveys as it tends to give a "halo effect" to the responses concerning the sponsor's products or services. There is no reason to conclude that this would be the case in this study, and identification gives prospects of substantially higher response rates. We shall assume that the bank will be identified in the initial telephone call for the appointment and the identification reaffirmed when the interviewer arrives.

Interviewer instructions are given in Figure 7-2. Our immediate concern, however, is with the interviewer schedule (Figure 7-3) and the self-administered questionnaire (Figure 7-4).[26]

The basic information desired is in the self-administered questionnaire. Note that a "funnel sequence" has been used moving from the "Did you borrow money in the last 12 months" general question at the beginning, up through the increasingly specific questions of "reasons why," "numbers of loans," and then to the most difficult question of "amounts borrowed." An easier question of "from whom" follows, and the questionnaire ends with a "more or less next year" prediction request.

25. Robert Ferber, *The Reliability of Consumer Reports of Financial Assets and Debts* (Urbana: Bureau of Economic and Business Research University of Illinois, 1966), pp. 60–64.

26. Certain parts of Figures 7-3 and 7-4 are borrowed rather freely from Appendix A of Robert Ferber, *ibid.* We are indebted to Professor Ferber and the Bureau of Business and Economic Research at the University of Illinois for permission to use them.

## INTERVIEWER INSTRUCTIONS

1. Interview both husband and wife if possible. If both cannot be interviewed and there is a choice, interview the husband (unless there is evidence the wife handles the families finances).

2. *Do not use the respondent's names.* Refer to them as "ma'am" and "sir."

3. Use the written materials for introduction and transition *as they are written.* Deviate only if it is necessary to do so.

4. *Read each question as it is written. If the respondent does not understand read it again. An explanation should be offered only if it is absolutely necessary.*

5. Make sure that the self-administered questionnaire is sealed in the envelope, preferably by the respondent. *Do not press for the respondent's name* (the questionnaire is serially numbered). Allow him to mail it if he insists but point out that you "can drop it in the mail box and save you the trouble." Mail the envelopes as soon as is convenient after the interview.

6. Record interviewer comments *after* the interview is completed. Extensive writing during the interview both delay it and may be threatening to the respondent.

7. Check all forms carefully after the interview to see that they have been filled out completely.

8. Return the personally administered interviews to the project director at the central office on Wednesday and Friday afternoons.

FIGURE 7–2    Interviewer instructions for extra reserve study

## INTERVIEWER SCHEDULE

Good (morning) (afternoon). I am＿＿＿＿＿＿＿＿＿＿＿＿＿from the Heritage Bank. (*show card*) You received a phone call a few days ago arranging an appointment for me to talk with you about household finances.

I am going to give you a form which asks most of the questions for which we would like information. (*Hand questionnaire on clipboard with pencil*). After you have finished answering them we will put the form in this envelope (*show envelope*) and seal it for mailing to the bank. Only the bank will have this information. Take as long as you need for filling it out and feel free to check your answers by looking at records if you need to.

(After the self-administered questionnaire is completed and sealed in the envelope, ask the questions below):

FIGURE 7–3    Interviewer schedule for extra reserve study

Classification Data

1. How many people in your family live here with you? _____ [  ]
2. Please tell me who they are. (Indicate number of children and other)

   Spouse _____ Children _____ Other _____ [  ]
3. What is the occupation of the main wage earner?_____ [  ]

   _____

4. Are there other members of the family who live here who work?

   Yes _____ No _____ [  ]
5. (If so) what are their occupations?_____ [  ]

   _____

(Fill in the following classification data, even for refusals and noncontacts)

*Type of Dwelling*

_____House              _____Apartment          [  ]

Approximate value  $_____    Approximate monthly rental  $_____

Condition of exterior_____    Condition of interior  _____

Condition of interior  _____

*Respondent Appraisal* (Fill in where applicable)

1. Approximate age of person interviewed._____
2. How would you describe the respondent's attitude in each of the following respects: (check below)

|  | Excellent | Good | Fair | Poor | Very Poor | Interviewer Comments |
|---|---|---|---|---|---|---|
| Cooperativeness | [  ] | [  ] | [  ] | [  ] | [  ] | _____ |
| Accuracy of information | [  ] | [  ] | [  ] | [  ] | [  ] | _____ |
| Completeness of information | [  ] | [  ] | [  ] | [  ] | [  ] | _____ |

3. What was the respondent's attitudes toward the use of records in supplying the figures requested?

   _____

4. Did you have the impression at any time that the respondent did not know the figures too well which he gave you?

   Yes _____ No _____ Not sure _____

   Explain:

   _____

FIGURE 7-3   (Continued)

148

5. Did you have the impression at any time that any figures were deliberately being "doctored?"

Yes _____ No _____ Not sure _____

Explain:

_____

## Summary

Please summarize briefly the overall reactions of the respondent to the interview. Include any information or observation which might be of interest.

_____

_____

_____

Identification Data (fill in where applicable)

1. Name of sample respondent _____

   Address _____

2. Contact Report

| when? | where? | |
| :---: | :---: | :---: |
| (date, day or time) | (Home, office or other) | Family Members Talked To |
| _____ | _____ | _____ |
| _____ | _____ | _____ |

Results:

| Int | Not Home | Too Busy | Ref. | Other (explain) |
| :---: | :---: | :---: | :---: | :---: |
| ____ | ____ | ____ | ____ | _____ |
| ____ | ____ | ____ | ____ | _____ |

3. Noncontact

   Reason:

   House Vacant _____ No such address _____ Death
   or illness _____ Out of town _____

   Other (explain) _____

   _____

4. Refusal: (Give reasons in detail)

   _____

   _____

5. Interviewer:

   _____

FIGURE 7-3 (Continued)

149

# THE HERITAGE BANK

Dear Depositor:

We are considering making a service available to depositors that will make it more convenient for them to borrow money when they need it. To determine whether such a service is needed we need to know the amounts and kinds of loans depositors made during a year. We will appreciate your answering the questions below.

*You need not give your name if you do not choose to do so. In order to make your information even more private, it will be sealed in the envelope which was shown you.*

1. Have you or members of your family living here borrowed money during the past twelve months? _____      [   ]

     _____ Yes      _____ No      _____ Not sure

If the answer to question 1 was "no" or "not sure" skip to question 6.

If the answer was "yes" continue with question 2.

2. For what uses were the loans made? (Check each item for which a loan was made.)

     _____ Automobile    _____ Doctor bills    _____ Clothing
     _____ Furniture    _____ House    _____ Vacation
     _____ Appliances    _____ Boat    _____ Christmas
     _____ Other (please specify)

3. How many loans were made? (Show *number* by each use of the loan.)

     _____ Automobile    _____ Doctor bills    _____ Clothing
     _____ Furniture    _____ House    _____ Vacation
     _____ Appliances    _____ Boat    _____ Christmas
     _____ Other (please specify

4. About how much was borrowed for each use? (Show *amounts* by each use of the loan. Consult your records if you wish.)

     _____ Automobile    _____ Doctor bills    _____ Clothing
     _____ Furniture    _____ House    _____ Vacation
     _____ Appliances    _____ Boat    _____ Christmas
     _____ other (please specify)

5. From whom did you make the loans for each use? (Show the *number* of loans from each type of lender for each use.)

| | Auto-mobile | Furni-ture | Appli-ances | Doctor bills | House | Boat | Clothing | Vaca-tion | Christ-mas |
|---|---|---|---|---|---|---|---|---|---|
| Bank | — | — | — | — | — | — | — | — | — |
| Store or dealer | — | — | — | — | — | — | — | — | — |
| Finance co. | — | — | — | — | — | — | — | — | — |

FIGURE 7–4   Self-administered questionnaire for extra reserve study

Credit union    __   __   __   __   __   __   __   __   __

Savings & loan   __   __   __   __   __   __   __   __   __

Other          __   __   __   __   __   __   __   __   __

6.   Do you think you will make fewer loans, more loans, or about the same number of loans during the next year as you did during the past one?

    _____ More     _____ Fewer     _____ About the same   [   ]

You may put your name below or not as you wish.

Name   _____

Please seal this in the stamped envelope given you. You may mail it or our representative will mail it if you like. Thank you for your assistance and cooperation.

Sincerely,

*Henry Cooper*

Henry Cooper
President,
The Heritage Bank

FIGURE 7–4   (Continued)

The question on "amount borrowed" (Question 4) was placed there because it was believed that respondent commitment might well have been rising to that point and fatigue will not have set in.

Note that Figure 7–2, when combined with the self-administered questionnaire of Figure 7–4, follows the general sequencing of (1) basic information, (2) classification information, (3) respondent appraisal, and (4) identification information.

## PRETESTING THE INSTRUMENT

The forms developed in the figures above will each require pretesting before final use. There are no doubt many opportunities for interpretive errors in Figure 7–4. For example, it is not clear whether "house" in Question 2 refers to "buying" or "repairing." This may not be of importance, but other potential interpretive errors may be highly important. They should be searched for carefully and the wording corrected when the source is found.

Pretesting should be carried out by administering the instrument to a group of people similar to those in the sample. If there is reason to believe that the people who work in the bank are similar to the depositors in their borrowing behavior and in their ability to read and interpret questions, they will comprise a convenient and satisfactory group for pretesting. A more cautious and expensive approach is to use a sampling plan similar to the one to be used in the final study to draw a pretest sample.

## INTERVIEWING IN OBJECTIVIST STUDIES

Interviewing is obviously an important part of all but mail surveys. Again, it is as difficult to generalize about the characteristics that make for good interviewing as it is for formulating good questionnaires. Interviewing in both objectivist and subjectivist studies is discussed in a subsequent section.

## Subjectivist Survey Research

Subjectivist methods of inquiry have lagged objectivist methods in acceptance. One of the earliest systematic statements of method in behavioral research was made by Emile Durkheim in *The Rules of Sociological Method*.[27] This book, still regarded as a classic statement of objectivism in behavioral research, was written in 1895. The subjectivist position was not stated in an equally well formulated manner for almost forty years. The book, *The Method of Sociology*,[28] was published by Florian Znaniecki in 1934 and is the subjectivist counterpart to Durkheim's *Rules*.

Znaniecki gets directly at the difference between objectivist and subjectivist surveys when he refers to the latter as always generating " 'somebody's,' never 'nobody's' data."[29] It is this element of investigator interpretation that distinguishes the two types of surveys most clearly.

## MODES OF SUBJECTIVIST SURVEYS

The requirement of getting at the latent as well as the manifest content of behavior usually requires a substantial investment of time with each respondent. The options in method are accordingly narrowed in most instances to those that involve personal interviewing.

27. Emile Durkheim, *The Rules of Sociological Method*, eighth edition, (New York: Free Press of Glencoe, Inc., 1950).
28. Florian Znaniecki, *The Method of Sociology* (New York: Holt, Rinehart, and Winston, Inc., 1934).
29. *Ibid.*, p. 3.

## DESIGN OF THE INSTRUMENT

The subjectivist investigator has essentially two approaches to attempting to uncover the underlying attitudes, aspirations, and motivations that shape behavior. He can use direct means of exploring in depth the aspect of behavior of interest, or he can try to obtain this information by indirect means. A combination of the two may of course also be used.

*Direct* means of obtaining information are, as their name implies, means which are designed to obtain only the information directly asked for. The question

> What is your opinion of buying things like refrigerators with a down payment and financing the rest?

is a direct question. It asks for an opinion of the respondent and no hidden implications are attached.

The question

> What is the opinion of your neighbors about buying things like refrigerators with a down payment and financing the rest?

may be either direct or indirect, depending upon how the answer is to be interpreted. If the answer is taken at face value, the question is obviously a direct one. It may be interpreted, however, as a projection of the opinion of the respondent on the situation posed; that his true feelings about buying on time are being imposed on the situation and passed on as the opinions of his "neighbors."

## DEPTH INTERVIEWS

The depth interview is a means of obtaining information which customarily employs both direct and indirect questioning. It involves a conversational type interview in which the interviewer probes in depth into areas that he perceives as being potentially productive in explaining behavior in the area in question.

Its effectiveness is highly dependent upon the level of interviewer skill. Skilled depth interviewers, in turn, are relatively expensive to use. They command high interviewer rates. They also require a substantial amount of time to conduct an interview. Study designs employing depth interviews are therefore likely to be more costly than those involving ordinary interviews.

## PROJECTIVE TESTS

Projective tests involve the presentation of an ambiguous, nonpersonal situation to the respondent, who is then asked to react to it in some

TABLE 7–2 Classification of projective techniques*

| Technique | Response requested |
|---|---|
| Construction | |
|  Thematic Apperception Test (TAT) | The respondent is asked to respond for or |
|  Item Substitution Test | to describe a character in a simulated situation. |
| Association | |
|  Word-association test | The respondent is asked to reply to a |
|  Rorschach Test | stimulus with the first word, image, or |
|  Cloud pictures | percept that occurs to him. |
|  Auditory projective techniques | |
| Completion | |
|  Sentence-completion test | The respondent is given an incomplete |
|  Picture completion study | expression, image, or situation and asked |
|  Psychodrama | to complete it however he chooses. |

*These and other projective techniques are discussed in Gardner Lindzey, *Projective Techniques and Cross Cultural Research* (New York: Appleton-Century-Crofts, Inc., 1961), chapter 3.

way. The assumption that underlies the test is that the reaction will involve an imposition or projection of the respondent's needs, motives, and values in clarifying the ambiguity. A useful classification of projective techniques is given in Table 7-2. All of these types of projective techniques are compatible with and have been used in survey research studies. Here we shall describe briefly the two construction techniques; descriptions of the other techniques and applications using them are available from other sources.[30]

*Thematic Apperception Test (TAT).* In one form of the TAT the respondent is asked to assume a role and to respond for a character in the situation with which he is presented. If the study of depositors were to include a section on attitudinal information on the use of installment credit, for example, the respondent might be presented with a cartoon depicting neighbors talking over the back fence. A conversational balloon over the head of one might say "Mary told me that the Smiths just bought a new color television on time." An empty balloon might appear over the head of the other and the respondent asked to fill in the response of the neighbor. In answering he will presumably project onto the situation his own feelings about such transactions.

  Other forms of the TAT involve only the giving of a visual stimulus to the respondent and asking him to characterize or describe it. Giving

30. For marketing research applications see especially Joseph W. Newman, *Motivation Research and Marketing Management* (Cambridge: Harvard University Graduate School of Business Administration, 1957). See also Darrell B. Lucas and Stuart H. Britt, *Measuring Advertising Effectiveness* (New York: McGraw-Hill Book Company, 1963), Chapter 6.

pictures of a sailboat and a motorboat to a respondent, for example, and asking him to characterize the owner of each, describe its uses, and whether or not it is likely that it was bought on an installment plan may well result in sharply differing sets of answers according to socio-economic strata.

*Item Substitution Test.* In this type of test, an experimental design is often used which requires that a part of the sample act as a control group and the other as a test group. The stimulus is a listing of items which is varied between the test and control group by substitution of items relevant to the study.

The study by Haire[31] is the classic of this type. Substituting Nescafé Instant Coffee" for "Maxwell House Coffee—drip grind" in an otherwise identical shopping list, he found that the "Maxwell House" housewife was perceived to be much cleaner, thriftier, and harder working than the "Nescafé" housewife.

If we were interested in attitudes toward installment credit, a similar technique could be used. A list of financial transactions for a hypothetical household for a year could be constructed. For the control group, the item "took $250 from savings to buy a new refrigerator" could be used for the control group with substitution of "took $25 from savings to buy new refrigerator with other $225 to be paid at $15 per month" for the test group. If the other items had no reference to installment buying and were kept the same, any strong attitudinal reactions to credit buying should emerge.

## Interviewing

While we have discussed objectivist and subjectivist methods as if they were mutually exclusive, as a practical matter most surveys contain some elements of both. It will be convenient to continue to segregate the two in discussing interviewing, however.

The least demanding interviewing situation is one in which a direct, structured questionnaire is used on which the opening comment, item explanations, and probe instructions are fully specified. We shall refer to this as an *enumerative* interview. It is clearly objectivist in nature.

The most demanding of interviews (from the standpoint of the interviewer) is the *depth* interview. As described earlier in the section on subjectivist surveys, the depth interviewer works in an unstructured, interactive interviewing situation in which he formulates questions, explanations, probes, and reinforcing comments as the interview proceeds.

31. Mason Haire, "Projective Techniques in Marketing Research," *Journal of Marketing,* vol. 14 (April, 1950), pp. 649–656. This study was done at a time (1949) when instant coffee was first being introduced. Sheth has since replicated it and found that taboos against instant coffee have now disappeared. See Jagdish N. Sheth, "A Review of Buyer Behavior," *Management Science,* vol. 12 (August, 1967), pp. 715–737.

It will be useful to compare and contrast these two types of interviews with respect to the criteria for interviewer performance.

## MEASURES OF INTERVIEWER PERFORMANCE

It would be pleasing to be able to report that the attributes of "good" interviewers have been identified and that we are able to predict the level of interviewer performance with a high degree of success. Unfortunately, such is not the case.

One of the leading studies of interviewer attributes is the one conducted by Axelrod and Cannell.[32] Three measures of interviewer effectiveness were used: ratings by field supervisors, by office administrative staff, and by coders. An index of interviewer effectiveness was constructed from these ratings for each interviewer. These were compared with measures of standard socioeconomic variables and the results of three widely used personality tests. The results were that the degree of the associations between predictor variables and performance were so low that the study proved to be of no help in selecting interviewers. Other studies have been equally unsuccessful in this area.

While we are not yet able to predict interviewer effectiveness with any degree of reliability, we can measure performance reasonably well. Interviewer performance can be measured usefully with respect to four aspects. These are

1. *Contact rate.* The contact rate is measured by the proportion of addresses or names with which the interviewer makes contact with an eligible respondent

2. *Response rate.* The response rate is measured by the proportion of contacts that result in interviews

3. *Completeness rate.* The completeness rate is measured by the proportion of information obtained to that desired

4. *Accuracy rate.* The accuracy rate is defined as the ratio of measured to true value

Each of these measures of effectiveness is discussed below with respect to enumerative and depth interviews.

*Contact Rate.* At least one study indicates that the contact rate is independent of level of experience of interviewers,[33] and it seems reasonable to assume it is independent of type of interview as well. Rather, contact rate

32. Morris Axelrod and Charles F. Cannell, "A Research Note on an Attempt to Predict Interviewer Effectiveness," *Public Opinion Quarterly,* vol. 23, no. 4, (Winter, 1959), pp. 571–575.
33. Bo W. Schyberger, "A Study of Interviewer Behavior," *Journal of Marketing Research,* vol. 4 (February, 1967), pp. 32–35.

in any given study seems likely to be a function of interviewer motivation and ingenuity, previous contacts to establish appointments, and, when appointments have not been made, the day of week and time of day of the call.

*Response Rate.* Obtaining responses after the contact is largely a matter of establishing a credible reason or reasons why the respondent should be willing to provide the information. Generally, such motivation arises from the help it will provide (a) the interviewer, (b) the respondent, and/or (c) some other person or group. (Kinsey's classic phrase, "it will help the doctors" is an example of the last of these).

It might be supposed that the *enumerative* interviewer has little effect on respondent willingness to cooperate, since he is largely constrained to a "script" covering both comment and questions throughout the interview. Two comments are relevant to such a supposition.

The first is that the implied assumption that the interviewer actually "sticks to the script" will not bear up very well under examination. Both experience and the results of at least one study using "planted" respondents suggest there are substantial deviations from script.[34] To the extent that such deviations do occur, the enumerative interviewer directly affects respondent motivation through the choice of *content* of motivational message.

Secondly, even though strict adherence to previously prepared materials is maintained, interviewer personality and skill will be reflected in the delivery of prepared materials in the same way that personality and acting skill are reflected in the delivery of lines by actors.

The depth interviewer will nonetheless need greater skill and tact to obtain as high a response rate as an enumerative interviewer. He is required to assure a potential respondent that it will be worthwhile to spend an hour or so in a discussion that may not seem to him to be at all important.

It has been suggested by several investigators that many people enjoy being interviewed. There is a feeling of importance associated with being asked for one's opinions, and it is pleasant to talk with someone who is supportive and interested in what one says. It is the interviewer's task to project this image of the forthcoming interview along with removing the threat of invasion of privacy to the extent that he can. Assurances of anonymity (which assurances must be strictly observed when given) are usually helpful in this last respect.[35]

*Completeness Rate.* The role of respondent is one for which no one has been trained and few are experienced. The good interviewer not only helps to motivate the respondent to cooperate in the interview but assists

34. *Ibid.*
35. An example of a response rate analysis is given in John B. Lansing and James N. Morgan, *Economic Survey Methods* (Ann Arbor: Institute for Social Research, 1971), pp. 255–268.

him in carrying out his role of respondent as well. He does this by making as clear as possible the general kinds of information required and the specific informational content of each question.

If the enumerative study interviewer is in fact constrained to using the precise wording of question explanations (as well as the questions), it might seem that there is little opportunity for the interviewer to affect either clarity of question or accessibility of content. However, it has been shown that attention span and understanding of verbal statements is increased as motivation level rises.[36] It has also been demonstrated that accessibility of information is increased with motivation.[37]

The observations on motivation and completeness rate made thus far are applicable to an in-depth interviewing situation but need to be extended. A skilled depth interviewer will be able to project acceptance and understanding of the views of the respondent that will encourage rather than inhibit responses. He will also be able to frame and to explain questions at a level and in a way that will be compatible with the verbal-skills level of the respondent.

*Accuracy Rate.* Accuracy in personal interviews was dealt with earlier in the discussion of reactive and interviewer induced errors (pp. 137–140).

It is apparent that one will not know the accuracy of the information obtained unless validation information is obtained. It was argued earlier (Chapter 4) that validation measures should be a part of every design. The measurement of interviewer performance is an added reason for validation measurements.

## CONTROL OF INTERVIEWER PERFORMANCE

Interviewer performance should be monitored through a system of call-backs as well as through the office measurements described above. Interviewers cheat, and they make mistakes. A carefully designed system of verification through sampling is usually a worthwhile expenditure of project funds.

## Observation

It has been observed that "there is still no man that would not accept dog tracks in the mud against the sworn testimony of a hundred eyewit-

36. Gertrude R. Schmeidler et al., "Motivation, Anxiety, and Stress in a Difficult Verbalizable Task," *Psychological Reports,* Vol. 19, no. 1 (February, 1965), pp. 247–255.
37. Theodore J. Doll, "Motivation, Reaction Time, and the Contents of Active Verbal Memory," *Journal of Experimental Psychology,* vol. 87, no. 1 (January, 1971), pp. 29–36.

nesses that no dog had passed by."[38] Yet we also know that for almost a hundred years sightings of the planet Uranus were reported by astronomers as evidence of a "new star." Observation is clearly not an infallible source of information.

Accuracy of observation is only one of the issues involved in its use as an informational source. Observation has many advantages as well as limitations as compared to asking as a means of obtaining information. The advantages include

1. *Directness.* One does not have to rely on reports but can obtain direct, firsthand information

2. *Naturalness.* It often permits the collection of data in typical behavioral situations

3. *Limited demands.* It requires less of the "respondent" than other methods

4. *Simultaneous occurrence and recording.* There is no necessary elapsed time between occurrence and recording of the behavior of interest

5. *Completeness.* Important data may emerge which would otherwise have not been asked for or described by the respondent

Clearly there are limitations to observation as a method of collecting information as well.

1. *Meausrement of effort.* "Posing" may occur when it is known that behavior is being observed

2. *Unpredictability of occurrence.* Some kinds of behavior of interest occur only sporadically and so are difficult to time for observation

3. *Privacy.* Some kinds of behavior are inaccessible to direct observation

4. *Interpretive error.* The margin for interpretive error is greater than in interviewing situations

This listing of advantages and limitations makes it apparent that observation can often be used to supplement and sometimes to supplant interviews as a source of behavioral information. It could be used as a corroborative method in the extra reserve study, for example. A sample of persons making small loans at the bank might be systematically observed for purposes of drawing inferences about attitudes toward borrowing money. Observation may also be used for verification; asking if one may see the contract for an appliance purchase on installment credit will provide an immediate check of accuracy of information given in an interview. Finally, it may be used as the primary informational source; one may observe what fraction of purchases are made using credit cards versus cash, for example.

38. W. L. Prosser, *Handbook of the Law of Torts,* third edition (St. Paul: West, 1964), p. 216.

There are many excellent descriptions of observation as an informational source. The discussion in Wieck[39] and Webb et al.[40] are especially recommended for a general background discussion. Those by Samli[41] and Wells and Lo Sciuto[42] are well worth reading for purposes of application.

## *Summary*

In this chapter we have been concerned with objectivist and subjectivist survey research and the various modes of each. The chapter was begun with a discussion of communication with respondents and the sources of errors it contains. Interpretive, reactive, and interviewer-induced errors were considered as they relate to communication as a means of obtaining information.

We then considered personal interviewing, telephone interviewing, and mail questionnaires as modes of objectivist surveys. The design of the data collection instrument was discussed with examples given.

The need for better means of getting at the latent as well as the manifest content of behavior has given use to subjectivist surveys. Both direct and indirect means of eliciting information on motivations, attitudes, and needs and wants were discussed. Depth interviews and projective techniques were described in this connection.

Interviewing in both objectivist and subjectivist surveys was then considered. The performance criteria of contact, response, completeness and accuracy rates were described as they apply to both objectivist and subjectivist interviews.

The chapter was concluded by a discussion of observation as a data gathering method.

### SELECTED BIBLIOGRAPHY

Hauck, Matthew and Stanley W. Steinkamp. *Survey Reliability and Interviewer Competence.* Urbana: Bureau of Economic and Business Research, Univer-

39. Karl E. Wieck, "Systematic Observational Methods," in Gardner Lindzey and Elliot Aronson, eds., *The Handbook of Social Psychology,* second edition, vol. 2 (Reading, Mass.: Addison-Wesley Publishing Co., 1968), Chapter 13.

40. Eugene J. Webb et al., *Unobtrusive Measures: Nonreactive Research in the Social Sciences* (Chicago: Rand-McNally & Co., 1966), Chapters 5 and 6.

41. A. Coskun Samli, "Observation as a Method of Fact Gathering in Making Decisions," *Business Perspectives,* vol. 4 (Fall, 1967), pp. 19–23. Reprinted in Gerald Albaum and M. Venkatesan, *Scientific Marketing Research* (New York: The Free Press, 1971), pp. 238–246.

42. William D. Wells and Leonard A. Lo Sciuto, "Direct Observation of Purchasing Behavior," *Journal of Marketing Research,* vol. 3 (August, 1966), pp. 227–234.

sity of Illinois, 1964. This book presents methodological findings focusing on the role of the interviewer in affecting the quality of data obtainable from personal interview surveys.

Hyman, Herbert et al. *Interviewing in Social Research.* Chicago: University of Chicago Press, 1954. An aging book that is still one of the best available sources on interviewing.

Lansing, John B. and James N. Morgan. *Economic Survey Methods.* Ann Arbor: Institute for Social Research, 1971. An authoritative book on the practice of obtaining economic data by survey. Chapter 4, "Methods of Data Collection," is an especially useful addition to the literature on objectivist survey procedures.

Lindzey, Gardner and Elliot Aronson, eds. *The Handbook of Social Psychology,* second edition, vol. 2, *Research Methods.* Reading, Mass.: Addison-Wesley Publishing Co., 1968. Especially Chapter 13, "Systematic Observational Methods" by Karl E. Wieck and Chapter 15, "Interviewing" by Charles F. Cannell and Robert L. Kahn. Each of these chapters is a carefully researched and well-written exposition of the topic with which it deals. Extensive bibliographies are provided at the end of both chapters as well.

Newman, Joseph W. *Motivation Research and Marketing Management.* Cambridge: Harvard University Graduate School of Business Administration, 1957. An early book on subjectivist methods as applied to marketing research. Several case studies are presented.

Payne, Stanley L. *The Act of Asking Questions.* Princeton: Princeton University Press, 1951. A book written with humor, and one that displays the extensive experience of the author. Highly recommended for persons who are involved or are about to become involved in questionnaire construction.

Scott, C. "Research on Mail Surveys," *The Journal of the Royal Statistical Society,* Series A, vol. 124 (1961). A comprehensive study of the use of mail questionnaires in England.

Webb, Eugene J. et al, *Unobtrusive Measures: Nonreactive Research in the Social Sciences.* Chicago: Rand-McNally & Co., 1966. A well-written book that makes a strong case for methods of research in which the respondent cannot contribute to error through having reacted to the measurement process. Observation is one such means of obtaining information and the discussion of it in Chapters 5 and 6 is highly recommended.

## QUESTIONS AND PROBLEMS

7.1. A merchant's association for a relatively small shopping center located in a metropolitan area of 125,000 population conducted a survey of shoppers. The survey was conducted with no interviewers present. Rather the questionnaires were merely placed on a table in the mall with a sign asking people to participate. The questionnaire shown on page 162 was used.

a. What interpretive and reactive errors are likely to arise? Explain.

b. Evaluate this survey and the questionnaire used as objectivist research.

c. If the questionnaire had been administered in the mall by personal interview, what errors in communication might arise? Explain.

## MARTIN MALL—QUICK ROAD MERCHANT'S ASSOCIATION
## SHOPPER'S SURVEY

In an attempt to serve you better, the Martin Mall—Quick Road Merchant's Association requests that you complete this questionnaire and deposit it in the special container marked *"Deposit Shopper's Survey Here"* located in the Mall. All information is strictly confidential and *you need not sign the Survey.* Your cooperation will be sincerely appreciated.

Check one:  Male _____     Female _____

1. Name of city or town in which you live _____
2. How long have you lived there?_____
3. Are you buying or renting a home? _____
4. How many automobiles in your household?_____
5. Husband's occupation? _____
6. Wife's occupation? _____
7. What is your annual income? (If both husband and wife work, please indicate total.) _____
8. What is your age? _____
9. Number of children in your family? _____
10. What are the ages of your children? _____
11. What radio station do you listen to most? _____
12. How often do you shop the Martin-Quick area? (Check one.)
    Weekly _____     Once or twice a month _____
    1–6 times a year _____     Only during special sales or events _____
13. Do you enjoy shopping the Martin-Quick area? Yes _____     No _____
14. In general, how would you rate the people who work the Martin-Quick shopping area on courtesy?
    Excellent _____     Good _____     Fair _____     Poor _____
    Very poor _____
15. In general, are you able to find what you are shopping for in the Martin-Quick area? _____
16. How much time per shopping trip do you spend in the Martin Mall-Quick Road shopping area? _____

7.2. "All things considered, in objectivist survey research the most valid, reliable, and economic approach is a questionnaire administered by personal interview." Comment.

7.3. Refer to the Heritage Bank example in this chapter. What changes would be necessary if the survey were conducted entirely by mail? By telephone?

7.4. There are many people who feel that projective techniques belong only in clinical psychology. Do you agree or disagree with this viewpoint? Present an argument to defend your position.

7.5. In practice, most surveys contain elements of both objectivist and subjectivist methods.

    a. Is this practice really desirable? Explain.

    b. Can interviews perform interviews involving enumerative and depth aspects in the same questionnaire equally well? Explain.

7.6. Discuss the statement: "Observation is a technique that is more effective in objectivist survey research than in subjectivist survey research."

# The Analysis Process

*Information* was defined earlier as recorded experience useful for making decisions. The marks that appear on boxes or the words written on questionnaires convey little information as such. These raw data must be compiled, analyzed, and interpreted carefully before their full meanings and implications can be understood.

*Analysis* can be viewed as the ordering, the breaking down into constituent parts, and the manipulating of data to obtain answers to the research question or questions underlying the survey project.[1] Tightly interwoven with analysis is interpretation; it is so closely related to analysis that it is a special aspect of analysis rather than a separate activity. The process of interpretation involves taking the results of analysis, making inferences relevant to the research relations studied, and drawing conclusions about these relations.[2] Since analysis represents the end of the research process (short of writing the report), everything done prior to this stage has been accomplished for the sole purpose of analysis. In a decisional setting, all conclusions, recommendations, and decisions are based upon the analysis of the data obtained from the survey project. This points to the need for taking analysis, or potential analysis, into consideration when planning the project.

1. Fred N. Kerlinger, *Foundations of Behavioral Research* (New York: Holt, Rinehart and Winston, Inc., 1964), p. 603.
2. *Ibid.*

The competent analysis of survey-derived data requires a blending of artistry and science, of intuition and informed insight, of judgment and statistical treatment, combined with a thorough knowledge of the context of the problem being investigated. It is apparent that some of these qualities can only be acquired by experience while others are heavily dependent upon the native abilities of the analyst. Still others can be acquired through education and training.

The general purpose of this chapter is to examine the processes by which the meanings and implications of survey data can best be extracted. The major procedural steps involved in the analysis of survey data will be discussed in some detail. Analytic techniques, which necessarily will receive a somewhat condensed treatment, are discussed in the next chapter.

## Major Steps in Analysis

The overall process of analyzing sample data and making inferences from them can be viewed as involving a number of separate and sequential steps:

1. *Sorting.* Establishing appropriate categories for the information desired and sorting the data into them
2. *Summarizing.* Making the initial counts of responses for each category and using summarizing measures to provide economy of description and so facilitate understanding
3. *Formulating additional hypotheses.* Using the inductions derived from the data concerning the relevant variables, their parameters, their difference, and relationships to suggest working hypotheses not originally considered
4. *Making inferences.* Reaching conclusions about the variables that are important, their parameters, their differences, and the relationships among them

While these steps have been shown as separate and there is an implication that they are sequential, in practice they sometimes tend to merge. They do not always follow in sequence; for example, the initial sorting of the data may suggest additional hypotheses that in turn require more and different sorting. Nor are all of the steps always required in a particular project; the study may be exploratory in nature, which means that it is designed to formulate hypotheses to examine in a later, full-scale project, for example. We now discuss each of these steps.

## *Sorting the Data into Categories*[3]

The sorting of data from respondents into categories involves a series of steps consisting of: (1) the establishment of categories, (2) the editing and coding of the responses, and (3) the tabulation of the data.

### ESTABLISHING CATEGORIES.

Analysis of any fairly large set of data, whether it is quantitative or qualitative in nature, requires that it be grouped into categories or classes. In dealing with data obtained from respondents, the basic questions concerning categorization should be asked and answered as early as possible during the project. Many of these questions will be resolved at the time the problem is formulated and the hypotheses to be examined specified. As the project progresses through the various stages, the classification scheme should continually be refined.

The establishment of categories prior to data collection has certain advantages. First, data collection forms may be improved, since the analyst must consider the alternative responses in more depth. Second, higher consistency of interpretation of responses and a reduction in editing problems is possible as investigators can be instructed in more detail. Third, precoding of collection forms is often possible, which can reduce both processing errors and costs.

Despite these advantages, sometimes establishing of categories can be done only after the data have been collected. This is likely to arise when open-end questions, unstructured interviews, and projective techniques are used. Establishing categories for unstructured responses is much more difficult than for structured responses (such as when dichotomous and multiple-choice questions are used).

Selecting categories is based upon both the purposes of the survey and the nature of the responses. To be useful, the resulting categories must meet certain conditions:

1. Within categories, responses are sufficiently similar that they can be considered the same

2. Between categories, responses are substantively different

3. Categories are based upon one, and only one relevant, dimension of the problem

4. Categories are mutually exclusive and collectively exhaustive

3. This section draws upon material contained in Paul E. Green and Donald S. Tull, *Research for Marketing Decisions* (Englewood Cliffs: Prentice-Hall, Inc., 1966), Chapter 10.

## EDITING AND CODING

Editing involves reviewing the data collected by investigators to insure maximum accuracy and unambiguity. *Coding*, on the other hand, occurs when responses are placed into data categories, and numbers or some other type of symbols are used to identify each response with its appropriate category.

*Editing.* Editing should be done as soon as possible after the data have been collected. In order that the data be treated consistently and uniformly, editing should be centralized. If the size of the sample is relatively small, it is desirable that only one person edit all the data for the entire project. For those projects whose size makes it necessary to use more than one editor, it is generally preferable to have each editor responsible for a different part of the data collection form. By doing this, each item on all forms is edited by the same person, which results in increased consistency of editing.

The editor should look at each collection form with respect to the following criteria that must be adhered to:

1. *Legibility.* Obviously, the data must be legible to be used. If a response is not presented clearly and clarification of it cannot be obtained from the person who recorded it, sometimes what it should say may be inferred from other data on the form. Where doubt exists about the meaning of a recorded response, it should be thrown out

2. *Completeness.* An omitted entry on a fully structured collection form may mean that no attempt was made to collect the data, that the respondent did not provide it (for whatever reason), or that the investigator simply did not record the data. If the investigator did not record the data, prompt editing and questioning of the investigator may provide the missing item. If an entry is missing because of either of the first two possible causes, there is not much that can be done, except to make another attempt to get the missing data. Obviously, this requires knowing why the entry is missing

3. *Consistency.* An entry that is inconsistent with others raises the question of which is correct. Inconsistencies in data should be resolved by questioning the investigator, if at all possible to do so. If this is not possible, then the inconsistent entries should be omitted

4. *Accuracy.* An editor should be alert to any indications of inaccuracies of the data. Of major importance is detecting any repetitive response patterns in the reports of individual investigators, since they may represent evidence of investigator bias or perhaps even dishonesty

*Coding.* Improper coding can cause poor analyses. Codes can be assigned to categories before the data are collected. This process, known as precoding, is particularly suitable when structured data collection forms are used. In contrast, when unstructured forms are used, *postcoding,* which is the assignment of codes to responses after the data are collected, is necessary.

Persons doing coding must be properly trained and supervised. Written instructions should be provided, and the coder should have first-hand knowledge of how the data is being collected. If the coder is familiar with what is involved in collection, interpretation of the data can be facilitated. If more than one person is doing the coding, it is desirable to compare the results of the various coders. This enables any inconsistencies to be brought out into the open. In addition to the obvious purpose of eliminating them, the discovery of inconsistencies sometimes points to the need for additional categories for data classification and sometimes may mean there is need to combine some of the categories.

## TABULATING

Tabulating, which is simply the counting of the number of responses in data categories, is the last step in the process of sorting the data into categories.

The most basic tabulation is the *simple tabulation,* also known as the *frequency distribution.* This type of tabulation consists of a count of the number of responses that occur in each of the data categories. For example, a simple tabulation of a survey of bank depositors' money borrowing habits might yield the following:

| Behavior | Number of Respondents |
|---|---|
| Presently borrowing | 513 |
| Have borrowed in the past | 106 |
| Have never borrowed | 795 |
| TOTAL | 1,414 |

This example shows tabulation for an attribute. A similar process occurs for tabulating a continuous measurement (that is, a variable). For a continuous measurement, the categories consist of the smallest intervals of data needed to solve the problem; the smallest possible interval is the unit of measurement. For instance a simple tabulation of the age of bank depositors might be:

| Age | Number of Respondents |
|-----|-----------------------|
| Under 35 | 359 |
| 35–54 | 589 |
| 55 & over | 466 |
| TOTAL | 1,414 |

If it was felt that tabulation should show individual ages, then the interval for each category would be the unit of measurement, that is, one year.

In contrast to the simple tabulation is the *cross tabulation,* which utilizes the simultaneous counting of the number of observations that occur in each of the data categories, based upon two or more factors. An example is given in Table 8–1. The use of cross tabulations in the analysis of the data will be discussed in Chapter 9.

There are many methods by which data can be tabulated. Which one should be used in a particular case depends upon such factors as (1) the number of categories of data, (2) the size of the sample, and (3) the amount and kind of analyses to be performed. Where few categories exist, a small sample has been used, and limited analysis performed, so-called hand tabulation is the quickest and most economic method. However, as there are increases in the number of categories, the size of the sample, and the amount and complexity of the required analysis, there comes a point at which computer tabulation becomes more productive and efficient. Once the data have been prepared for use of the computer (a costly and time consuming activity), the tabulation and running of analytic calculations can be done quickly and accurately. That is, the ease of using the computer for analysis is a prime reason for tabulating the data by computer. Many computer programs combine both the necessary tabulations and the technique of analysis into a single process.

TABLE 8–1   Cross tabulation of money borrowing habits by age of respondent*

| Borrowing habit | Age | | | |
|-----------------|----------|-------|-----------|-------|
| | Under 35 | 35-54 | 55 & over | Total |
| Presently borrowing | 147 | 230 | 136 | 513 |
| Have borrowed in the past | 36 | 34 | 36 | 106 |
| Have never borrowed | 176 | 325 | 294 | 795 |
| TOTAL | 359 | 589 | 466 | 1,414 |

*Hypothetical data.

## Summarizing Categorized Data

Summarization so as to facilitate the understanding and analysis of data is only partly accomplished by their tabulation into frequency distributions. Also desirable is to summarize data further by computing descriptive measures of them: relative measures, such as the percentage of depositors who have borrowed money on a short-term basis; averages, such as the mean amount borrowed; and the amount of variation in the distribution, such as the range or standard deviation of the amount borrowed.

The use of the word *descriptive* for these measures is somewhat misleading because it implies that their only role is to describe the distribution from which they were computed. While this is one of the roles they occupy, they are also used for drawing inferences and making decisions. That is, in many instances they are crucial for testing hypotheses.

When used properly, descriptive statistical measures reduce a set of data into simple, precise, and meaningful figures. Occasionally it is possible to reduce a distribution of data into summary measures that, for purposes of decision making, can be substituted for the entire distribution. These summary measures are known as certainty equivalents.

Descriptive measures can be classified into two broad types. The first type measures the central values of the distribution. These measures are known as *measures of central tendency*. The other type deals with the extent and kind of variation in the data, and is known as *measures of dispersion*. Table 8–2 defines these summary measures and indicates the minimum level of measurement needed for proper use of each.

## Formulating Additional Hypotheses

As stated earlier, the objectives of the study and the hypotheses to be examined should be—to the extent feasible—clearly stated and agreed upon at the outset. These objectives and hypotheses shape and mold the study; they determine the kind of information that is required, the specific data that are to be collected, and the kind of analysis that will be necessary.

However, a project will usually turn up new hypotheses, regardless of the rigor with which it was thought through and planned. New hypotheses are suggested at many stages of the project, ranging from data collection through the final interpretation of the findings.

In Chapter 2 it was pointed out that scientific method has been viewed in its simplest form as consisting of four sequential steps: (1) problem formulation; (2) hypothesis formulation; (3) devising one or more tests for the hypotheses; and (4) testing the hypotheses. It should be noted that hypothesis formulation precedes the collection of information to test it.

TABLE 8–2   Summary measures of one-dimensional distributions

---

*Measures of Central Tendency:*

---

*Arithmetic Mean*—the point on a scale around which the values of a distribution balance. For a probability distribution, the arithmetic mean is called the expected value of the distribution. The level of measurement must be at least interval.

*Median*—the midpoint of the data in the distribution. The minimum level of measurement is ordinal.

*Mode*—the typical or most frequently occurring value in the distribution. Nominal measurement is all that is necessary.

---

*Measures of Dispersion:*

---

*Range*—the extreme values of the distribution. Measurement must be at least ordinal.

*Semi-interquartile Range*—calculated as one-half of the difference between the extreme values of the middle 50 percent of the values in the distribution. Measurement must be at least ordinal.

*Variance*—the mean of the squared deviations of the individual measurements from the arithmetic mean of the distribution. Measurements must be at least intervally scaled.

*Standard Deviation*—a measure that is useful because it is one of the terms included in the equation of the normal distribution. It is calculated as the square root of the variance, and, thus, requires at least interval measurement.

*Coefficient of Variation*—an abstract measure without a base unit; it is the ratio of the standard deviation to the arithmetic mean $(\sigma/\mu)$. Interval measurement is a minimum requirement.

---

Rigorous standards of investigation require that this be the case. Thus, the data that suggest the hypothesis should *not* be used to test it.

We do not disagree with these standards of objective evidence for hypothesis testing. However, it is important to note that information suggesting a new hypothesis may be sufficiently compelling to result in a high prior probability's being attached to the new hypothesis' being correct. On a practical basis this prior probability may be sufficiently high to make it uneconomic to test the new hypothesis. The expected value of the additional information may be less than the cost of acquiring it.

When new hypotheses are formulated during the project, it is desirable to expand the analysis to examine them to the extent that the data permit. At one extreme, it may be possible to show that the new hypothesis is not supported by the data and that no further investigation should be considered. At the other extreme, it may turn out that strong supportive evidence is provided by other portions of the data and that a high prior probability of its being correct will result. Between these extremes may be the outcome that the new hypothesis is neither supported nor rejected by the data. In this event additional collection of information may be indicated.

A more extreme position is taken by Hanan Selvin and Alan Stuart; they feel that in survey research, it is rarely possible to formulate precise hypotheses independently of the data.[4] This means that most survey research is essentially exploratory in nature. Rather than having a single predesignated hypothesis in mind, the analyst works with many diffuse and ill-defined hypotheses. The added cost of an extra question is so low that the same survey can be used to investigate many problems without increasing the total cost very much. On a typical survey project, therefore, the analyst alternates between analyzing the data and formulating hypotheses. Obviously, there are exceptions to all general rules and phenomena. Selvin and Stuart, therefore, designate three practices of survey analysts:

1. *Snooping.* The process of testing from the data all of a predesignated set of hypotheses
2. *Fishing.* The process of using the data to choose which of a number of predesignated variables to include in a explanatory model
3. *Hunting.* The process of searching through a body of data and looking at many relations in order to find those worth testing (that is, there is no predesignation)

The position taken by Selvin and Stuart may be reasonable for basic research but may not be practical for decisional research. Time and other pressures seem to require that snooping and perhaps fishing are useful in decision research. Rarely, can the decision maker afford the luxury of hunting. Again, it simply reduces to the question of cost versus value.

## Making Inferences

Once the data have been tabulated and summary measures calculated, it may be desirable to analyze them to determine whether observed differences between categories are indicative of actual differences or whether they occurred as the result of chance variation in the sample. In some studies, on the other hand, it may be sufficient simply to know the value of certain parameters of the population, such as the mean usage of our product per consuming unit, or the proportion of stores carrying our brand, or the preferences of housewives concerning alternative styles or designs of a new product. Even in these cases, however, it is desirable that the decision maker know about the underlying associated factors involved, if not for purposes of the immediate problem, then for use in solving later problems. In other cases, it is necessary to analyze the relationships of the variables and attrib-

4. Hanan C. Selvin and Alan Stuart, "Data-Dredging Procedures in Survey Analysis," *The American Statistician* (June, 1966), pp. 20–23.

utes involved to determine behavioral correlates and causal relationships. Knowledge of these relationships will enhance the ability to make reliable predictions of the results of making changes in controllable variables.

As pointed out in Chapter 2, the broad objective of testing of hypotheses underlies all decisional research. Often this can be done directly. At times, however, estimation may be necessary. Thus, while estimation may be useful in itself in basic research, in decisional research it is done only when necessary for the testing of a hypothesis. In both estimation and hypothesis testing, *inferences* are made about the population of interest on the basis of information from a sample. We now discuss estimation and hypothesis testing as each relates to making inferences.

## ESTIMATION

In estimation, the researcher is interested in estimating the value of a characteristic of the population (that is, a parameter), which may be a variable or attribute, from the information provided by a sample. The value calculated is called a *statistic*.

The procedure used in estimation is quite simple. A sample is chosen, the data are collected, the relevant statistic is calculated, and an estimate is made of the corresponding population parameter on the basis of this statistic. Only by chance or coincidence, however, will an estimate be the same as the true population parameter. It may vary as a result of either bias or variable errors being present. It will be recalled from Chapters 2 and 4 that there are several potential sources of error in estimates. There are nonsampling errors that arise from imperfections of measurements made, the sampling frame used, the selection process, the inability to contact all of the sample of respondents selected, and refusals from some of the sample contacted. There is also the sampling error resulting from the chance specification of respondents according to the sampling plan.

Suppose for the moment that we have only sampling error present and that the sampling plan is such as to give an unbiased estimate. The best single estimate we could get of the parameter is the sample value: this is called a *point estimate*. If, for example, a bank conducted a survey of a sample of its depositors and found that the mean amount borrowed during the past year was $100, this would be a point estimate of the population mean. If the estimate were unbiased, it would be the best single point estimate of the population mean that could be made from the survey data.

It is often more useful to have the estimate in the form of a range of values within which the true value is believed to lie. This range, which is called a *confidence interval*, designates an interval within which the true population will lie in a determinate proportion of cases. Through the use of probability theory, for a sampling distribution that is known, and when nonsampling errors are negligible, we can calculate the probability that the true population parameter lies within the interval of the sample estimate plus and minus a specified amount. As discussed in Chapter 2, this amount is determined by the standard error of the sampling distribution.

For example, suppose a bank conducted a survey on a sample of its depositors and found that the mean amount borrowed during the past year was $100 (that is, $\overline{X} = \$100$) and that the standard error calculated from the sample standard deviation was $20 (that is, $\hat{\sigma}_x = \$20$). Assuming that the population of depositors is a normal distribution and that the only error is from sampling, we can say that there is a 68 percent chance that the true population value of the mean amount borrowed ($\mu$) lies within the interval $\overline{X} \pm \hat{\sigma}_x$. Thus, in the hypothetical survey stated above, $\mu$ lies within the interval $80–120 with a probability $p = .68$.

## HYPOTHESIS TESTING

In general, the testing of hypotheses is concerned with (1) determining whether a population value differs from a critical value, (2) determining whether certain populations or sections of a population differ from one another in particular characteristics, or (3) inferring relationships among variables and/or attributes. The validity of sample-based inferences about the population is judged on the basis of statistical significance tests. For example, a hypothesis stating a relevant difference may be postulated. The question arising after a survey is done is whether the sample result tends to discredit or support the hypothesis. The criterion by which to judge validity is to determine whether any observed differences actually exist in the population (that is, is statistically significant) or whether the difference occurred as a result of sampling variations.

The general approach to statistical significance tests is much the same as that used in estimation. A "region of acceptance" around a hypothetical or true parameter is determined in much the same way as a confidence interval (or credible interval). The region of acceptance is an interval over which the corresponding values of similar samples taken from the same population have a specified probability of fluctuating due to sampling variations. As in the case of estimation, the region of acceptance is stated as a certain multiple of the standard error.

*Illustration of an Objectivist Test.* An illustration of a test, using the extra reserve example to provide the test situation, will be helpful at this point. We shall suppose that a bank is interested in determining whether the mean amount which would be borrowed per year by depositors through the plan, $\mu$, would exceed the amount required by the bank to break even, $\bar{\mu}$. If $\mu > \bar{\mu}$, the plan will be initiated. Otherwise the plan will not be implemented. If $\bar{\mu} = \$100$, the null hypothesis, $H_o$, is

$$H_o: \mu \leq \$100$$

The bank conducts a sample survey of size $n = 50$ using an objectivist procedure which provides the following data: $\bar{X} = \$125$; $s = \$175$; and $\alpha = .10$.

The sampling distribution for the test can be identified by specifying (a) that it is normal and (b) the mean and standard error of it. The mean is specified by the null hypothesis. We make an unbiased estimate of the standard error of mean as follows:

$$\hat{\sigma}_{\bar{X}} = \frac{s}{\sqrt{n-1}} = \frac{\$175}{\sqrt{50-1}} = \frac{\$175}{7} = \$25$$

The 10 percent risk of falsely rejecting a true hypothesis (that is, $\alpha = .10$), translates to the requirement that the sample mean equal or exceed the population mean plus 1.28 standard errors. This is equal to $132 ($100 + 1.28 \times \$25$). Since the sample mean was $125, we conclude that we cannot reject the hypothesis.

It is instructive to calculate the likelihood $p(\bar{X} = \$125 \mid \mu = \$100)$. The number of standard errors represented by $(\bar{X} - \mu)$ is

$$Z = \frac{\bar{X} - \mu}{\hat{\sigma}_{\bar{X}}} = \frac{\$125 - 100}{\$25} = 1.0$$

The area to the right of $+1.0$ standard errors as determined from a normal distribution table is 0.158. Thus, if we rejected the hypothesis that $\mu = \$100$ on the basis of a sample mean of $125 (obtained from a simple random sample of size 50 and with a sample standard deviation of $175), we would be running a risk of slightly less than 16 percent of falsely rejecting a true hypothesis.

*Illustration of a Bayesian Test.*  It will be useful to illustrate a Bayesian test of an hypothesis by applying it to the example just used for the objectivist test. The circumstances of the test are as follows:

$$H_o: \mu = \$100 \qquad n = 50$$
$$\bar{X} = \$125 \qquad \hat{\sigma}_x = \$25$$
$$s = \$175$$

Now suppose that before the research is conducted, the information obtained by the investigator from an experience survey and other sources has led him to conclude that the mean number of dollars per year that will be borrowed by individual depositors through the "extra reserve" plan, $\mu_o$, is $145. He decides that the distribution is normal and that there is a 95 percent probability that the true value of the mean lies between $105 and $185. This is a 95 percent *credible interval.* The standard deviation of this prior distribution, $\hat{\sigma}_{\bar{o}}$, is approximately $20, since 95.4 percent of the area of a normal distribution lies in the area bounded by two standard deviations on each side of the mean. This prior distribution is shown in Figure 8-1.

As indicated by the formula given in Chapter 2, the posterior density is determined as

$$\text{posterior density} = \frac{(\text{prior density})(\text{likelihood})}{\Sigma[(\text{prior density})(\text{likelihood})]}$$

This calculation simplifies to formulae for determining the posterior mean and posterior standard deviation when the distributions are normal.[5] The formula for the posterior mean is

$$\mu_1 = \frac{\mu_o(1/\sigma_o{}^2) + \bar{X}(1/\hat{\sigma}_{\bar{X}}{}^2)}{1/\sigma_o{}^2 + 1/\hat{\sigma}_{\bar{X}}{}^2} \tag{8.1}$$

and the posterior standard deviation is given by

$$\sigma_1 = \frac{1}{\sigma_o{}^2} + \frac{1}{\hat{\sigma}_{\bar{X}}{}^2} \tag{8.2}$$

where

$\mu_o$ = prior mean
$\bar{X}$ = sample mean
$\sigma_o$ = prior standard deviation
$\hat{\sigma}_{\bar{X}}$ = estimated standard error of sampling distribution

For the present example, the posterior mean is calculated from (8.1) as

$$\mu_1 = \frac{\$145\dfrac{1}{(\$20)^2} + \$125\dfrac{1}{(\$25)^2}}{\dfrac{1}{(\$20)^2} + \dfrac{1}{(\$25)^2}} = \$137.20$$

5. For a derivation of these formulae see Robert Schlaifer, *Probability and Statistics for Business Decisions* (New York: McGraw-Hill Book Co., 1959). These formulae are also presented and discussed in Ben M. Enis and Charles L. Broome, *Marketing Decisions: A Bayesian Approach* (New York: Intext Educational Publishers, 1971), Chapter 5.

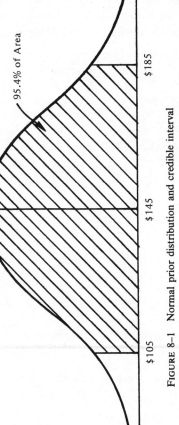

FIGURE 8–1   Normal prior distribution and credible interval

Using 8.2, the posterior standard deviation is determined as

$$\sigma_1 = \cfrac{1}{\cfrac{1}{(\$20)^2} + \cfrac{1}{(\$25)^2}} = \$15.62$$

The three distributions are shown in Figure 8-2. It will be observed that the posterior mean lies between the sampling and prior distribution means ($100 < $137.20 < $145). *This will always be the case.* It may also be noted that the posterior distribution is more "peaked" than either the sampling or the prior distribution. This reflects a smaller standard deviation than either of the two ($15.62 < $20, $25), and this also is an invariant result of combining sampling and prior distributions.

The posterior distribution permits conditional probability statements concerning population values, given sampling and prior information. In our example, these probabilities are of the form $p(\mu \mid \mu_1)$. In testing the hypothesis $H_o$: $\mu = \$100$ we are therefore treating $\mu$ as a *random variable*. Allowing only a 10 percent chance of incorrectly concluding that the true mean is greater than $\mu$ when in fact it is not, the critical value is determined from the posterior distribution as

$$\begin{aligned} C = \mu_1 - Z\sigma_1 &= \$137.20 - (1.28 \times \$15.62) \\ &= \$137.20 - 19.99 \\ &= \$117.21 \end{aligned}$$

We must therefore *reject* the null hypothesis.

*Conditions of Use.* The use of Bayesian tests of hypotheses has been limited almost exclusively to decisional research. The reason for this is clear; the results of the test are jointly dependent upon the sample evidence *and* the prior distribution. Acceptance of the test outcome therefore requires agreement with the prior distribution.

A necessary condition for use of a Bayesian hypothesis test is that the analyst be able to obtain a prior distribution from the decision maker. This may prove easier to assume in textbooks than it is to accomplish in an executive office. Bayesian analysis is still new enough that most executives have had no formal exposure to it. It is therefore not unusual that they do not understand it. For those who do not, impatience may be the reaction when a seemingly complex and not very meaningful series of questions is asked them.

A second problem that arises less frequently is that the decision maker does understand the procedure but does not agree that it is useful. Many professional statisticians remain strongly traditional with respect to the testing of hypotheses.

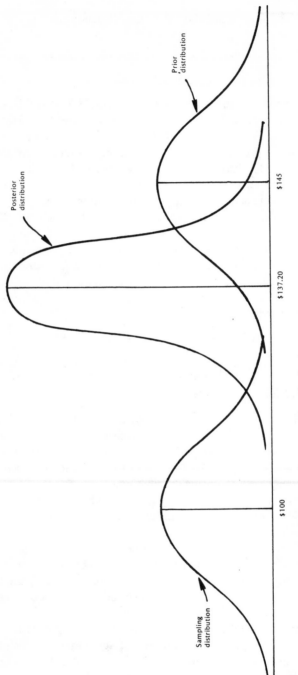

FIGURE 8-2  Prior, posterior, and sampling distributions

180

A situation that is sometimes considered to be a problem is that of multiple decision makers. How can one obtain a prior distribution from the board of directors or the executive committee when there is no unanimity of prior judgment?

One answer to this question is that one should not attempt to obtain a prior distribution. Rather, one should proceed on a series of individual hypothesis tests to see if in fact differences in prior judgments make any difference in the decision based upon the test results. If they do not, there is no problem. If the differing prior distributions do result in differing decisions, a form of sensitivity analysis results. The area of difference in prior judgment that caused the difference in test outcome will have been identified and discussion can be focused on it.

*Level of Significance.* A question that continually plagues analysts is "What should be the significance level used in hypothesis testing?" This involves specifying the value of $\alpha$, which is the allowable amount of Type I error (or the probability that we will incorrectly reject $H_o$).

Significance levels are—or, at any rate, should be—set as a result of (a) cost of error and (b) decision rule used. There are substantial differences between basic and decisional research in assignment of error costs and there *may* be differences in choice of decision rule as well. The result is that the levels of significance used in a basic research project may be entirely inappropriate for those in a decisional research project dealing with the same problem.

There is a pronounced and, to our way of thinking, laudable tradition of conservatism in basic research. This tradition results in the requirement that a high level of probability be demonstrated that the effects being investigated do in fact stem from the operation of the hypothesized causal agents before any such conclusion is drawn.

This tradition has resulted in the standard procedure in basic research of testing hypotheses in which it is assumed that no differential effects exist; that is, null hypotheses are usually tested. Further, this conservative tradition has resulted in the practice of keeping the error of falsely rejecting the null hypothesis at a low level. This is to say that the Type I error has been traditionally considered to be more important than the Type II error and, correspondingly, that it is more important to have a low $\alpha$ than a low $\beta$. The basic researcher typically assigns higher costs to a Type I than to a Type II error.

In decisional research, the costs are assigned by the consequences of the errors. The cost of foregoing gain as a result of a Type II error may be even greater than the loss from making a Type I error, depending upon the situation and the decision rule being used.[6] To an expected value decision maker the value of the information he receives from the project is reduced as the costs of making Type I and Type II errors, weighted by $\alpha$ and $\beta$ respectively, rise.

In basic research the usual practice is to predesignate a level of $\alpha$, with no real concern about $\beta$. For decisional research, we can approach the significance level problem in one of two ways:

1. If we are unable to formulate an alternative hypothesis specifying a magnitude of difference that would affect the decision to be made, the level of $\alpha$ at which significance occurs can be reported

2. If a relevant magnitude of difference can be specified as an alternative hypothesis, then for certain types of problems we can estimate $\beta$ for corresponding levels of $\alpha$.[7] The decision maker can then determine the necessary balance between desired $\alpha$ and $\beta$ levels

## Summary

This chapter has dealt with the process of analysis of survey data. The four major steps in the analysis process were identified and examined in some detail. These activities are: (1) sorting the data into categories; (2) summarizing the categorized data; (3) formulating additional hypotheses; and (4) making inferences.

Concerning the last step, inferences can be made pertaining to differences between or among categories of data and relationships among variables and attributes. Making inferences involves both estimation and hypothesis testing. Concerning the testing of hypotheses, we discussed the problem of determining significance levels in decisional research.

This chapter provides the necessary background for our discussion of techniques of analysis next in Chapter 9.

6. Not all decision situations have these types of consequences of making errors. There are situations where making a Type I error may lead to an opportunity cost (for example, a foregone gain) and a Type II error may create a direct loss. For example, suppose an investigator had to decide which one of two alternative measuring instruments to use in measuring attitudes toward an extra reserve plan. One instrument was a "proven" one, with a reasonably high degree of pragmatic validity. The other instrument was newly developed, but the cost of administering it was less than the "proven" one. In this type of decisional situation, and an hypothesis of no difference, a Type I error could lead to an opportunity cost, since the investigator would have decided to keep using the higher cost instrument. On the other hand, a Type II error could create direct monetary loss depending upon the management decisions made on the basis of data provided by an "invalid" instrument.

7. See Enis and Broome, op. cit., pp. 79–83, and Gerald E. Thompson, Statistics for Decisions: An Elementary Introduction (Boston: Little, Brown and Company, 1972), Chapters 11 and 12.

## SELECTED BIBLIOGRAPHY

Cartwright, Dorwin P. "Analysis of Qualitative Material." pp. 421–470 in Leon Festinger and Daniel Katz, eds. *Research Methods in the Behavioral Sciences.* New York: Holt, Rinehart and Winston, 1953. A thorough presentation of the analysis process involved in treating symbolic or "qualitative" material.

Labovitz, Sanford. "Criteria for Selecting a Significance Level: A Note on the Sacredness of .05." *The American Sociologist,* vol. 3, no. 3 (August, 1968), pp. 220–222. A discussion of eleven more or less independent criteria that can be considered in determining an appropriate $\alpha$ level for testing hypotheses.

Selltiz, Claire et al. *Research Methods in Social Relations.* New York: Holt, Rinehart and Winston, revised edition, 1959. Chapter 11 of this excellent book on research methodology discusses the procedures used in analysis and interpretation. The end result is a very readable treatment of the major steps in the analysis process.

Thompson, Gerald E. *Statistics for Decision: An Elementary Introduction.* Boston: Little, Brown and Company, 1972. An easily readable and understandable nonmathematical introduction to Bayesian statistical methods that integrates the main methods of "classical" statistics.

## QUESTIONS AND PROBLEMS

8.1. We have suggested that analysis be taken into consideration in the planning stage of a survey project. Explain how this can be done for each of the major steps in the analysis process.

8.2. Decide which measure or measures of central tendency is/are appropriate in each of the following situations.

a. You have made a study of family incomes in a market area and have found that the range is from $2,285 to $423,690 for the year

b. A company planning to market only one size of a product makes a study of the distribution of sales for the industry by size of the product

c. You have made a study of the amount of the charges per customer for a cleaning establishment for the past month. The owner has estimated the number of customers his cleaning firm will serve during the next month and wishes to estimate total revenues

d. You have made the same calculation twelve times and have arrived at a total of three different answers. You do not have time for additional rechecking

8.3. Decide which measure or measures of dispersion is/are appropriate in each of the following situations.

a. You wish to indicate the dispersion in family incomes in a market area during a given year.

b. You wish to indicate the dispersion in retail gasoline prices for the same grade of gasoline in a given marketing area

*8.4. The marketing manager of a company that has developed an "improved" industrial product in the "operating supply" category had decided that he will market this product if the average monthly purchase is at least 80 units. A

survey of a simple random sample of 65 buyers indicates the following: $\overline{X} = 82$ and $s = 4$.

   a.  Based upon an objectivist's approach, should the product be marketed? Explain

   b.  Would your answer change if the minimum needed was 82 units and $\overline{X} = 80$? Explain.

   c.  Explain how this question could be answered using a Bayesian approach. What additional data would be needed to use the Bayesian model?

   8.5.  What is your position on the so-called significance level controversy? Discuss fully.

# Techniques of Analysis

In Chapter 8 we looked at the overall process of analysis. In this chapter we extend the treatment of analysis and consider various statistical and mathematical techniques that can be applied to survey data for purposes of estimation and hypothesis testing. Our major concern is with determining differences between parameters and relationships among variables. The major emphasis of this chapter is on univariate and bivariate techniques. However, a relatively brief discussion is included of some of the more popular multivariate techniques.

## Determining Differences

The concept of the sampling distribution of a statistic was discussed in Chapter 3. We now extend the discussion to cover *differences* in statistics. The sampling distribution of the differences in two sample statistics is the probability distribution of the differences in the two statistics of all possible pairs of samples of given size $n_A$ and $n_B$ drawn, respectively, from universe A and universe B.

### STANDARD ERROR OF DIFFERENCES

For samples that are independent and randomly selected, the standard error of the differences in means is calculated in the following way:

$$\hat{\sigma}_{\bar{X}_A - \bar{X}_B} = \sqrt{\frac{\hat{\sigma}_A^2}{n_A} + \frac{\hat{\sigma}_B^2}{n_B}} \qquad (9.1a)$$

when the standard deviations of each of the populations must be estimated, which is the usual case in survery research. The calculations for $\hat{\sigma}_A$ and $\hat{\sigma}_B$ are made in the manner shown in Chapter 3. For relatively small samples, the resulting formula for the estimated standard error is

$$\hat{\sigma}_{\bar{X}_A - \bar{X}_B} = \sqrt{\frac{s_A^2}{n_A - 1} + \frac{s_B^2}{n_B - 1}} \qquad (9.1b)$$

If $n_A$ and $n_B$ are quite large, then the correction factor

$$\frac{n}{n - 1}$$

need not be used, and $s_A$ and $s_B$ can be used as direct estimates of the population standard deviations (that is, $s_A = \hat{\sigma}_A$ and $s_B = \hat{\sigma}_B$). Taking this into account, formula (9.1b) becomes

$$\hat{\sigma}_{\bar{X}_A - \bar{X}_B} = \sqrt{\frac{s_A^2}{n_A} + \frac{s_B^2}{n_B}} \qquad (9.1c)$$

For proportions, the standard error of the differences is derived somewhat similar to that for the mean. Specifically,

$$\hat{\sigma}_{p_A - p_B} = \sqrt{\hat{\sigma}_A^2 + \hat{\sigma}_B^2} \qquad (9.2a)$$

when the individual population standard deviations must be estimated. When large samples are used, and $\hat{\sigma}_A^2$ and $\hat{\sigma}_B^2$ are derived as shown in Chapter 3, we get

$$\hat{\sigma}_{p_A - p_B} = \sqrt{\frac{p_A(1 - p_A)}{n_A} + \frac{p_B(1 - p_B)}{n_B}} \qquad (9.2b)$$

For small samples, $\hat{\sigma}_{pA}^2$ and $\hat{\sigma}_{pB}^2$ must be multiplied by the correction factor $n_i / n_i - 1$, and (9.2b) becomes

$$\hat{\sigma}_{pA - pB} = \sqrt{\frac{p_A(1 - p_A)}{n_A - 1} + \frac{p_B(1 - p_B)}{n_B - 1}} \qquad (9.2c)$$

The formulas given above for the standard error of the difference between two means and proportions can be applied either for purposes of estimation or hypothesis testing.

## ESTIMATION

In addition to estimating population means or proportions, we often are interested in comparing the parameters of two populations. For instance, a bank might want to compare the potential success of two alternative plans for an extra reserve plan. Two samples of depositors could be randomly and independently drawn, and each group presented with one of the plans and asked how much might be borrowed. We would make inferences concerning the difference as measured by the difference in mean amount that might be borrowed under each of the plans.

This example postulates two populations, $A$ and $B$. The point estimate of the difference between the two means $(\mu_A - \mu_B)$, is $(\overline{X}_A - \overline{X}_B)$. However, as we mentioned in the last chapter, often we are interested in an interval estimate, which involves placing a confidence interval around the point estimate. When the sample sizes are large (that is, $n_A$, $n_B > 30$), a confidence interval for $(\mu_A - \mu_B)$ with confidence coefficient $(1-\alpha)$ can be calculated from

$$(\overline{X}_A - \overline{X}_B) \pm Z_{\alpha/2} \hat{\sigma}_{\overline{X}_A - \overline{X}_B} \qquad (9.3)$$

where $Z_{\alpha/2}$ is taken from the Normal Probability Distribution table (Appendix Table 2) and

$$\hat{\sigma}_{\overline{X}_A - \overline{X}_B}$$

is derived from Formula 9.1d. The interval estimate for differences in proportions is arrived at similarly. For example, suppose that two samples were drawn of size $n_A = n_B = 100$, and the following statistics were derived concerning amount of money that would be borrowed under each plan:

$$\overline{X}_A = \$885 \qquad\qquad \overline{X}_B = \$390$$
$$s_A{}^2 = \$36{,}800 \qquad\qquad s_B{}^2 = \$47{,}200$$

It is desired that a confidence interval of .99 be placed around the difference in mean amount that would be borrowed. The point estimate of $(\mu_A - \mu_B)$ is $(\overline{X}_A - \overline{X}_B) = \$885 - \$390 = \$495$. The .99 confidence interval using formula (9.3) is

$$(\overline{X}_A - \overline{X}_B) \pm 2.58 \sqrt{\frac{\$36{,}000}{100} + \frac{\$47{,}200}{100}}$$

or

$$\$495 \pm 2.58\ (\$28.98)$$

Thus, the difference in mean amount that will be borrowed is estimated to lie between \$420.23 and \$569.77.

If, in the above illustration, the sample sizes for $A$ and $B$ were small ($< 30$), then to construct a confidence interval around the point estimate $(\mu_A - \mu_B)$, the Student $t$ distribution must be used instead of the normal distribution. Doing this, we get a confidence interval, with coefficient $(1-\alpha)$ from the formula

$$(\overline{X}_A - \overline{X}_B) \pm t_{\alpha/2} \hat{\sigma}_{\overline{X}_A - \overline{X}_B} \qquad (9.4)$$

where $t_{\alpha/2}$ is taken from the table of critical values of the $t$ distribution (Appendix Table 3) and

$$\hat{\sigma}_{\overline{X}_A - \overline{X}_B}$$

is calculated from Formula 9.1b.

Suppose that in the above example of two types of extra reserve plans we had derived the same statistics

$$\overline{X}_A = \$885$$

$$\overline{X}_B = \$390$$

$$\hat{\sigma}_{\overline{X}_A} - \overline{X}_B = \$28.98$$

*from samples of size* $n_A = n_B = 15$. In this case, we use Formula 9.4 for a .99 confidence interval $\$495 \pm 2.76(\$28.98)$ where $t_{\alpha/2}$ is the $t$ value corresponding to $(n_A + n_B - 2)$ degrees of freedom. The difference in mean amount that will be borrowed in this situation will lie between \$415.02 and \$574.98.

## TESTING OF HYPOTHESES

When applying the formulas above for hypotheses testing concerning parameters, the following conditions must be met:

1. Samples must be independent
2. Individual items in samples must be drawn in a random manner
3. The population being sampled must be normally distributed[1]
4. For small samples, the population variances are equal
5. The data must be at least intervally scaled

When these five conditions are met, or at least can be reasonably assumed to exist, the traditional method of hypothesis testing utilizes the following procedure:

1. The null hypothesis ($H_o$) is specified that there is no difference between the parameters of interest in the two populations; any observed difference occurred solely because of sampling variation. For problems involving differences in means, the null and alternative ($H_1$) hypotheses are

$$H_o: \mu_A - \mu_B = 0$$
$$H_1: \mu_A - \mu_B \neq 0$$

and for problems involving differences in proportions

$$H_o: \pi_A - \pi_B = 0$$
$$H_1: \pi_A - \pi_B \neq 0$$

2. The alpha risk is established
3. A $Z$ value is calculated by the appropriate adaptation of the $Z$ formula.[2] For the means, $Z$ is calculated in the following way:

---

1. This is not necessarily true for Formula 9.3, according to the Central Limit Theorem, if $n$ is large enough.
2. This assumes that large samples are used. For small samples, the Student $t$ distribution must be used, and for means, $t$ comes from

$$t = \frac{(\overline{X}_A - \overline{X}_B) - (\mu_A - \mu_B)}{\hat{\sigma}_{\overline{X}_A - \overline{X}_B}} = \frac{(\overline{X}_A - \overline{X}_B) - 0}{\hat{\sigma}_{\overline{X}_A - \overline{X}_B}}$$

Significance is determined from the table of the $t$ distribution, which is interpreted with $(n_A + n_B - 2)$ degrees of freedom.

$$Z = \frac{(\bar{X}_A - \bar{X}_B) - (\mu_A - \mu_B)}{\hat{\sigma}_{\bar{X}_A - \bar{X}_B}} = \frac{(\bar{X}_A - \bar{X}_B) - 0}{\hat{\sigma}_{\bar{X}_A - \bar{X}_B}} \qquad (9.5a)$$

and for proportions

$$Z = \frac{(p_A - p_B) - (\pi_A - \pi_B)}{\hat{\sigma}_{p_A - p_B}} = \frac{(p_A - p_B) - 0}{\hat{\sigma}_{p_A - p_B}} \qquad (9.5b)$$

4. The probability of the observed difference of the two sample statistics having occurred by chance is determined from a table of the normal distribution (or the $t$ distribution)

5. If the probability of the observed difference's having occurred by chance is *greater* than the alpha risk, the null hypothesis is accepted; it is concluded that the parameters of the two universes are not significantly different. If the probability of the observed differences having occurred by chance is *less* than the alpha risk, the null hypothesis is rejected; it is concluded that the parameters of the two populations differ significantly

In a decisional situation, the procedure explained above will be modified. Strictly speaking, null hypotheses are not necessarily tested according to a predetermined alpha level. Rather, the value of $\alpha$ at which significance occurs is determined, and the decision maker balances this with the cost involved in making a Type I error, taking into account the associated beta risk (which can be estimated if we can attach a meaningful magnitude of difference to $H_1$) and the cost of making a Type II error. We discussed this relationship in Chapter 8.

An example will illustrate the traditional application of this procedure.

*Example of Testing for Significance of Differences in Two Means.* Suppose that a survey of short-term money borrowing behavior has been made among urban (population $A$) and rural (population $B$) families. The average amount of money borrowed by a random sample of 400 urban families was found to be $32 with a standard deviation of $10; for a random sample of 225 rural families the average was $30.80 with a standard deviation of $9. In looking at the results of the study the question arises, do urban families actually borrow more money, or is the difference of $1.20 in the sample means caused by sampling variation?

The data necessary for conducting a significance test can be summarized:

$$\overline{X}_A = \$32.00 \qquad \overline{X}_B = \$30.80$$
$$s_A = \$10.00 \qquad s_B = \$\ 9.00$$
$$n_A = 400 \qquad n_B = 225$$

We now follow the steps outlined above.

1. The following null and alternative *hypotheses* are established:

$$H_0: \mu_A - \mu_B = 0$$
$$H_1: \mu_A - \mu_B > 0$$

2. The *alpha* risk is set at, say, .05

3. Since a large sample test is called for, the *Z value* is calculated after determining the standard error in differences in means. In this case we use Formula 9.1c, since $s_A$ and $s_B$ can be used as direct estimates of $\hat{\sigma}_A$ and $\hat{\sigma}_B$

$$\hat{\sigma}_{\overline{X}_A - \overline{X}_B} = \sqrt{\frac{(10.0)^2}{400} + \frac{(9.0)^2}{225}} = \$0.781$$

The Z value is then calculated from (9.5a) as

$$Z = \frac{(32.0 - 30.8) - 0}{.781} = +1.54$$

4. The probability of the observed differences of the sample means having occurred due to sampling variation is determined by finding the area under the normal curve that falls to the right of the point $Z = +1.54$ (one-tail test). Consulting Table 2 in the Appendix, we find this area to be 0.0618

5. Comparing this calculated probability of the observed differences of means having occurred by sampling variation with the alpha risk indicates that the former is greater and that the null hypothesis should, therefore, be accepted. That is, there is no difference between urban and rural families concerning the average amount of money borrowed. It should be noted that, had $\alpha = .10$, the null hypothesis should be rejected, which means that the observed difference of means is not due solely to sampling variation at that level of allowable alpha risk. In a decisional setting, the decision maker has to determine whether this probability ($p = .06$) is low enough for him to conclude, on pragmatic grounds, that the urban and rural families do not differ in their behavior

To illustrate the small sample test, let us assume the same values for the following:

$$\overline{X}_A \qquad \overline{X}_B \qquad \hat{\sigma}_{\overline{X}_A - \overline{X}_B}$$

Furthermore, we assume that the values for $s_A$ and $s_B$ are such that we get

$$\hat{\sigma}_{\overline{X}_A - \overline{X}_B} = \$0.781$$

when $n_A = 15$ and $n_B = 12$. To test for the significance of the difference in means, we must calculate $t$ from the formula given in footnote 2:

$$t = \frac{(32.0 - 30.8) - 0}{0.781} = 1.54$$

The critical value of $t$ can be obtained from Table 3 of the Appendix. In this case, for $\alpha = .05$, we determine the critical value of $t$ for $(n_A + n_B - 2) = 25$ degrees of freedom to be 1.708 (one-tailed test). Since the calculated $t < 1.708$ we cannot reject $H_o: \mu_A - \mu_B = 0$.

*Example of Testing for Differences in Proportions.* To test for the significance of the differences in proportions, we must modify the above procedure. For two populations, say $A$ and $B$, one test of the hypothesis $\pi_A = \pi_B$ (Formula 9.5b is another test) involves finding approximate confidence intervals by

$$p_A - p_B + Z_{1/2\alpha} \sqrt{\frac{p_A(1-p_A)}{n_A} + \frac{p_B(1-p_B)}{n_B}} < \pi_A - \pi_B$$

$$< p_B + Z_{1-1/2} \sqrt{\frac{p_A(1-p_A)}{n_A} + \frac{p_B(1-p_B)}{n_B}} \qquad (9.6)$$

when the samples are relatively large (that is, $n_A p_A$, $n_B p_B$, $n_A(1-p_A)$, $n_B (1-p_B)$ are all larger than 5). If these limits cover zero there would be no reason to reject the hypothesis ($H_o: \pi_A = \pi_B$ or $\pi_A - \pi_B = 0$) at whatever $\alpha$ level of significance is used. If they do not cover zero, $H_o$ should be rejected. There is no contradiction between this confidence interval approach and (9.5b) for testing $H_o: \pi_A = \pi_B$

To illustrate, suppose that a bank conducts a survey concerned with determining attitudes toward an extra reserve plan. Random samples of 600 depositors (population *A)* and 600 nondepositors (population *B)* are drawn. Assuming that attitudes are measured by an interval scale such as Thurstone differential scale, the results show that 43 percent of the depositors have a favorable attitude toward the plan, while only 52 percent of the nondepositors are so inclined. Is the difference between the two groups significant at the .05 level? To answer the question, we determine the 95 percent confidence limits from (9.6) as follows:

$$.52 - .43 + 1.96 \sqrt{\frac{(.52)(.48)}{600} + \frac{(.43)(.57)}{600}} < \pi_A - \pi_B$$

$$< .52 - .43 - 1.96 \sqrt{\frac{(.52)(.48)}{600} + \frac{(.43)(.57)}{600}}$$

This gives the limits

$$-.1455 < \pi_A - \pi_B < -.0345$$

Since these limits do not cover zero, we reject the hypothesis.[3]

For decisional purposes this approach may be less desirable than the Z-test approach of (9.5b) since it requires that the decision maker predesignate a critical $\alpha$ level. Thus, not all of the potentially available information that might be helpful in making a decision is obtained. On the other hand, *the confidence interval approach is useful to a risk-averting decision maker.*

*Inferences about Population Variances.*[4] In order to make inferences about population means or differences in means, estimates of the population variance ($\sigma^2$) or differences in variances ($\sigma_A^2 - \sigma_B^2$) are fundamental. In addition, there are operational conditions where $\sigma^2$ is the main objective of the investigation, although this concern is more prevalant in experimental research than in survey research. Nevertheless, there are times, for instance, when the survey analyst is concerned with the precision of his measuring instrument. The following discussion will deal first with a single variance and with two variances second.

1. For a single variance the unbiased estimator of the population variance is

$$\hat{\sigma}^2 = \frac{n}{n-1} s^2$$

This statistic has a probability distribution with mean equal to $\sigma^2$, which

---

3. Wilfrid J. Dixon and Frank J. Massy, Jr., *Introduction to Statistical Analysis* (New York: McGraw-Hill Book Co., second edition, 1957), pp. 232–234. This approach is based upon independent samples. When the samples are dependent (or the proportions correlated), another test must be used.

4. Our discussion is based upon material contained in William Mendenhall and James E. Reinmuth, *Statistics for Management and Economics,* (Belmont, California: Duxbury Press, 1971), pp. 235–244.

is independent of the population mean, but which possesses a distribution for each sample size, and each value of $\sigma^2$.

If a sample is drawn randomly from a normally distributed population, the distribution of $\sigma^2$ is the well-known chi-square ($X^2$) distribution. For any given $n$, there are $(n-1)$ degrees of freedom associated with $\sigma^2$. To test the null hypothesis concerning a population variance,

$$H_o: \sigma^2 = \bar{\sigma}^2$$

we use the following statistic:

$$\chi^2 = \frac{(n-1)\hat{\sigma}^2}{\bar{\sigma}^2} \qquad (9.7)$$

If $\sigma^2$ is significantly greater than the hypothesized value, $\bar{\sigma}^2$, then $X^2$ will be large and will fall toward the upper end of the distribution. To determine the significance of the calculated value of $X^2$, we look at the table of critical values of the statistic (Table 5 of the Appendix), and interpret in the same manner as the $t$-table. The test should be a one- or two-tailed statistical test, depending upon the alternative hypothesis chosen. However, since it is desirable for $\sigma^2$ to be small, a one-tailed test seems best. To reject $H_o$ on the "low" side is probably not too realistic. To illustrate this test, suppose than an analyst believes that his intervally scaled attitudinal measuring instrument provides attitude measurements with a standard deviation, $\sigma = 2$. During a survey the following measurements are obtained: 4.1, 5.2, 10.2, 7.8, 2.2. We want to test the null hypothesis:

$$H_o: \sigma^2 = (2)^2 = 4$$

against the alternative

$$H_1: \sigma^2 > 4$$

The estimated population variance is $\hat{\sigma}^2 = 9.88$. Using Formula 9.7, we test $H_o$ as follows (using a one-tailed test):

$$\chi^2 = \frac{(n-1)\hat{\sigma}^2}{\bar{\sigma}^2} = \frac{(5-1)(9.88)}{4} = 9.88$$

The critical value of $X^2$ for $\alpha = .05$ and (5-1) degrees of freedom is $X^2 = 9.49$. Since the calculated statistic exceeds the critical value, we reject $H_o$. From a decisional point of view, we determine that the probability at which significance occurs is ($p \simeq .044$), which means that there is a slightly more than 4 percent chance that an error has been made in rejecting $H_o$ and accepting $H_1$.

2.There may be times when the analyst wants to compare the precision of alternative measuring devices. One way to handle this is to compare two population variances, $\sigma_A^2$ and $\sigma_B^2$, using the ratio of the unbiased estimators $\sigma_A^2/\sigma_B^2$.

If independent random samples from two normal populations with equal variances (that is $\sigma_A^2 = \sigma_B^2$) are drawn, then $\sigma_A^2/\sigma_B^2$ has a probability distribution known as the $F$ distribution. The shape of this distribution is nonsymmetrical and depends upon the number of degrees of freedom associated with $\sigma_A^2$ and $\sigma_B^2$. To test the null hypothesis,

$$H_o: \sigma_A^2 - \sigma_B^2 = 0$$

we use the statistic

$$F = \frac{\hat{\sigma}_A^2}{\hat{\sigma}_B^2} \tag{9.8}$$

When using this test, $\sigma_A^2$ is interpreted as the larger sample variance. Critical values of the $F$ distribution are tabled with separate degrees of freedom for each $\sigma_i^2$ (see Table 4 in the Appendix). The degrees of freedom $(n_1-1)$ listed horizontally in the table refer to the sample variance in the numerator of Formula 9.8, while those listed vertically $(n_2-1)$ refer to the variance in the denominator. If the calculated $F$ is greater than or equal to the tabled value $[F_\alpha (n_1-1, n_2-1)]$, then we reject $H_o$ at $\alpha$.

Suppose that we are interested in comparing the precision of the measuring instrument mentioned in the previous section ($\sigma_A^2 = 9.88$, $n = 5$) with another instrument designed to measure the same type of attitude. The measurements obtained from the second instrument are 4.7, 5.1, 3.5, 4.2, 5.0. The estimated variance of the second instrument is $\sigma_B^2 = .43$. We want to test the hypothesis $H_o: \sigma_A^2 - \sigma_B^2 = 0$. To conduct this test we use Formula 9.8

$$F = \frac{9.88}{.43} = 22.99$$

The critical value of $F$ with (5–1, 5–1) degrees of freedom at $\alpha = .01$ is $F = 15.98$. Since our calculated $F$ exceeds the critical value, we reject $H_o$ and can say that the precisions of the two instruments differ. There is less than a 1 percent chance that this conclusion is wrong.

Although our discussion has been concerned with two variances, this need not be the case. Treating variances of two populations in the manner indicated above is a special case of the more general technique of analysis of variance (ANOVA), which is used most often in experimental research.[5]

*Nonparametric Tests.* When the assumptions for using the $t$ and $F$ tests cannot be met, a *nonparametric* test must be used, that is, a test for

5. See Keith Cox and Ben Enis, *Experimentation for Marketing Decisions* (New York: Intext Educational Publishers, 1969).

which no knowledge or assumptions concerning population parameters are required. For intervally scaled data, there are certain relatively powerful nonparametric tests that are appropriate. For illustrative purposes, we mention two of these tests.

If the samples are independent, then the *randomization test* is useful for testing the significance of the difference between means.[6] With this test, the exact probability under the null hypothesis associated with our observations can be determined. This can be done even though we cannot assume normal populations or homogeneity of variances in the populations. This nonparametric test is as powerful as the *t* test (the most powerful parametric test).[7]

Another nonparametric test for intervally scaled measurements is the *Walsh test.* This is a powerful test which can be used if we can assume that the observed difference scores in two related samples are drawn from symmetrical (not normal) populations. With symmetrical populations, the mean is an accurate measure of central tendency and is equal to the median. When compared to the *t* test, power-efficiency of the Walsh Test, which varies with *n* (the number of matched pairs) and $\alpha$, generally is 95 percent.

There are several good textbooks dealing with nonparametric methods which may be consulted for more detailed description of these and other nonparametric methods. An especially well-written example is the work by Siegel.[8]

## TESTING NONINTERVALLY SCALED MEASUREMENTS

When the data collected are at best ordinally scaled, then the statistical significance tests discussed above are not applicable. Moreover, the use of the mean and variance as measures of central tendency and dispersion, respectively, is not correct. However, it is not uncommon that these measures are used on ordinal data. As pointed out in Chapter 3, the basis for using such measures with ordinal data is pragmatic. That is, they appear to work in certain instances. This means that ordinal measurements are being treated as if they were interval measurements.

With nominal and ordinal data it is not possible to give exact measures of population parameters in most situations. Notable exceptions are the

6. There is also a randomization test for dependent samples; a different procedure is followed.

7. The concept of power or power-efficiency is concerned with the amount of increase in sample size which is necessary to make one statistical test as powerful as another. The analyst can avoid meeting some of the assumptions of the parametric tests without losing power by selecting another test and drawing a larger *n*. Thus, the meaning of the power-efficiency of the randomization test is that the sample does not have to be larger than that required for the *t* test.

8. Sidney Siegel, *Nonparametric Statistics for the Behavioral Sciences* (New York: McGraw-Hill Book Co., 1956).

median, mode, and population proportions with ordinal data and the mode and population proportions with nominal data. Often, however, our interest centers on hypotheses concerning the form of the population frequency distribution or hypotheses that involve comparing populations. Thus, nonparametric statistical methods, rather than parametric methods, must be used.

There are many nonparametric tests. Which one is appropriate for analyzing a set of survey data depends upon the level of measurement of the data, the number of samples that are involved, and, for multiple samples, whether they are independent or related. A listing of selected tests is given in Table 9–1. We cannot discuss all of these tests. Those that are discussed are intended to be illustrative of those most commonly used to analyze survey data pertaining to a marketing problem. The previously cited work by Siegel is one source for a detailed discussion of all these tests.[9]

*Chi-Square Analysis.* Chi-square analysis is an appropriate test for nominally scaled data. That is, when the data collected consist of frequencies in two or more discrete categories, the $X^2$ test is suitable for analyzing the data.

In the one sample case, the technique involves testing for goodness-of-fit. This means that the $X^2$ test can test whether a significant difference exists between an observed number of responses in each category and an expected

TABLE 9–1    Selected nonparametric statistical tests for one- and two-sample cases

| | Level of Measurement | |
| --- | --- | --- |
| Sample cases | Nominal | Ordinal |
| One-sample | Binomial test | Kolmogorov-S mirnov one-sample test |
| | $X^2$ one-sample test | One-sample runs test |
| Two-sample related samples | McNemar test for the significance of changes | Sign test Wilcoxon matched-pairs signed-ranks test |
| Independent samples | Fischer exact probability test $X^2$ test for two independent samples | Median test Mann-Whitney U test Kolmogorov-Smirnov two-sample test Wald-Wolfowitz runs test |

Source: Adapted from S. Siegel, *Nonparametric Statistics for the Behavioral Sciences* (New York: McGraw-Hill Book Company, 1956).

9. *Ibid.*

number based on $H_o$. Thus, the expected frequencies can be deduced from the null hypothesis.

The test statistic is

$$\chi^2 = \sum_{i=1}^{m} \frac{(O_i - E_i)^2}{E_i}$$

where

$O_i$ = observed number of cases in $i$th category
$E_i$ = expected number of cases in $i$th category
$m$ = number of categories

The sampling distribution of $\chi^2$ under $H_o$ follows the chi-square distribution with $(m-1)$ degrees of freedom. Critical values of $\chi^2$ are presented in Table 5 of the Appendix. These critical values are the maximum values likely to occur as a result of sampling error, given $\alpha$ and degrees of freedom. If the calculated $\chi^2$ exceeds the critical value at $\alpha$ level of significance, $H_o$ is rejected. In a decisional setting, however, it is best to determine the $\alpha$ at which $\chi^2_{calc.}$ becomes significant.

The $\chi^2$ test can be used also to test the significance of differences between two independent groups. Usually, the hypothesis of concern is that the two groups differ with respect to some characteristic as measured by the relative frequency with whch group members are placed in categories. The test of this hypothesis involves comparing the proportion of cases from one group in the various categories with the proportions from the other group. For instance, a bank may be interested in comparing men and women depositors with respect to their attitudes toward having an "extra reserve" plan available.

Essentially, the $\chi^2$ test for two independent samples is carried out by comparing an observed set of data with another set computed on the assumption of $H_o$—that is, on the assumption that there is no relationship between any of the distributions or between any of the means of classification; the only difference is caused by sampling.[10] It is a test of *independence* between row and column effects from a contingency table. Chi-square is calculated by using Formula 9.9. However, in the two-sample case the definitions of the terms differ from those previously mentioned as follows:

$i$ = $i$th cell in the contingency table
$O_i$ = observed value for cell $i$
$E_i$ = expected value for cell $i$

---

10. The null hypothesis is not limited to populations of no relationship. Any hypothetical relationship can be used to compare two populations. See Robert Ferber, *Market Research* (New York: McGraw-Hill Book Co., 1949), pp. 270 ff.

$m$ = number of cells ($r \times c$) in which $r$ is the number of rows and $c$ is the number of columns.

Significance is determined in the same way as the one-sample case, except that the degrees of freedom are $(r-1)(c-1)$. To calculate the expected frequency for each cell ($E_i$), multiply the two marginal totals common to a particular cell, and divide the product by the total number of cases, $n$.

When the number of observations in a cell are less than 10 (or where a $2 \times 2$ contingency table is involved), a correction factor must be applied to Formula 9.9. This gives

$$\chi^2 = \sum_{i=1}^{m} \frac{(|O_i - E_i| - {}^1/_2)^2}{E_i} \qquad (9.10)$$

where the term $\frac{1}{2}$ is the *continuity correction,* which adjusts for the use of a continuous distribution to estimate probability in a discrete distribution.[11]

An example will illustrate the use of this popular technique. Suppose we want to test whether men and women depositors differ with respect to attitude toward an extra reserve service. Table 9–2 shows the frequencies with which a sample of men and a sample of women are categorized as having "favorable" or "unfavorable" attitudes. The null hypothesis is that attitude is independent of sex, which means that the proportion of women depositors who have favorable attitudes is the same as the proportion of men who have favorable attitudes, etc. Given this $H_o$, the expected frequency for each cell is calculated by multiplying the marginal totals common to a cell and dividing by $n$ to obtain $E_i$. For example, the expected frequency for the upper right-hand cell in Table 9–2 is

$$E = \frac{(93)(135)}{200} \cong 63$$

The approximate expected frequency for each of the four cells in Table 9–2 is shown in Table 9–3. Using Formula 9.10, the computation of $\chi^2$ is simple:

$$\chi^2 = \frac{(|41 - 30| - .5)^2}{30} + \frac{(|52 - 63| - .5)^2}{63} + \frac{(|24 - 35| - .5)^2}{35}$$

$$+ \frac{(|83 - 72| - .5)^2}{72}$$

$$= 3.675 + 1.750 + 3.150 + 1.531$$

$$= 10.106$$

11. William S. Peters and George W. Summers, *Statistical Analysis for Business Decisions* (Englewood Cliffs: Prentice-Hall, Inc., 1968), pp. 270, 276.

TABLE 9–2   Sex and attitudes toward extra reserve service

|              | Men | Women | Total |
|--------------|-----|-------|-------|
| Favorable    | 41  | 52    | 93    |
| Unfavorable  | 24  | 83    | 107   |
| TOTAL        | 65  | 135   | 200   |

TABLE 9–3   Sex and attitude: expected frequencies

|              | Men | Women | Total |
|--------------|-----|-------|-------|
| Favorable    | 30  | 63    | 93    |
| Unfavorable  | 35  | 72    | 107   |
| TOTAL        | 65  | 135   | 200   |

To determine the significance of $X^2 = 10.106$ with $(2-1)(2-1) = 1$ degree of freedom, we go to Table 5 of the Appendix, which shows that it is significant at the .01 level ($X^2_{.01} = 6.64$). Thus, we reject $H_o$ of no difference at $\alpha = .01$, which in a decisional context means that it is at least 99 percent probable that this is the case. Had the calculated $X^2$ been lower, then the probability of there being no difference also would be lower.

In order to use properly the $X^2$ rest, the following conditions must generally hold:

1. Sample observations are independent
2. Sample units are randomly drawn
3. The data must be in original units, not in percentages or ratios
4. A maximum of one-fifth of the cells have an expected frequency of less than 5, and none have less than 1

*Wilcoxon Rank Sum Test.* For dependent samples in which the data are collected in matched pairs, the Wilcoxon "T" test can be used. This test takes into account both the direction of differences within pairs of observations and the relative magnitude of the differences. The Wilcoxon matched-pairs signed-ranks tests gives more weight to pairs showing large differences between the two measurements than to a pair showing a small difference. To use this test, measurements must be at least ordinally scaled within pairs. In addition, ordinal measurement must hold for the differences between pairs.

This test has many practical applications in survey research. For instance, it may be used to test whether a promotional campaign has had an effect on attitudes. An ordinal scaling device, such as a semantic differential, can be used to measure attitudes toward, say, a bank. Then, after a special promotional campaign, the same sample would be given the same scaling device. Changes in values of each scale could be analyzed by this Wilcoxon test.

*Mann-Whitney U Test.* With ordinal measurement and two independent samples, the Mann-Whitney U test may be used to test whether the two groups are from the same population. This is a relatively powerful nonparametric test, and is an alternative to the *t* test, when the analyst cannot meet the assumptions of the *t* test or when measurement is at best ordinal. Both one- and two-tailed tests can be conducted. As compared to the *t* test, the Mann-Whitney U has power-efficiency of about 95 percent.

## SOME GENERAL COMMENTS ON HYPOTHESIS TESTING

The overall procedure discussed in the preceding pages is a valid one for determining whether there is a significant difference between parameters of two categories of data. With the increasing usage of marketing research and the resulting cumulation of sample data over time, this technique is particularly useful for determining the conditional probabilities of an actual change in the parameters of interest (market share, proportion of the market using, mean usage per consuming unit, proportion of readers or viewers, etc.) when the observed differences in the sample values are given.

Viewed from the standpoint of decision making, however, the form of the analysis which the significance test takes is not as useful as it can be. For decision-making purposes, there are at least two major shortcomings of the traditional test of significance: (1) it deals only with the *conditional probabilities of making errors* and does not formally balance these probabilities against the costs of the errors, and (2) the prior probability distribution is disregarded.[12]

# Relationships among Variables

The ideal situation for purposes of estimation and prediction is to have exact, deterministic relationships between variables which are expressed in quantitative terms. The true nature of the relationship between variables in marketing is hidden to an extent (a) by the fact that, generally, only samples of data are being used for analysis; (b) by the effects of extraneous variables that have not been explicitly introduced into the analysis; (c) the relation-

12. The conditional probability distribution developed in the sampling distribution of two statistics is highly useful for decision making in certain classes of problems using the Bayesian approach, however.

ship may be probabilistic rather than deterministic; and (d) by the important complication that such relationships among marketing variables change over time. Although these problems are recognized, it is often highly useful to approximate the functional relationships between variables and express them in quantitative terms.

Many "informal" and mathematical techniques have been developed for measuring the kinds and extent of relationships in the data to be analyzed. Our concern here is with a relatively short discussion of two of the informal techniques and the mathematical techniques of regression analysis and correlation analysis. We also consider briefly some of the increasingly popular multivariate techniques of analysis of data.

## INFORMAL ANALYSIS OF RELATIONSHIPS

The simplest way to examine the relationships between or among variables is through ordering them into arrays. The cross-tabulation table discussed in Chapter 8 is one form of a data array of two or more variables. If a graphic presentation is desired, the scatter diagram or regular line chart may be used, particularly when two variables are involved.

As defined earlier, a cross-tabulation table is formed by the simultaneous counting of the number of observations that occur in each of the data categories in two or more informational sets. Table 8–1 presented earlier is an example of a cross-tabulation. In analyzing these data our concern is the affect of age upon money borrowing habits. Informal analysis would involve simply examining these data to try to assess whether there is a meaningful association between the two variables.

In attempting to answer the question of whether or not there is a causal relationship between age and money borrowing behavior, it must be remembered that the answer, whether "Yes" or "No," would be conditional. That is, the answer would depend upon the apparent extent of association, and whether there are other variables which, if introduced into the analysis, would substantially alter the association observed. For instance, the incorporation of income or occupation might affect the association between age and borrowing behavior.

Instead of presenting the array of data in two informational sets in tabular form, it can be presented graphically. One type of graphic array is called a scatter diagram. To illustrate, suppose that the survey of 1,414 depositors mentioned in Chapter 8 also yielded data concerning the number of times money was borrowed during the past six months, and the extent of television viewing. The bank has been advertising its services by using television as a medium. In this situation we are interested in assessing the effect of television advertising on money borrowing behavior. We assume that the data obtained for 10 depositors are as shown in Table 9–4. The

TABLE 9–4 Television exposure and money borrowing behavior in past six months for sample of ten depositors

| Depositor | Television exposure (mean hours per week) | Number of times borrowed money |
|---|---|---|
| 1 | 13.2 | 2 |
| 2 | 0.0 | 1 |
| 3 | 18.6 | 3 |
| 4 | 8.8 | 0 |
| 5 | 12.3 | 2 |
| 6 | 28.3 | 4 |
| 7 | 0.0 | 0 |
| 8 | 23.5 | 5 |
| 9 | 5.6 | 1 |
| 10 | 1.5 | 2 |

corresponding scatter diagram is shown in Figure 9–1. (The complete scatter diagram for the example shown would include the ungrouped data from all of the 1,414 depositors included in the sample.) As indicated, television exposure is assumed to be the independent variable and number of times money borrowed the dependent variable.

The scatter diagram is a valuable aid in assessing relationships between two variables. As a general rule, it should be prepared before any mathematical analysis of relationships is done in order to obtain a clearer understanding of the nature and degree of the association involved.

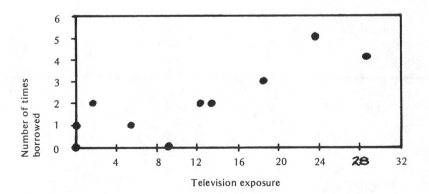

FIGURE 9–1 Scatter diagram for television exposure and number of times money borrowed by ten depositors

## REGRESSION ANALYSIS[13]

In regression analysis, a *regression equation* is derived which measures the degree of change in the dependent variable that is associated with changes in one or more independent variables. For example, suppose that a bank with fourteen branches has obtained data for the immediately preceding six-month period for each of the branches' market area on the dependent variable "money borrowed" *(Y)* and the independent variables advertising expenditures $(X_1)$ and "personal selling" expenditures $(X_2)$. These data are shown in Table 9–5. Regression analyses of the following kinds could be made:

1. *Simple regression.* An analysis of the relationship between money borrowed and any one of the independent variables. This relationship may be either *linear* or *curvilinear.* The linear regression equation will be of the general form

$$\hat{Y}_C = a + bX$$

TABLE 9–5  Amount of money borrowed, advertising expenditures, and personal selling expenditures for 14 branches of a bank

| Branch | Amount borrowed ($100,000) $Y$ | Advertising expenditure ($1,000) $X_1$ | Personal selling expenditure ($1,000) $X_2$ |
|---|---|---|---|
| 1 | 13 | 4.0 | 3.5 |
| 2 | 7 | 4.0 | 3.5 |
| 3 | 4 | 9.0 | 8.5 |
| 4 | 1 | 4.0 | 8.5 |
| 5 | 3 | 4.0 | 3.5 |
| 6 | 2 | 4.0 | 3.5 |
| 7 | 5 | 4.0 | 3.5 |
| 8 | 12 | 9.0 | 8.5 |
| 9 | 9 | 12.5 | 12.5 |
| 10 | 6 | 4.0 | 3.5 |
| 11 | 8 | 12.5 | 12.5 |
| 12 | 14 | 12.5 | 12.5 |
| 13 | 10 | 12.5 | 12.5 |
| 14 | 11 | 9.0 | 8.5 |

13. A detailed discussion of regression analysis is given in Mendenhall and Reinmuth, *op. cit.,* Chapter 12; and Peters and Summers, *op. cit.,* Chapters 14, 15.

Where $\hat{Y}_C$ is the estimated conditional level of the dependent variable for a given value of the independent variable $X$, $a$ is the intercept of $Y$ when $X$ is zero, and $b$ is the slope of the line—that is, the change in $Y_C$ that is associated with a unit change in $X$.[14] If the bank conducted a simple regression of amount of money borrowed and advertising expenditures, the resulting linear regression equation (using the method of least-squares) is

$$Y = 2.981 + .603X_1$$

2. *Multiple regression.* An analysis of the relationship between money borrowed and two or more of the independent variables. The linear regression relationship is of the general form[15]

$$Y_C = a + b_1X_1 + b_2X_2 + \ldots + b_nX_n$$

Using the data in Table 9–5, we get the following multiple regression equation

$$Y = 3.378 + 1.575X_1 - 1.012X_4$$

How may regression analysis be used? Probably the major purpose is to predict the value of a dependent variable from estimates or values of independent variables. In our example, decisions will have to be made for the coming period concerning the amount of advertising and personal selling expenditures in each of the branch market areas. Simple regression analyses can assist in measuring the effects of any of these variables on money borrowed and, by so doing, improve the prediction of the effects of changes in these independent variables. For instance, in the regression of money borrowed and advertising expenditures, each additional $1,000 spent on advertising should yield an additional $603 in money borrowed. Multiple regression analysis also can be a useful technique for determining the joint effects of the independent variables. What this amounts to is that regression analyses is one way of quantifying the problem situation model relating desired outcome to certain variables.

14. One form of curvilinear univariate regression equation has the formulation

$$\hat{Y}_c = a + b_1X + b_2X^2 + \ldots + b_nX^n$$

Many formulations are possible, however.

15. For the *curvilinear multivariate* regression equation, the formulation will depend upon which of the independent variables are nonlinear with respect to $Y$ and the type of nonlinearity which is present. If the relationship is second degree in, say, only $X_1$, the equation becomes

$$Y_C = a + b_1X_1^2 + b_2X_2 + \ldots + b_nX_n$$

## CORRELATION ANALYSIS[16]

In our discussion above we considered the nature of relationships. Knowing the nature of the relationship is not very useful until one knows the extent of it as well. We may have found that money borrowed varies directly, and in a linear fashion, with advertising expenditures, but to what extent do the points vary around the regression line? Obviously, if all the data points fall on the regression line, the relationship and the predictions made from it are likely to be much more useful than if there is wide variation of the points around the line.

*The Parametric Case.* For data that are at least intervally scaled and which come from a bivariate or multivariate normal population, the summary measure used for determining the "closeness of fit" is the *coefficient of determination, $r^2$*. This coefficient is a measure of the extent to which the regression line "explains" the original variance observed in the data

$$r^2 = \frac{\text{explained variance}}{\text{total variance}}$$

This means that $r^2$ is a measure of that part of the total variance of the dependent variable ($Y$) that is "accounted for" or "explained" by knowing the value of the independent variable or variables, $X_i$. The square root of this coefficient, $r$, is the *coefficient of correlation*. If the regression line does not "explain" all of the variance, the points in the scatter will not all lie on the line, and $r$ will fall between $-1.0$ and $+1.0$. For a linear regression, the sign of $r$ is the same as the sign of the slope of the regression line. A positive value for $r$ means that the line slopes upward to the right, while a negative value indicates that it slopes downward to the right.

For linear relationships, the following types of correlation coefficients may be calculated:

1. *Simple correlation coefficient.* A measure of the degree of linear association between two variables; for example, a measurement of the degree of association between money borrowed and advertising expenditure. In the example used above, $r = .554$

2. *Partial correlation coefficient.* A measure of the degree of linear association between the dependent and one of the independent variables in a multivariate analysis when the effects of the other variables in the analysis are held constant; for example, if a multivariate analysis were being run between money borrowed and the two independent variables, a partial correlation coefficient could be determined of the linear association between

16. Some of the sources in which a detailed discussion of correlation techniques is given include R. Frank, A. Kuehn, and W. Massy, *Quantitative Techniques in Marketing Analysis* (Homewood, Ill.: Richard D. Irwin, Inc., 1962), pp. 69–78; Peters and Summers, *op. cit.,* Chapter 16; and Ferber, *op. cit.,* Chapters 11, 12.

money borrowed and, say, advertising expenditure when the effect of the other independent variable is held constant

3. *Multiple correlation coefficient.* A measure of the linear association between the dependent variable and two or more independent variables. In the example used above, multiple $r = .638$

Similar coefficients may be calculated for curvilinear relationships.

On occasion it may be desirable to estimate the population value of the correlation coefficient, rho ($\rho$), in the universe or to test the significance of the coefficient. A problem arises in that the sampling distribution of the correlation coefficient is not normal when $r$ is large. The problem can be handled by transforming the sampling relationship of $r$ into a logarithmic function. This is called the $z$ transformation, and it normalizes the skewness of the correlation measures.

When $\rho$ is around zero, the sampling distribution of $r$ tends to be normal. Thus, we can test the significance of $r$ in terms of whether its true value might be zero (that is, $H_o: \rho = 0$). When $N$ is small, the $t$ distribution is an appropriate model for testing simple and partial correlation coefficients. The $t$ statistic is calculated from

$$t = r \sqrt{\frac{N - m}{1 - r^2}} \tag{9.11}$$

where $N$ is the number of sets of measures and $m$ is the number of variables. The calculated value of $t$ is compared to the critical value obtained from Table 3 of the Appendix, with $(N - m)$ degrees of freedom. To illustrate this test we use the simple correlation that was determined for the relationship between amount of money borrowed and advertising expenditures by a bank. Since $r = .554$, we test $H_o: \rho = 0$ by

$$t = .554 \sqrt{\frac{14 - 2}{1 - (.554)^2}} = .554 \sqrt{17.316} = 2.305$$

In Table 3 of the Appendix, we see that $t = 2.179$ for $(14 - 2)$ degrees of freedom at $\alpha = .025$ (one-tailed test). Since our calculated $t$ is greater, we can reject $H_o$ with little probability that we are wrong, and conclude that $r$ is significantly greater than zero.

When $N$ is large, the significance of the sample correlation coefficient ($H_o: \rho = 0$) is determined by

$$Z = r\sqrt{N - 1} \tag{9.12}$$

which is a test for the standard normal deviate. Using the cumulative normal distribution, the relevant probability can be determined. For the partial correlation coefficient, the $z$ transform must be used when $N$ is large.

There are excellent sources that can be consulted for a more detailed exposition of the significance of $r$.[17]

*Nonparametric Measures.* When measurements are nominally or ordinally scaled, the measures of association discussed above cannot be used. Consequently, nonparametric measures must be used. Moreover, even if the data are intervally scaled, if population normality is questionable, nonparametric methods must be used because they make no assumption about the shape of the population.

1. *Contingency coefficient.* The contingency coefficient $C$ is a descriptive measure of association applicable when working with nominal measurement. The coefficient measures the extent of association between two sets of attributes. The categories need not be continuous nor ordered in any way. The data are derived from a random sample of the population, and we are concerned with whether the attributes are associated in the population from which the sample is drawn. An example is a determination of degree of association of, say, political party affiliation and area of the country in which one lives.

To compute $C$, the measurements on the two attributes are arranged into a contingency table of frequencies which may be of any size. The degree of association is calculated by

$$C = \frac{\chi^2}{n + \chi^2}$$

where $\chi^2$ is derived by applying the two-sample version of Formula 9.9 or Formula 9.10, and $n$ is the total size of the sample.

An example will be helpful. Suppose a bank wants to know if the attitude of depositors toward an "extra reserve" plan is associated with their income. A survey is run, and the data obtained from a sample of 146 depositors is categorized as shown in Table 9–6. The numbers in parentheses in each cell are the expected frequencies under the null hypothesis that there is no correlation in the population. We compute $\chi^2$ in the usual way and get $\chi^2 = 22.68$. Now, $C$ is computed

$$C = \sqrt{\frac{22.68}{146 + 22.68}} = 0.37$$

To test the significance of $C$ ($H_o$: $C_p = 0$), we use simply the usual $\chi^2$ test for independence. Thus, by looking at Table 5 in the Appendix, we determine that a $\chi^2 \geq 22.68$ with $(3-1)(3-1) = 4$ degrees of freedom has

17. See Howard L. Balsley, *Quantitative Research Methods for Business and Economics* (New York: Random House, 1970), pp. 189–196; and Ferber, *op. cit.,* Chapter 13.

TABLE 9–6   Frequency of depositors' attitudes in three income classes

| Attitude | Income Class | | | Total |
| | I | II | III | |
|---|---|---|---|---|
| Favorable | $14^{(14.2)}$ | $14^{(23.5)}$ | $24^{(14.2)}$ | 52 |
| Neutral | $16^{(14.2)}$ | $23^{(23.5)}$ | $13^{(14.2)}$ | 52 |
| Unfavorable | $10^{(11.5)}$ | $29^{(19.0)}$ | $3^{(11.5)}$ | 42 |
| TOTAL | 40 | 66 | 40 | 146 |

probability of occurrence under $H_o$ of less than .001. We could then be quite confident in concluding that attitude and income are related in the population of depositors.

There are limitations to the contingency correlation coefficient. First, although the lower limit of $C$ is zero, the upper limit varies with the size of the contingency table and never reaches unity. Second, because of the variability in range of values, contingency correlation coefficients cannot be compared with each other unless they are based upon contingency tables of the same size. Even so, this measure is extremely useful because it may be used without the stringent assumptions and requirements of other measures.

2. *Rank correlation coefficient.* When the data are *ordinally scaled,* rank correlation techniques can be used to measure the association between two sets of data. All that is required is that two order series exist—that is, objects or individuals can be ranked in two ordered variables.

The best-known and easiest technique is that involving use of the Spearman rank correlation coefficient, $r_s$.[18] We show the use of this measure by an example. Suppose a sales manager evaluates his salesmen by two different methods (performance index and a new method). Since the new method is easier to use, the manager wants to know if it will yield the same relative results as the "proven" existing method. The scores have been transformed into rankings so that each salesman has two rankings. Table 9–7 shows the rankings.

To measure the extent of rank correlation we use the statistic

$$r_s = 1 - \frac{6 \sum\limits_{i=1}^{N} d_i^2}{N(N^2 - 1)} \tag{9.14}$$

18. Another measure which gives comparable results is the Kendall rank correlation coefficient, $\tau$ (tau). One advantage to $\tau$ is that it can be generalized to a partial correlation coefficient. See Siegel, *op. cit.,* pp. 213–229.

TABLE 9–7   Ranks on two methods of evaluation

| Salesman· | Rank | | $d_i$ | $d_i^2$ |
| :---: | :---: | :---: | :---: | :---: |
| | Performance index (X) | New method (Y) | | |
| A | 8 | 6 | 2 | 4 |
| B | 4 | 7 | −3 | 9 |
| C | 1 | 2 | −1 | 1 |
| D | 6 | 3 | 3 | 9 |
| E | 2 | 1 | 1 | 1 |
| F | 10 | 8 | 2 | 4 |
| G | 5 | 5 | 0 | 0 |
| H | 3 | 9 | −6 | 36 |
| I | 7 | 4 | 3 | 9 |
| J | 9 | 10 | 1 | 1 |
| | | | $\Sigma d_i^2 =$ | 74 |

where $N$ is the number of pairs of ranks and $d$ is the difference between the two rankings for an individual (that is, $X - Y$). Applying Formula 9.14 to our example, we get

$$r_s = 1 - \frac{6(74)}{10(100 - 1)} = .55$$

If the subjects whose scores were used in computing $r_s$ were randomly drawn from a population, we can test the significance of the obtained value. The null hypothesis is that the two variables are not associated, and, thus, the true value of $\rho$ is zero. Under $H_o$ any observed value would be due to chance. When $N \geq 10$, significance can be tested using the statistic

$$t = r_s \sqrt{\frac{N - 2}{1 - r_s^2}} \qquad (9.15)$$

which is interpreted from the table of the Student $t$ distribution with $(N-2)$ degrees of freedom. For our example, we calculate

$$t = .55 \sqrt{\frac{10 - 2}{1 - (.55)^2}} = 1.870$$

Looking at the table of critical values of $t$, we find that $p > .10$ (two-tailed test) for $(10 - 2 = 8)$ degrees of freedom. Thus, if a strict $\alpha$ level is to be

adhered to (.10 or less) we accept $H_o$ and conclude that it is unlikely a correlation exists between the scores from the two evaluation methods.

Another approach to testing significance involves the use of a table of critical values of $r_s$ (Table 6 in the Appendix). This approach is necessary when $N < 10$, and is much easier for larger samples than applying Formula 9.15. If an observed value of $r_s$ equals or exceeds the value in the table, the observed value is significant.

One final point concerning the use of the Spearman rank correlation coefficient is warranted. At times, tied observations will exist. When this happens, each of them is assigned the average of the ranks which would have been assigned in the absence of ties. If the proportion of ties is small, their effect on $r_s$ is minute. If large, however, a correction factor must be applied.[19]

3. *Rank correlation for more than two sets of rankings.* The Spearman rank correlation coefficient is limited to measuring correlation between only two sets of rankings. If an analyst wants to measure the relationship between three or more rankings of $N$ things, the nonparametric *Kendall coefficient of concordance, W,* can be used. This measure is useful in looking at the extent of agreement among several sets of judges, such as used in developing scaling instruments, or simply the association among many variables, which are at best ordinally scaled. We shall not discuss this measure further but refer the reader to the writings of Siegel.[20]

*A Concluding Remark.* How may correlation analysis be used in survey research? We have already pointed out the need to know the degree of the relationship between variables as well as its nature for predictive purposes. In the example concerning bank market areas, if a number of regression equations have been derived for, say, profits, interest earned, and money borrowed, each with different combinations of independent variables, the coefficient of determination of each relationship can be calculated to determine which provides the best explanation of the observed values of the dependent variables. Or we may simply need to know the degree of association between variables without being directly concerned with the nature of the relationship. In any event, correlation analysis, alone or together with regression analysis, may be useful in quantifying the problem situation model.

## MULTIVARIATE TECHNIQUES

Marketing problems are inherently multidimensional. To approach, understand, and solve these problems, analysts are turning increasingly to

19. *Ibid.,* pp. 206–210.
20. *Ibid.,* pp. 229–238.

*multivariate analysis,* which can be defined simply as any simultaneous analysis of three or more variables. Our discussion has been centered around univariate and bivariate analysis, although we have mentioned two types of multivariate techniques: multiple regression and correlation, and, in Chapter 6, multidimensional scaling. At this point, we discuss additional multivariate techniques that are being used increasingly to tackle marketing problems and analyze survey data: (1) cluster analysis; (2) discriminant analysis; and (3) factor analysis.[21] Along with advancements in computer technology has come the development of programs that enable the analyst to tackle multidimensional problems using these techniques.

*Cluster Analysis.* Cluster analysis includes a set of techniques designed to identify objects, individuals, or variables which are similar with respect to some criteria or characteristics. The resulting clusters should be highly homogeneous within clusters and highly heterogeneous between clusters. Geometrically the objects within a cluster should be located close to each other while objects in different clusters should be far from each other.

Cluster analysis is often referred to as numerical taxonomy. It consists of a set of numerical procedures for classifying objects. The major purpose is to describe *natural* groupings that occur in large masses of data. Thus the techniques have use for the orderly classification of multivariate phenomena. Thus categories may be set that can be analyzed further by other techniques.

Given a set of objects, each of which can be described by a measurement on each of a set of characteristics, and assuming that we are interested in natural groupings, the problem reduces to the following general question: How should objects be assigned to groups so there will be homogeneity within groups and as much heterogeneity among groups as possible? To solve this problem, we need a *proximity measure* to summarize the similarity of profiles according to the characteristics of concern and a procedure for grouping the objects on the basis of the proximity measure.[22]

Concerning proximity measures, there are three general types that can be used. They are as follows:

21. Two excellent sources that provide broad coverage of multivariate techniques in marketing situations are Jagdish N. Sheth, "Multivariate Analysis in Marketing," *Journal of Advertising Research* vol. 10, no. 1 (February, 1970), pp. 29–39, and David A. Aaker, ed., *Multivariate Analysis in Marketing: Theory and Application* (Belmont, Calif.: Wadsworth Publishing Co., Inc., 1971). These two works are sources of references for more specific treatments.

22. A good overview of these techniques is Ronald E. Frank and Paul E. Green, "Numerical Taxonomy in Marketing Analysis: A Review Article," *Journal of Marketing Research,* vol. 5, no. 1 (February, 1968), pp. 83–98.

1. Distance measures
2. Correlation measures
3. Similarity measures for attribute data

Which of these measures of pair-wise proximity is best to use in a situation will depend upon the level of which measurement of the characteristics takes place (the input data can be at any level). For instance, similarity measures are often used when the characteristics of each object are nominally measured. Once the proximity measure has been decided upon, we must select a method for grouping. There are many varied computer programs available for this task.

We can illustrate cluster analysis by a simple example. The problem is to group a set of twelve branches of a bank into three clusters of four branches each according to the characteristics of the number of men who have borrowed money $(X_1)$ and the number of women who have borrowed money $(X_2)$. The branches are plotted in two dimensions in Figure 9-2. We use a distance measure of proximity, based on Euclidean distances in space

$$d_{jk} = \sqrt{(X_{1j} - X_{1k})^2 + (X_{2j} - X_{2k})^2}$$

where $j$ and $k$ are any two branches. Branches 2 and 10 appear to be the closest together. The first cluster is formed by finding the midpoint between branches 2 and 10 and computing the distance of each branch from this midpoint. The two closest branches (6 and 8) are then added to give the desired sized cluster. The other clusters are formed in a similar manner. When more than two dimensions (that is, characteristics) are involved, a computer program must be used for measuring distances and the clustering process.

Other questions that we have not considered in our brief discussion are: (1) What descriptive measures are appropriate for summarizing the characteristics of each group? (2) Are the groups formed really different from each other? (3) How many clusters should be formed? and (4) How do we handle characteristics that are measured in different units and at different levels of measurement? Although we have ignored these somewhat technical questions and problems because of space limitations, they, and many others, must nevertheless be answered when using cluster analysis.

*Discriminant Analysis.* In discriminant analysis the dependent variable is nominal—that is, it is categorical. The predictive problem in this type of analysis is to use a set of independent variables as the basis of predicting to which category of the dependent variable a subject belongs. That is, objects can be classified into one of two or more mutually exclusive and

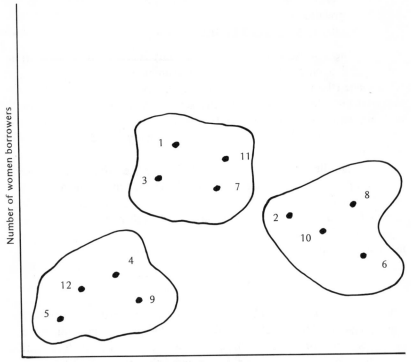

FIGURE 9–2   Clustering of bank branches

exhaustive categories by a set of predictor variables. For example, a marketing manager may want to classify consumers as either buyers or nonbuyers
on the basis of their income, age, occupation, size of home, etc. In addition
to prediction, discriminant analysis is useful for understanding group differences. Before a discriminant function can be fitted, however, the analyst
must be able to classify a priori the objects of concern into mutually exclusive and exhaustive categories.

The analysis involves a transformation of scores on individuals on a
set of independent predictor variables into a so-called discriminant score.[23]
For two groups, each individual's discriminant score, $D_i$, is a linear function
of the predictor variables.

$$D_i = b_o + b_1 X_{1i} + b_2 X_{2i} + \ldots + b_n X_{ni} \qquad (9.16)$$

where $X_{ji}$ is the $i$th individual's score on the $j$th variable and $b_j$ is the
discriminant coefficient for the $j$th variable. A classification boundary be-

23. See Donald G. Morrison, "On the Interpretation of Discriminant Analysis," *Journal of Marketing Research,* vol. 6, no. 2 (May, 1969), pp. 156–163.

tween the two groups, $D_{crit.}$, can be identified as being midway between the means of the function for each of the two groups. To classify an individual, if $D_i > D_{crit.}$ the individual belongs in one group, while if $D_i < D_{crit.}$ the individual goes into the other group.

Thus, the results of a discriminant analysis assist in answering three basic questions:

1. Which predictor variables are good discriminators?
2. How well do these variables discriminate among the groups?
3. What decision rule should be used for classifying individuals?[24]

It is true that the answers are subject to interpretation. Nonetheless, answers to these questions are required in any marketing problem involving differential treatment among groups. Imperfect information is usually (not always, but usually) preferable to no information.

To answer the first question, we recognize that the more a variable affects $D_i$, the better it discriminates. If the predictor variables are of the same units (dollars, years, etc.), the $b$'s can be used directly to determine which are the better discriminating variables, since the sign and size of the $b$'s determine the effect of the variables $X_j$. In this case, clearly the $X_j$'s with the larger $b_j$'s are the better discriminators. If, however, the predictor variables are not of the same units, a very likely situation, then we must standardize (normalize) the variables by dividing each variable by its standard deviation. The discriminant coefficient, $b_j^*$, derived from using standardized variables can then be used to determine which variables are good discriminators. If it is not possible to standardize the predictor variables, $b_j^*$ can be derived from[25]

$$b_j^* = b_j \sigma_j \qquad (9.17)$$

To determine how well the predictor variables discriminate among groups, we look at a classification table that relates the actual distribution among the groups to the distribution that arises from application of the discriminant function. It should be recognized that allowances must be made for the proportion of objects that would be correctly classified by chance. Another matter of concern relating to the extent of correct classification is the possibility of upward bias. A typical "canned" discriminant analysis computer program uses all of the observations to calculate the function and then classifies all these same individuals with the function. One way to avoid the upward biases that can occur by this approach is to develop the discriminant function with a subset of the observations and then use the function to classify the remaining individuals.

Finally, the decision rule used for classification involves economic

24. *Ibid.*, pp. 158–159.
25. *Ibid.*, pp. 159–160.

considerations. Very simply, misclassification costs must enter the decision concerning the classification of individuals.

*Factor Analysis.* *Factor analysis* is a term describing a number of methods or techniques to analyze the intercorrelation within a set of variables. Its major purpose is to summarize the information contained in a number of original variables (for example, responses or scores of individuals on a set of variables) into a smaller set of new latent variables with a minimum loss of information—that is, to remove the redundancy in the original data.[26] These new variables are called *factors*. A factor, then, is a linear combination of the observed (that is, original manifest variables $(X_j)$)

$$F = a_1 X_1 + a_2 X_2 + \ldots + a_n X_n \qquad (9.18)$$

From any given set of manifest variables, a number of factors may be derived. For instance, six variables may reduce to two factors, as follows:

$$F_1 = a_{11} X_1 + a_{21} X_2$$
$$F_2 = a_{32} X_3 + a_{42} X_4 + a_{52} X_5 + a_{62} X_6$$

In actuality, each factor has coefficients for all the observed variables but they are zero or close to zero for the variables not grouped in a factor.

Factor analysis is a complex form of multivariate analysis, requiring the use of computer programs. There are many different techniques that can be used. Each individual is assigned a *factor score* as a result of his scores on the observed variables

$$F_i = a_1 X_{1i} + a_2 X_{2i} + \ldots + a_n X_{ni} \qquad (9.19)$$

For the *i*th individual, there will be as many factor scores as there are factors. When the factor scores are correlated with the observed manifest variable scores of the individuals in a sample, the resulting correlation is a *factor loading*. With $n$ variables and $m$ factors, there will be a total of $(n \times m)$ factor loadings. Factor loadings are useful in determining which manifest variables can be grouped in each factor and in determining how many factors should be extracted. When a large set of variables is factored, a number of factors may be derived. Factor loadings are used in determining what percent of the total variance is summarized by a factor. If an additional factor adds only a small percentage of total variance, it may be desirable to discard it and stop factoring. There are other stoppping criteria as well.[27]

26. Ronald E. Frank and Paul E. Green, *Quantitative Methods in Marketing* (Englewood Cliffs: Prentice-Hall, 1967), p. 75.
27. See William D. Wells and Jagdish N. Sheth, "Factor Analysis in Marketing Research," in Aaker, *op. cit.*, pp. 218–219.

Factor analysis has been used widely in marketing research. In general, there are at least four distinct ways in which the technique appears to be useful:[28]

1. Finding a set of dimensions that are latent in a much larger set of variables. This is the classical approach to factor analysis, in which all that is needed are the factor loadings. An example is the work of Osgood and his associates with the semantic differential in identifying the major factors of evaluation, activity and potency. Unfortunately, in most analyses, factors are not easily labeled

2. Grouping people into distinctly different groups existing within a larger population. Factor loadings are all that is necessary for the analysis. This is a form of cluster analysis

3. Identifying certain variables from a much larger set of independent variables that are likely for subsequent types of analysis such as regression or discriminant analysis. In this use, factor loadings are not ends in themselves. An example of this type of use is the study conducted by Twedt on the relationship between readership of an advertisement and a set of predictor variables.[29] Through factor analysis, three major factors were extracted. A set of three predictor variables, one for each of the three factors was used in a multiple regression designed to predict readership. This process has the obvious advantage of removing any effects of multicollinearity from the regression analysis

4. Creating a new set of variables from the common parts of a set of original variables that can subsequently be used in regression or discriminant analysis

*A Concluding Note.* The brief discussion above of the three multivariate techniques and that earlier for multiple regression is intended to describe what these techniques are and what they are capable of doing. The salient characteristics of the four techniques are summarized in Table 9-8. These, of course, do not represent all of the multivariate techniques that are available, although they are the ones being used most widely. One additional technique that warrants further attention is *canonical analysis*. This technique is appropriate where more than one criterion (dependent variable) is of concern to the analyst, for it is an extension of multiple regression for two sets of measurements: a criterion set and a predictor set. Canonical analysis is most useful when the analyst is interested in the overall association between the sets of variables, which must be intervally scaled. Those independent variables that contribute most to the overall relation can be

---

28. William F. Massy, "What is Factor Analysis?" in Aaker, *op. cit.,* pp. 241–245.
29. Dik Warren Twedt, "A Multiple Factor Analysis of Advertising Readership," *Journal of Applied Psychology,* vol. 37, no. 3 (June, 1952), pp. 207–215.

TABLE 9–8   Selected multivariate techniques of analysis

| Technique | Purpose | Level of measurement | Number of criterion variables |
|---|---|---|---|
| Cluster analysis | Classify a population of entities into a small number of mutually exclusive and exhaustive groups based on the similarities of profiles among entities. | Any level (input data) | None |
| Factor analysis | Analyze intercorrelations within a set of variables and reduce to a smaller set of latent variables. | Interval | None |
| Discriminant | Predict an entity's likelihood of belonging to a particular class or group based on several prediction variables. | Nominal (dependent variable)<br><br>Any level (independent variables) | One |
| Multiple regression | Predict the variability in a dependent variable based on its covariance with all independent variables. | Interval (dependent variable)<br><br>Any level (independent variables) | One |

isolated. Also, indications are provided concerning which of the dependent variables are most affected.[30]

## Summary

This chapter has discussed statistical and mathematical techniques used to analyze survey data. The primary concern has been with determining differences in parameters and analyzing relationships among variables.

Concerning differences, we first developed formulas for the standard error that are necessary for both estimation and the testing of hypotheses. Both parametric and nonparametric methods for hypothesis testing were presented. Throughout our discussion we pointed out the relevant differences in approach for basic and decisional research.

Our discussion of relationships between variables considered regression analysis, parametric and nonparametric correlation analysis, and selected multivariate techniques.

30. See Aaker, *op. cit.,* pp. 155–173 and Mark I. Alpert and Robert A. Peterson, "On the Interpretation of Canonical Analysis," *Journal of Marketing Research,* vol. 9, no. 2 (May, 1972), pp. 187–192.

## SELECTED BIBLIOGRAPHY

Aaker, David A., ed. *Multivariate Analysis in Marketing: Theory and Application.* Belmont, California: Wadsworth Publishing Co., Inc., 1971. A collection of excellent articles covering the major techniques of multivariate analysis.

Draper, N. and H. Smith. *Applied Regression Analysis.* New York: John Wiley & Sons, Inc., 1966. A mathematical treatment of basic linear regression models. Prerequisite mathematical background is at the level of introductory calculus.

Mendenhall, William and James E. Reinmuth. *Statistics for Management and Business.* Belmont, Calif.: Duxbury Press, 1971. An introductory level book covering statistical inference and analytical methods used in specific experimental situations. The prerequisite mathematical background needed is at the level of college algebra.

Morrison, Donald F. *Multivariate Statistical Methods.* New York: McGraw-Hill Book Co., 1967. A somewhat mathematical treatment of multivariate methods.

Peters, William S. and George W. Summers. *Statistical Analysis for Business Decisions.* Englewood Cliffs: Prentice-Hall, Inc., 1968. A book providing a thorough grounding and reference source to the concepts and methods of application of probability and statistics to business decision-making situations.

Siegel, Sidney. *Nonparametric Statistics for the Behavioral Sciences.* New York: McGraw-Hill Book Co., 1956. Although somewhat old, this book explains nonparametric techniques in a clear and easily understandable way.

## QUESTIONS AND PROBLEMS

*9.1 A manufacturer wants to determine whether his "improved" product appeals more to women than to men. A survey is conducted of a group of women and a group of men and each person is asked how many units she or he might purchase during a one-month time period. The samples are randomly selected. The following data are obtained:

|  | Men | Women |
|---|---|---|
| Sample size | 25 | 25 |
| Total number of units expected to be bought | 50 | 61 |
| Sample standard deviation | 0.6 | 0.8 |

a. Is there a significant difference in the mean number of expected purchases between men and women?

b. Construct an interval estimate around the difference in means between the two groups

c. How would your solution in (a) differ according to your using basic and decisional approaches to answering the question?

*9.2 A manufacturer of a household cleaner (EXAM) conducted a survey in two cities, using a randomly selected sample of 600 households in each city. The following data were obtained:

|                                              | City 1 | City 2 |
|----------------------------------------------|--------|--------|
| Had EXAM in the house:                       |        |        |
| Regular size                                 | 20%    | 24%    |
| Large size                                   | 16     | 28     |
| Tried EXAM in past 4 weeks for:              |        |        |
| Painted woodwork                             | 23%    | 24%    |
| Painted walls                                | 19     | 17     |
| Linoleum floors                              | 12     | 25     |
| Attitude toward EXAM for cleaning floors     |        |        |
| (users only):                                |        |        |
| Housewives made:                             |        |        |
| Favorable comments only                      | 40%    | 37%    |
| Unfavorable comments only                    | 9      | 13     |
| Both favorable and unfavorable               |        |        |
| comments                                     | 47     | 42     |
| No specific comment                          | 4      | 8      |
|                                              | 100%   | 100%   |

What inferences can you make based on these data? Explain.

*9.3 In analyzing its sales records for a metropolitan area, a company derives the following information concerning the size distribution of its customers, by locality:

| Customer Size (Sales volume) | Number of Central City Customers | Number of Suburban Customers |
|------------------------------|----------------------------------|------------------------------|
| Under $250,000               | 20                               | 30                           |
| $250,000 to $1,000,000       | 18                               | 40                           |
| Over $1,000,000              | 40                               | 52                           |

To what extent are size and location related? Is this significant?

9.4 In which ways are regression analysis and correlation analysis related to each other? In which ways are they independent of each other? Explain.

9.5 Parametric and nonparametric measures of correlation use data in different forms. Under what conditions might the problem represented by the data in Table 9–7 be treated as a parametric correlation problem? Explain.

9.6 For each of the following situations indicate the mutivariate techniques that would be most helpful to an analyst. Also, explain how you would conduct the analysis.

a. A manufacturer wishes to develop a profile of his customers so that he can predict whether a potential customer may, in fact, become an actual customer

b. A company desires to know which of its 20 salesmen are similar to each other, and which ones differ

c. An analyst wants to know which of 18 possible independent variables should be included in a multiple regression model

# Answers to

# Selected Problems

## CHAPTER 3

3.2 A sample size of 1600 is required for the portion of the problem dealing with the mean number of flights. For the part of the problem concerning the proportion originating in New York, a sample size of 900 is needed. Since both estimates are to be made from the same set of data, a sample of 1600 is required.

3.3 a. The interval estimate is 20.0 ± 8.0 percent.

    b. The interval estimate is

$$.25 \pm \sqrt{\frac{100}{99}} \ (.08) \text{ lbs.} \approx .25 \pm .08 \text{ lbs.}$$

3.4 The same size

3.5 (a,b)

| Stratum | Sample Size | Interval Estimate |
|---|---|---|
| 0 – $10,000 | 200 | $\overline{X}_1 \pm \$28.28$ |
| $10,001 – 15,000 | 400 | $\overline{X}_2 \pm \$40.00$ |
| $15,001 – 20,000 | 400 | $\overline{X}_3 \pm \$80.00$ |

## CHAPTER 4

4.5 a. .0136.

    b. Yes.

## CHAPTER 6

6.3 $S_A = -.35$, $S_B = .29$, $S_C = -.06$

## CHAPTER 8

8.4 a. To answer this question we test the null hypothesis $H_o: \mu \leq 80$. To see whether $\overline{X} = 82$ is significantly greater than 80, we compare it to

$$\mu + Z_\alpha \hat{\sigma}_{\overline{X}}.$$

For instance, for

$$\alpha = .0001, \mu + Z_\alpha \hat{\sigma}_{\overline{X}}$$

is 81.85 (80 + 3.70 × ½). Since the sample mean exceeds this value, we reject $H_o$. Thus, under the conditions stated, the product should be marketed.

b. The product should not be marketed in this case, since the sample mean does not exceed the population mean. This means that $H_o$ cannot be rejected.

## CHAPTER 9

9.1 (a,c) The null hypothesis to be tested is $H_o: \mu_A - \mu_B = 0$. Using the data in the problem, we get

$$\hat{\sigma}_{X_A - X_B} = .20$$

$$Z = 2.2.$$

The probability that the observed difference (2.44 − 2.00) occurred by chance (for a $Z$ value of 2.2) is .014. Thus, for $\alpha = .05$ the null hypothesis is rejected, whereas for $\alpha = .01$ it is accepted. In a decisional setting, the decision maker must decide if $p = .014$ is a small enough probability of making a Type I error for him to infer that there is a significant difference in expected purchase between men and women.

b. The interval estimate (when $\alpha = .05$) is:

$$\overline{X}_A - \overline{X}_B \pm Z_{\alpha/2}\, \hat{\sigma}_{\overline{X}_A - \overline{X}_B}$$

$$(2.44 - 2.00) \pm 1.96 \sqrt{\frac{.64}{25} + \frac{.36}{25}}$$

$$.440 \pm 1.96(.20)$$

$$.440 \pm .392$$

9.2 The null hypothesis to be tested is $H_o: \pi_1 - \pi_2 = 0$. For $\alpha = .05$, the following results are obtained:

Had EXAM in the house:
Regular size
$$-0.0870 < \pi_1 - \pi_2 < +0.0070 \qquad\qquad \text{accept } H_o$$
Large size
$$-0.1670 < \pi_1 - \pi_2 < -0.0730 \qquad\qquad \text{reject } H_o$$
Tried EXAM in past 4 weeks for:
Painted Woodwork
$$-0.0590 < \pi_1 - \pi_2 < +0.0390 \qquad\qquad \text{accept } H_o$$
Painted Walls
$$-0.0231 < \pi_1 - \pi_2 < +0.0631 \qquad\qquad \text{accept } H_o$$
Linoleum Floors
$$-0.1731 < \pi_1 - \pi_2 < +0.0869 \qquad\qquad \text{reject } H_o$$

Attitude toward EXAM for cleaning floors (users only):

Favorable comments only
$$-0.025 < \pi_1 - \pi_2 < +0.085 \qquad\qquad \text{accept } H_o$$
Unfavorable comments only
$$-0.075 < \pi_1 - \pi_2 < -0.005 \qquad\qquad \text{reject } H_o$$
Both favorable and unfavorable comments
$$-0.006 < \pi_1 - \pi_2 < +0.106 \qquad\qquad \text{accept } H_o$$
No specific comments
$$-0.067 < \pi_1 - \pi_2 < -0.013 \qquad\qquad \text{reject } H_o$$

9.3 The Contingency Correlation Coefficient is $C = .011$. Under the null hypothesis $H_o: C_P = 0$, chi-square is calculated to be $\chi^2 = 2.323$. $\chi^2$ with $(3-1)(2-1) = 2$ degrees of freedom has probability of occurence under $H_o$ of greater than .30. Thus, it is highly likely that size and locality are not related.

# Appendix

```
44 17 81 63 93 91 52 43 50 74 61 99 02 19 94 26 77 28 14 95 39 22 25 30 53
88 67 13 65 42 16 55 42 78 81 12 66 58 07 30 20 59 47 14 96 78 59 58 69 07
53 18 13 47 12 81 71 93 43 14 45 90 39 29 77 47 92 81 23 69 70 56 79 90 60
88 57 56 97 96 24 63 95 32 41 90 43 48 61 52 05 74 80 89 89 12 76 37 73 88
49 37 69 38 27 16 62 64 95 32 63 31 18 12 21 68 08 84 16 48 33 93 67 46 98
66 00 15 15 06 86 14 07 76 69 84 86 58 40 08 58 63 87 36 88 19 90 93 66 23
17 07 89 49 45 65 08 01 23 92 30 67 99 66 81 88 60 41 47 47 28 53 64 08 12
73 99 60 72 28 09 19 34 62 10 49 62 95 68 60 91 13 06 88 83 46 64 87 59 24
11 33 21 44 43 15 91 22 07 59 28 42 12 76 76 20 27 24 24 70 78 93 67 51 61
43 08 41 21 85 32 51 09 47 54 45 23 51 66 66 50 44 27 63 67 16 08 28 32 25
57 56 85 67 62 97 61 49 23 51 35 95 77 49 03 10 42 91 43 94 50 57 03 49 38
62 38 42 48 72 35 81 64 85 19 29 39 03 71 60 19 86 80 21 92 34 33 81 80 35
21 73 14 67 12 30 23 68 19 78 55 90 37 25 71 03 99 59 12 51 47 82 45 25 58
75 65 33 81 82 13 23 96 76 82 86 23 82 51 50 64 17 55 28 41 95 03 63 62 95
61 13 17 91 71 77 05 72 82 73 67 52 45 97 77 51 16 78 93 01 91 17 66 61 26
72 56 13 65 11 38 13 00 50 56 82 68 31 33 12 41 61 84 23 92 13 13 55 38 14
97 53 14 68 19 44 44 70 74 30 71 09 35 63 80 55 10 31 95 97 17 11 39 44 32
35 79 16 21 57 81 75 53 33 60 94 77 79 29 49 07 85 47 83 12 22 55 88 46 13
22 64 20 80 44 28 22 09 90 58 41 06 16 23 35 36 38 02 23 49 46 95 65 00 07
87 88 39 37 23 99 34 19 32 45 33 73 30 66 95 80 65 92 68 67 31 91 29 79 83
50 76 04 65 30 15 56 76 70 61 88 39 27 70 46 09 46 73 04 97 55 24 55 10 12
02 76 80 86 96 52 36 34 74 80 76 33 60 20 92 29 77 41 81 94 05 73 64 28 13
34 36 90 26 29 39 20 76 95 42 67 34 58 69 47 56 81 35 65 86 23 82 53 24 47
```

225

Table 1 (Continued)

```
69 47 26 60 28 33 65 51 63 91 41 07 85 54 48 47 89 89 28 16 53 63 25 95 88
36 14 60 08 90 71 30 34 43 18 96 70 86 34 51 06 51 11 14 03 33 67 85 71 90
62 16 07 76 94 09 32 30 74 76 86 78 75 52 70 37 57 13 08 29 32 23 91 70 56
75 46 96 99 49 03 54 14 38 20 58 77 01 14 85 16 66 99 28 95 46 57 76 48 08
32 53 72 54 45 60 27 95 50 61 94 74 24 19 78 12 00 75 85 97 32 75 62 45 62
66 09 42 47 16 57 33 42 44 67 41 75 32 43 09 79 78 39 01 27 21 30 48 49 20
12 56 30 19 62 47 50 43 45 05 13 13 79 58 36 73 10 71 17 77 56 92 66 44 72
93 63 44 66 76 44 76 82 75 38 09 46 79 96 66 80 57 46 23 99 32 05 27 34 43
99 96 86 08 57 19 62 73 25 37 61 76 95 17 07 61 40 57 34 44 54 85 84 40 08
92 95 55 56 71 43 33 26 00 73 43 15 01 66 82 74 35 10 28 92 17 90 92 95 63
88 77 70 08 13 16 60 87 60 67 80 97 39 58 27 90 59 22 75 49 43 63 83 03 90
71 43 59 44 65 08 48 18 95 88 73 16 98 95 53 70 49 86 71 25 87 37 88 73 79
81 71 50 68 32 00 95 95 39 17 83 77 07 95 65 90 61 10 52 48 74 48 32 49 54
85 35 17 54 65 57 99 07 07 65 21 93 79 91 42 77 75 10 96 19 13 78 19 34 56
97 98 88 17 00 58 81 12 61 35 25 42 21 18 68 84 37 73 30 88 85 19 59 16 47
40 50 04 89 66 51 21 91 82 71 15 80 17 88 38 27 49 65 30 34 49 28 22 14 67
22 73 51 48 82 14 87 85 46 89 19 46 67 54 20 61 33 11 68 14 55 25 25 25 92
21 29 99 31 69 64 45 42 00 84 18 46 43 44 30 16 40 07 95 26 63 24 69 37 48
18 09 80 67 79 82 33 35 05 92 31 34 64 39 62 35 51 99 31 87 41 61 85 97 94
26 72 96 60 46 44 75 28 54 62 38 92 97 05 53 34 53 64 56 43 93 64 05 68 42
66 28 80 86 71 43 11 46 59 63 17 27 36 56 92 37 11 11 86 57 44 98 34 87 82
62 99 58 99 85 78 25 10 31 75 63 00 87 08 78 22 12 12 52 85 49 86 18 07 70
55 60 57 69 48 19 41 83 50 67 59 12 99 19 02 00 28 19 08 11 96 28 36 61 43
76 62 89 95 48 58 09 12 03 61 59 06 54 85 46 84 63 96 51 96 65 12 98 54 11
94 66 26 20 23 40 59 39 40 32 15 16 54 81 79 63 12 78 47 16 58 70 58 97 02
50 73 51 48 98 54 66 93 14 37 81 30 87 07 65 99 55 12 72 94 81 51 49 09 37
94 11 04 04 22 92 49 83 08 57 01 85 53 53 23 75 41 14 29 11 66 15 93 94 90
97 87 81 59 36 66 29 96 73 78 67 53 01 98 78 74 15 70 42 62 68 10 52 98 34
46 50 73 23 03 04 37 49 13 66 97 24 11 63 83 18 23 87 99 66 21 91 79 12 63
43 85 00 91 54 39 67 34 53 17 21 10 43 16 80 81 09 79 08 82 51 07 40 95 83
18 20 00 87 87 11 61 72 26 45 62 83 74 27 48 29 35 71 96 66 24 78 91 94 06
68 94 94 68 84 27 04 78 14 17 14 84 79 82 01 96 90 62 31 73 19 12 96 97 05
04 19 46 04 41 94 03 09 64 84 26 45 84 77 37 82 23 36 75 78 06 25 19 44 15
18 58 79 01 03 59 56 25 50 68 29 21 93 72 00 20 31 12 49 91 03 44 85 01 90
26 87 32 08 99 64 30 36 58 90 58 70 80 67 30 42 75 00 20 65 26 58 88 47 67
90 20 49 76 36 22 43 33 57 79 13 28 77 43 95 15 19 29 43 38 90 92 24 43 00
68 93 78 50 75 23 01 32 08 15 82 88 68 41 71 56 17 53 39 40 70 98 59 39 46
23 61 67 72 61 78 97 23 52 21 04 28 70 85 52 07 48 39 83 91 49 36 55 45 83
36 81 30 45 20 87 66 57 46 10 63 90 44 51 16 34 99 76 43 99 29 73 43 68 75
64 82 04 03 25 82 97 21 68 67 47 59 76 41 65 23 03 25 96 48 23 25 04 85 76
67 92 73 22 99 94 89 62 03 72 78 24 18 67 17 97 70 95 77 12 27 85 69 67 31
05 45 92 49 35 00 70 97 89 69 11 90 73 09 40 37 10 16 23 31 67 28 57 94 01
33 29 57 36 32 45 53 75 40 28 99 21 70 95 70 42 17 58 80 35 02 21 44 63 12
91 42 82 67 44 48 86 50 23 86 56 80 70 72 60 20 71 43 46 05 08 23 02 87 65
24 98 47 67 18 87 74 90 59 94 35 56 47 21 76 38 48 64 71 93 50 38 79 12 10
62 91 99 52 60 90 70 65 91 82 81 09 39 55 97 31 79 48 61 18 48 33 50 08 00
74 58 79 34 74 09 90 75 69 72 05 17 86 75 39 43 84 44 89 66 61 55 09 08 27
76 88 26 52 23 09 90 35 96 91 04 09 24 83 47 12 27 77 65 87 07 99 92 92 70
40 32 79 41 51 66 56 78 85 99 92 43 96 55 24 50 07 25 50 35 77 62 65 21 17
15 32 70 90 68 94 21 44 85 64 37 87 37 68 64 14 45 65 33 14 33 99 83 60 23
14 03 62 04 19 90 20 87 62 99 75 87 38 39 63 70 30 92 95 93 65 23 13 78 10
10 16 42 17 06 50 75 65 87 66 47 88 93 43 63 18 79 80 71 72 36 69 63 64 76
76 10 61 42 98 08 79 97 47 21 36 73 41 15 98 69 51 74 85 37 84 64 20 56 78
```

226

TABLE 1 (Continued)

```
76 64 86 33 02 31 69 29 80 60 37 96 26 82 91 51 09 25 36 03 01 81 96 43 58
12 08 69 72 19 33 85 11 82 00 36 41 49 01 52 88 83 67 24 33 70 25 83 15 32
17 09 08 27 40 24 74 94 96 25 27 35 35 73 17 84 51 32 38 58 83 35 76 24 39
19 51 82 15 97 67 34 68 30 63 93 81 92 16 33 96 68 90 19 69 88 10 19 71 22
48 78 53 97 59 06 30 77 81 40 76 26 03 70 23 49 42 74 88 57 56 32 97 26 94
82 48 64 20 53 92 57 27 74 81 09 90 32 58 36 14 85 12 16 54 27 32 26 71 66
91 97 69 13 86 24 39 93 08 64 95 56 58 19 13 41 59 88 63 15 80 22 60 56 59
21 56 45 40 34 36 44 90 23 28 81 61 81 25 54 43 24 44 75 11 70 89 74 04 15
62 79 34 61 32 84 21 05 19 80 88 54 74 84 55 32 27 49 18 23 45 25 89 98 06
78 93 03 74 39 29 08 50 96 65 62 11 00 14 82 72 01 09 59 30 91 36 26 30 28
35 76 20 37 49 39 99 24 56 78 44 32 72 47 21 19 95 60 37 55 62 26 53 86 35
19 81 41 93 93 30 03 10 58 40 09 31 73 53 60 22 57 53 38 13 31 58 31 08 72
71 68 80 73 01 62 28 98 63 19 06 32 01 26 40 75 27 84 77 63 15 74 45 23 49
33 22 70 16 56 71 25 46 61 83 86 34 09 11 76 32 02 45 53 26 80 12 74 72 00
83 64 94 95 67 57 88 02 50 62 87 96 14 27 52 14 86 89 72 84 47 26 54 94 59
34 60 89 24 72 76 00 75 11 30 01 20 20 25 51 76 98 57 64 03 12 10 28 95 47
63 45 68 29 76 71 39 86 25 46 54 85 51 12 76 66 50 59 56 96 08 45 60 66 87
74 45 10 02 32 43 94 15 40 05 37 34 18 24 07 67 73 98 41 97 69 82 56 84 18
19 44 92 80 72 75 72 29 18 36 58 88 46 84 77 67 03 32 13 02 95 77 67 83 44
66 26 00 28 33 50 26 29 48 43 31 71 16 86 41 19 06 50 17 09 72 69 45 12 06
40 37 11 16 01 80 90 67 29 56 19 63 96 60 41 60 98 94 39 06 03 24 36 59 19
58 56 02 17 51 76 00 91 90 62 11 71 77 33 80 07 57 69 89 22 89 05 80 22 45
24 17 15 80 77 91 26 32 93 18 43 53 27 16 03 66 89 63 41 86 50 24 81 45 04
36 96 51 56 70 62 79 07 56 97 33 08 57 02 91 55 65 93 99 07 97 41 29 61 72
```

TABLE 2 Normal probability distribution (Values of P corresponding to Z for the normal curve)

| $Z$ | Area from mean to $Z$ | Area in larger portion | Area in smaller portion |
|------|------|------|------|
| 0.00 | .0000 | .5000 | .5000 |
| 0.02 | .0080 | .5080 | .4920 |
| 0.04 | .0160 | .5160 | .4840 |
| 0.06 | .0239 | .5239 | .4761 |
| 0.08 | .0319 | .5319 | .4681 |
| 0.10 | .0398 | .5398 | .4602 |
| 0.12 | .0478 | .5478 | .4522 |
| 0.14 | .0557 | .5557 | .4443 |
| 0.16 | .0636 | .5636 | .4364 |
| 0.18 | .0714 | .5714 | .4286 |
| 0.20 | .0793 | .5793 | .4207 |
| 0.22 | .0871 | .5871 | .4129 |
| 0.24 | .0948 | .5948 | .4052 |
| 0.26 | .1026 | .6026 | .3974 |
| 0.28 | .1103 | .6103 | .3897 |
| 0.30 | .1179 | .6179 | .3821 |
| 0.32 | .1255 | .6255 | .3745 |
| 0.34 | .1331 | .6331 | .3669 |
| 0.36 | .1406 | .6406 | .3594 |
| 0.38 | .1480 | .6480 | .3520 |
| 0.40 | .1554 | .6554 | .3446 |
| 0.42 | .1628 | .6628 | .3372 |
| 0.44 | .1700 | .6700 | .3300 |
| 0.46 | .1772 | .6772 | .3228 |
| 0.48 | .1844 | .6844 | .3156 |
| 0.50 | .1915 | .6915 | .3085 |
| 0.52 | .1985 | .6985 | .3015 |
| 0.54 | .2054 | .7054 | .2946 |
| 0.56 | .2123 | .7123 | .2877 |
| 0.58 | .2190 | .7190 | .2810 |
| 0.60 | .2257 | .7257 | .2743 |
| 0.62 | .2324 | .7324 | .2676 |
| 0.64 | .2389 | .7389 | .2611 |
| 0.66 | .2454 | .7454 | .2546 |
| 0.68 | .2517 | .7517 | .2483 |
| 0.70 | .2580 | .7580 | .2420 |
| 0.72 | .2642 | .7642 | .2358 |
| 0.74 | .2704 | .7704 | .2296 |
| 0.76 | .2764 | .7764 | .2236 |
| 0.78 | .2823 | .7823 | .2177 |
| 0.80 | .2881 | .7881 | .2119 |

Source: Adapted from *Handbook of Mathematical Functions With Formulas, Graphs, and Mathematical Tables,* U.S. Department of Commerce, National Bureau of Standards, Applied Mathematics Series 55, June 1964, pp. 966-972.

TABLE 2 (Continued)

| Z | Area from mean to Z | Area in larger portion | Area in smaller portion |
|---|---|---|---|
| 0.82 | .2939 | .7939 | .2061 |
| 0.84 | .2995 | .7995 | .2005 |
| 0.86 | .3051 | .8051 | .1949 |
| 0.88 | .3106 | .8106 | .1894 |
| 0.90 | .3159 | .8159 | .1841 |
| 0.92 | .3212 | .8212 | .1788 |
| 0.94 | .3264 | .8264 | .1736 |
| 0.96 | .3315 | .8315 | .1685 |
| 0.98 | .3365 | .8365 | .1635 |
| 1.00 | .3413 | .8413 | .1587 |
| 1.02 | .3461 | .8461 | .1539 |
| 1.04 | .3508 | .8508 | .1492 |
| 1.06 | .3554 | .8554 | .1446 |
| 1.08 | .3599 | .8599 | .1401 |
| 1.10 | .3643 | .8643 | .1357 |
| 1.12 | .3686 | .8686 | .1314 |
| 1.14 | .3729 | .8729 | .1271 |
| 1.16 | .3770 | .8770 | .1230 |
| 1.18 | .3810 | .8810 | .1190 |
| 1.20 | .3849 | .8849 | .1151 |
| 1.22 | .3888 | .8888 | .1112 |
| 1.24 | .3925 | .8925 | .1075 |
| 1.26 | .3962 | .8962 | .1038 |
| 1.28 | .3997 | .8997 | .1003 |
| 1.30 | .4032 | .9032 | .0968 |
| 1.32 | .4066 | .9066 | .0934 |
| 1.34 | .4099 | .9099 | .0901 |
| 1.36 | .4131 | .9131 | .0869 |
| 1.38 | .4162 | .9162 | .0838 |
| 1.40 | .4192 | .9192 | .0808 |
| 1.42 | .4222 | .9222 | .0778 |
| 1.44 | .4251 | .9251 | .0749 |
| 1.46 | 4279 | .9279 | .0721 |
| 1.48 | .4306 | .9306 | .0694 |
| 1.50 | .4332 | .9332 | .0668 |
| 1.52 | .4357 | .9357 | .0643 |
| 1.54 | .4382 | .9382 | .0618 |
| 1.56 | .4406 | .9406 | .0594 |
| 1.58 | .4429 | .9429 | .0571 |
| 1.60 | .4452 | .9452 | .0548 |
| 1.62 | .4474 | .9474 | .0526 |
| 1.64 | .4495 | .9495 | .0505 |
| 1.66 | .4515 | .9515 | .0485 |
| 1.68 | .4535 | .9535 | .0465 |
| 1.70 | .4554 | .9554 | .0446 |
| 1.72 | .4573 | .9573 | .0427 |
| 1.74 | .4591 | .9591 | .0409 |
| 1.76 | .4608 | .9608 | .0392 |

TABLE 2 (Continued)

| $Z$ | Area from mean to $Z$ | Area in larger portion | Area in smaller portion |
|------|------|------|------|
| 1.78 | .4625 | .9625 | .0375 |
| 1.80 | .4641 | .9641 | .0359 |
| 1.82 | .4656 | .9656 | .0344 |
| 1.84 | .4671 | .9671 | .0329 |
| 1.86 | .4686 | .9686 | .0314 |
| 1.88 | .4699 | .9699 | .0301 |
| 1.90 | .4713 | .9713 | .0287 |
| 1.92 | .4726 | .9726 | .0274 |
| 1.94 | .4738 | .9738 | .0262 |
| 1.96 | .4750 | .9750 | .0250 |
| 1.98 | .4761 | .9761 | .0239 |
| 2.00 | .4772 | .9772 | .0228 |
| 2.02 | .4783 | .9783 | .0217 |
| 2.04 | .4793 | .9793 | .0207 |
| 2.06 | .4803 | .9803 | .0197 |
| 2.08 | .4812 | .9812 | .0188 |
| 2.10 | .4821 | .9821 | .0179 |
| 2.12 | .4830 | .9830 | .0170 |
| 2.14 | .4838 | .9838 | .0162 |
| 2.16 | .4846 | .9846 | .0154 |
| 2.18 | .4854 | .9854 | .0146 |
| 2.20 | .4861 | .9861 | .0139 |
| 2.22 | .4868 | .9868 | .0132 |
| 2.24 | .4875 | .9875 | .0125 |
| 2.26 | .4881 | .9881 | .0119 |
| 2.28 | .4887 | .9887 | .0113 |
| 2.30 | .4893 | .9893 | .0107 |
| 2.32 | .4898 | .9898 | .0102 |
| 2.34 | .4904 | .9904 | .0096 |
| 2.36 | .4909 | .9909 | .0091 |
| 2.38 | .4913 | .9913 | .0087 |
| 2.40 | .4918 | .9918 | .0082 |
| 2.42 | .4922 | .9922 | .0078 |
| 2.44 | .4927 | .9927 | .0073 |
| 2.46 | .4931 | .9931 | .0069 |
| 2.48 | .4934 | .9934 | .0066 |
| 2.50 | .4938 | .9938 | .0062 |
| 2.52 | .4941 | .9941 | .0059 |
| 2.54 | .4945 | .9945 | .0055 |
| 2.56 | .4948 | .9948 | .0052 |
| 2.58 | .4951 | .9951 | .0049 |
| 2.60 | .4953 | .9953 | .0047 |
| 2.62 | .4956 | .9956 | .0044 |
| 2.64 | .4959 | .9959 | .0041 |
| 2.66 | .4961 | .9961 | .0039 |
| 2.68 | .4963 | .9963 | .0037 |
| 2.70 | .4965 | .9965 | .0035 |
| 2.72 | .4967 | .9967 | .0033 |
| 2.74 | .4969 | .9969 | .0031 |

TABLE 2 (Continued)

| Z | Area from mean to Z | Area in larger portion | Area in smaller portion |
|---|---|---|---|
| 2.76 | .4971 | .9971 | .0029 |
| 2.78 | .4973 | .9973 | .0027 |
| 2.80 | .4974 | .9974 | .0026 |
| 2.82 | .4976 | .9976 | .0024 |
| 2.84 | .4977 | .9977 | .0023 |
| 2.86 | .4979 | .9979 | .0021 |
| 2.88 | .4980 | .9980 | .0020 |
| 2.90 | .4981 | .9981 | .0019 |
| 2.92 | .4982 | .9982 | .0018 |
| 2.94 | .4984 | .9984 | .0016 |
| 2.96 | .4985 | .9985 | .0015 |
| 2.98 | .4986 | .9986 | .0014 |
| 3.00 | .4987 | .9987 | .0013 |
| 3.05 | .4989 | .9989 | .0011 |
| 3.10 | .4990 | .9990 | .0010 |
| 3.15 | .4992 | .9992 | .0008 |
| 3.20 | .4993 | .9993 | .0007 |
| 3.25 | .4994 | .9994 | .0006 |
| 3.30 | .4995 | .9995 | .0005 |
| 3.35 | .4996 | .9996 | .0004 |
| 3.40 | .4997 | .9997 | .0003 |
| 3.45 | .4997 | .9997 | .0003 |
| 3.50 | .4998 | .9998 | .0002 |
| 3.55 | .4998 | .9998 | .0002 |
| 3.60 | .4998 | .9998 | .0002 |
| 3.65 | .4999 | .9999 | .0001 |
| 3.70 | .4999 | .9999 | .0001 |
| 3.75 | .4999 | .9999 | .0001 |
| 3.80 | .4999 | .9999 | .0001 |
| 3.85 | .4999 | .9999 | .0001 |
| 3.90 | .4999 | .9999 | .0001 |
| 3.95 | .4999 | .9999 | .0001 |
| 4.00 | .4999 | .9999 | .0001 |
| 4.20 | .4999 | .9999 | .0001 |
| 4.40 | .4999 | .9999 | .0001 |
| 4.60 | .4999 | .9999 | .0001 |
| 4.80 | .4999 | .9999 | .0001 |
| 5.00 | .4999 | .9999 | .0001 |

TABLE 3    Percentiles of the *t* distribution (one- and two-tailed tests)*

| d.f. | P = .90 (.45) | .80 (.40) | .70 (.35) | .60 (.30) | .50 (.25) | .40 (.20) | .30 (.15) | .20 (.10) | .10 (.05) | .050 (.025) | .02 (.01) | .01 (.005) |
|---|---|---|---|---|---|---|---|---|---|---|---|---|
| 1 | .158 | .325 | .510 | .727 | 1.000 | 1.376 | 1.963 | 3.078 | 6.314 | 12.706 | 31.821 | 63.657 |
| 2 | .142 | .289 | .445 | .617 | .816 | 1.061 | 1.386 | 1.886 | 2.920 | 4.303 | 6.965 | 9.925 |
| 3 | .137 | .277 | .424 | .584 | .765 | .978 | 1.250 | 1.638 | 2.353 | 3.182 | 4.541 | 5.841 |
| 4 | .134 | .271 | .414 | .569 | .741 | .941 | 1.190 | 1.533 | 2.132 | 2.776 | 3.747 | 4.604 |
| 5 | .132 | .267 | .408 | .559 | .727 | .920 | 1.156 | 1.476 | 2.015 | 2.571 | 3.365 | 4.032 |
| 6 | .131 | .265 | .404 | .553 | .718 | .906 | 1.134 | 1.440 | 1.943 | 2.447 | 3.143 | 3.707 |
| 7 | .130 | .263 | .402 | .549 | .711 | .896 | 1.119 | 1.415 | 1.895 | 2.365 | 2.998 | 3.499 |
| 8 | .130 | .262 | .399 | .546 | .706 | .889 | 1.108 | 1.397 | 1.860 | 2.306 | 2.896 | 3.355 |
| 9 | .129 | .261 | .398 | .543 | .703 | .883 | 1.100 | 1.383 | 1.833 | 2.262 | 2.821 | 3.250 |
| 10 | .129 | .260 | .397 | .542 | .700 | .879 | 1.093 | 1.372 | 1.812 | 2.228 | 2.764 | 3.169 |
| 11 | .129 | .260 | .396 | .540 | .697 | .876 | 1.088 | 1.363 | 1.796 | 2.201 | 2.718 | 3.106 |
| 12 | .128 | .259 | .395 | .539 | .695 | .873 | 1.083 | 1.356 | 1.782 | 2.179 | 2.681 | 3.055 |
| 13 | .128 | .259 | .394 | .538 | .694 | .870 | 1.079 | 1.350 | 1.771 | 2.160 | 2.650 | 3.012 |
| 14 | .128 | .258 | .393 | .537 | .692 | .868 | 1.076 | 1.345 | 1.761 | 2.145 | 2.624 | 2.977 |
| 15 | .128 | .258 | .393 | .536 | .691 | .866 | 1.074 | 1.341 | 1.753 | 2.131 | 2.602 | 2.947 |
| 16 | .128 | .258 | .392 | .535 | .690 | .865 | 1.071 | 1.337 | 1.746 | 2.120 | 2.583 | 2.921 |
| 17 | .128 | .257 | .392 | .534 | .689 | .863 | 1.069 | 1.333 | 1.740 | 2.110 | 2.567 | 2.898 |
| 18 | .127 | .257 | .392 | .534 | .688 | .862 | 1.067 | 1.330 | 1.734 | 2.101 | 2.552 | 2.878 |
| 19 | .127 | .257 | .391 | .533 | .688 | .861 | 1.066 | 1.328 | 1.729 | 2.093 | 2.539 | 2.861 |
| 20 | .127 | .257 | .391 | .533 | .687 | .860 | 1.064 | 1.325 | 1.725 | 2.086 | 2.528 | 2.845 |
| 21 | .127 | .257 | .391 | .532 | .686 | .859 | 1.063 | 1.323 | 1.721 | 2.080 | 2.518 | 2.831 |
| 22 | .127 | .256 | .390 | .532 | .686 | .858 | 1.061 | 1.321 | 1.717 | 2.074 | 2.508 | 2.819 |
| 23 | .127 | .256 | .390 | .532 | .685 | .858 | 1.060 | 1.319 | 1.714 | 2.069 | 2.500 | 2.807 |
| 24 | .127 | .256 | .390 | .531 | .685 | .857 | 1.059 | 1.318 | 1.711 | 2.064 | 2.492 | 2.797 |
| 25 | .127 | .256 | .390 | .531 | .684 | .856 | 1.058 | 1.316 | 1.708 | 2.060 | 2.485 | 2.787 |
| 26 | .127 | .256 | .390 | .531 | .684 | .856 | 1.058 | 1.315 | 1.706 | 2.056 | 2.479 | 2.779 |
| 27 | .127 | .256 | .389 | .531 | .684 | .855 | 1.057 | 1.314 | 1.703 | 2.052 | 2.473 | 2.771 |
| 28 | .127 | .256 | .389 | .530 | .683 | .855 | 1.056 | 1.313 | 1.701 | 2.048 | 2.467 | 2.763 |
| 29 | .127 | .256 | .389 | .530 | .683 | .854 | 1.055 | 1.311 | 1.699 | 2.045 | 2.462 | 2.756 |
| 30 | .127 | .256 | .389 | .530 | .683 | .854 | 1.055 | 1.310 | 1.697 | 2.042 | 2.457 | 2.750 |
| ∞ | .12566 | .25335 | .38532 | .52440 | .67449 | .84162 | 1.03643 | 1.28155 | 1.64485 | 1.95996 | 2.32634 | 2.57582 |

*The *p* in parentheses is for a one-tailed test.

Source: Taken from R. A. Fisher, *Statistical Methods for Research Workers*, 14th Edition, 1970, published by Oliver and Boyd, Edinburgh. Reproduced by permission of the author and publishers.

**TABLE 4** Percentiles of the F distribution 5% (top line of pair) and 1% (bottom line of pair)

$n_1$ degrees of freedom (for greater mean square)

| $n_2$ | 1 | 2 | 3 | 4 | 5 | 6 | 7 | 8 | 9 | 10 | 11 | 12 | 14 | 16 | 20 | 24 | 30 | 40 | 50 | 75 | 100 | 200 | 500 | ∞ |
|---|---|---|---|---|---|---|---|---|---|---|---|---|---|---|---|---|---|---|---|---|---|---|---|---|
| 1 | 161 | 200 | 216 | 225 | 230 | 234 | 237 | 239 | 241 | 242 | 243 | 244 | 245 | 246 | 248 | 249 | 250 | 251 | 252 | 253 | 253 | 254 | 254 | 254 |
|  | 4,052 | 4,999 | 5,403 | 5,625 | 5,764 | 5,859 | 5,928 | 5,981 | 6,022 | 6,056 | 6,082 | 6,106 | 6,142 | 6,169 | 6,208 | 6,234 | 6,258 | 6,286 | 6,302 | 6,323 | 6,334 | 6,352 | 6,361 | 6,366 |
| 2 | 18.51 | 19.00 | 19.16 | 19.25 | 19.30 | 19.33 | 19.36 | 19.37 | 19.38 | 19.39 | 19.40 | 19.41 | 19.42 | 19.43 | 19.44 | 19.45 | 19.46 | 19.47 | 19.47 | 19.48 | 19.49 | 19.49 | 19.50 | 19.50 |
|  | 98.49 | 99.00 | 99.17 | 99.25 | 99.30 | 99.33 | 99.34 | 99.36 | 99.38 | 99.40 | 99.41 | 99.42 | 99.43 | 99.44 | 99.45 | 99.46 | 99.47 | 99.48 | 99.48 | 99.49 | 99.49 | 99.49 | 99.50 | 99.50 |
| 3 | 10.13 | 9.55 | 9.28 | 9.12 | 9.01 | 8.94 | 8.88 | 8.84 | 8.81 | 8.78 | 8.76 | 8.74 | 8.71 | 8.69 | 8.66 | 8.64 | 8.62 | 8.60 | 8.58 | 8.57 | 8.56 | 8.54 | 8.54 | 8.53 |
|  | 34.12 | 30.82 | 29.46 | 28.71 | 28.24 | 27.91 | 27.67 | 27.49 | 27.34 | 27.23 | 27.13 | 27.05 | 26.92 | 26.83 | 26.69 | 26.60 | 26.50 | 26.41 | 26.35 | 26.27 | 26.23 | 26.18 | 26.14 | 26.12 |
| 4 | 7.71 | 6.94 | 6.59 | 6.39 | 6.26 | 6.16 | 6.09 | 6.04 | 6.00 | 5.96 | 5.93 | 5.91 | 5.87 | 5.84 | 5.80 | 5.77 | 5.74 | 5.71 | 5.70 | 5.68 | 5.66 | 5.65 | 5.64 | 5.63 |
|  | 21.20 | 18.00 | 16.69 | 15.98 | 15.52 | 15.21 | 14.98 | 14.80 | 14.66 | 14.54 | 14.45 | 14.37 | 14.24 | 14.15 | 14.02 | 13.93 | 13.83 | 13.74 | 13.69 | 13.61 | 13.57 | 13.52 | 13.48 | 13.46 |
| 5 | 6.61 | 5.79 | 5.41 | 5.19 | 5.05 | 4.95 | 4.88 | 4.82 | 4.78 | 4.74 | 4.70 | 4.68 | 4.64 | 4.60 | 4.56 | 4.53 | 4.50 | 4.46 | 4.44 | 4.42 | 4.40 | 4.38 | 4.37 | 4.36 |
|  | 16.26 | 13.27 | 12.06 | 11.39 | 10.97 | 10.67 | 10.45 | 10.27 | 10.15 | 10.05 | 9.96 | 9.89 | 9.77 | 9.68 | 9.55 | 9.47 | 9.38 | 9.29 | 9.24 | 9.17 | 9.13 | 9.07 | 9.04 | 9.02 |
| 6 | 5.99 | 5.14 | 4.76 | 4.53 | 4.39 | 4.28 | 4.21 | 4.15 | 4.10 | 4.06 | 4.03 | 4.00 | 3.96 | 3.92 | 3.87 | 3.84 | 3.81 | 3.77 | 3.75 | 3.72 | 3.71 | 3.69 | 3.68 | 3.67 |
|  | 13.74 | 10.92 | 9.78 | 9.15 | 8.75 | 8.47 | 8.26 | 8.10 | 7.98 | 7.87 | 7.79 | 7.72 | 7.60 | 7.52 | 7.39 | 7.31 | 7.23 | 7.14 | 7.09 | 7.02 | 6.99 | 6.94 | 6.90 | 6.88 |
| 7 | 5.59 | 4.74 | 4.35 | 4.12 | 3.97 | 3.87 | 3.79 | 3.73 | 3.68 | 3.63 | 3.60 | 3.57 | 3.52 | 3.49 | 3.44 | 3.41 | 3.38 | 3.34 | 3.32 | 3.29 | 3.28 | 3.25 | 3.24 | 3.23 |
|  | 12.25 | 9.55 | 8.45 | 7.85 | 7.46 | 7.19 | 7.00 | 6.84 | 6.71 | 6.62 | 6.54 | 6.47 | 6.35 | 6.27 | 6.15 | 6.07 | 5.98 | 5.90 | 5.85 | 5.78 | 5.75 | 5.70 | 5.67 | 5.65 |
| 8 | 5.32 | 4.46 | 4.07 | 3.84 | 3.69 | 3.58 | 3.50 | 3.44 | 3.39 | 3.34 | 3.31 | 3.28 | 3.23 | 3.20 | 3.15 | 3.12 | 3.08 | 3.05 | 3.03 | 3.00 | 2.98 | 2.96 | 2.94 | 2.93 |
|  | 11.26 | 8.65 | 7.59 | 7.01 | 6.63 | 6.37 | 6.19 | 6.03 | 5.91 | 5.82 | 5.74 | 5.67 | 5.56 | 5.48 | 5.36 | 5.28 | 5.20 | 5.11 | 5.06 | 5.00 | 4.96 | 4.91 | 4.88 | 4.86 |
| 9 | 5.12 | 4.26 | 3.86 | 3.63 | 3.48 | 3.37 | 3.29 | 3.23 | 3.18 | 3.13 | 3.10 | 3.07 | 3.02 | 2.98 | 2.93 | 2.90 | 2.86 | 2.82 | 2.80 | 2.77 | 2.76 | 2.73 | 2.72 | 2.71 |
|  | 10.56 | 8.02 | 6.99 | 6.42 | 6.06 | 5.80 | 5.62 | 5.47 | 5.35 | 5.26 | 5.18 | 5.11 | 5.00 | 4.92 | 4.80 | 4.73 | 4.64 | 4.56 | 4.51 | 4.45 | 4.41 | 4.36 | 4.33 | 4.31 |
| 10 | 4.96 | 4.10 | 3.71 | 3.48 | 3.33 | 3.22 | 3.14 | 3.07 | 3.02 | 2.97 | 2.94 | 2.91 | 2.86 | 2.82 | 2.77 | 2.74 | 2.70 | 2.67 | 2.64 | 2.61 | 2.59 | 2.56 | 2.55 | 2.54 |
|  | 10.04 | 7.56 | 6.55 | 5.99 | 5.64 | 5.39 | 5.21 | 5.06 | 4.95 | 4.85 | 4.78 | 4.71 | 4.60 | 4.52 | 4.41 | 4.33 | 4.25 | 4.17 | 4.12 | 4.05 | 4.01 | 3.96 | 3.93 | 3.91 |
| 11 | 4.84 | 3.98 | 3.59 | 3.36 | 3.20 | 3.09 | 3.01 | 2.95 | 2.90 | 2.86 | 2.82 | 2.79 | 2.74 | 2.70 | 2.65 | 2.61 | 2.57 | 2.53 | 2.50 | 2.47 | 2.45 | 2.42 | 2.41 | 2.40 |
|  | 9.65 | 7.20 | 6.22 | 5.67 | 5.32 | 5.07 | 4.88 | 4.74 | 4.63 | 4.54 | 4.46 | 4.40 | 4.29 | 4.21 | 4.10 | 4.02 | 3.94 | 3.86 | 3.80 | 3.74 | 3.70 | 3.66 | 3.62 | 3.60 |
| 12 | 4.75 | 3.88 | 3.49 | 3.26 | 3.11 | 3.00 | 2.92 | 2.85 | 2.80 | 2.76 | 2.72 | 2.69 | 2.64 | 2.60 | 2.54 | 2.50 | 2.46 | 2.42 | 2.40 | 2.36 | 2.35 | 2.32 | 2.31 | 2.30 |
|  | 9.33 | 6.93 | 5.95 | 5.41 | 5.06 | 4.82 | 4.65 | 4.50 | 4.39 | 4.30 | 4.22 | 4.16 | 4.05 | 3.98 | 3.86 | 3.78 | 3.70 | 3.61 | 3.56 | 3.49 | 3.46 | 3.41 | 3.38 | 3.36 |
| 13 | 4.67 | 3.80 | 3.41 | 3.18 | 3.02 | 2.92 | 2.84 | 2.77 | 2.72 | 2.67 | 2.63 | 2.60 | 2.55 | 2.51 | 2.46 | 2.42 | 2.38 | 2.34 | 2.32 | 2.28 | 2.26 | 2.24 | 2.22 | 2.21 |
|  | 9.07 | 6.70 | 5.74 | 5.20 | 4.86 | 4.62 | 4.44 | 4.30 | 4.19 | 4.10 | 4.02 | 3.96 | 3.85 | 3.78 | 3.67 | 3.59 | 3.51 | 3.42 | 3.37 | 3.30 | 3.27 | 3.21 | 3.18 | 3.16 |
| 14 | 4.60 | 3.74 | 3.34 | 3.11 | 2.96 | 2.85 | 2.77 | 2.70 | 2.65 | 2.60 | 2.56 | 2.53 | 2.48 | 2.44 | 2.39 | 2.35 | 2.31 | 2.27 | 2.24 | 2.21 | 2.19 | 2.16 | 2.14 | 2.13 |
|  | 8.86 | 6.51 | 5.56 | 5.03 | 4.69 | 4.46 | 4.28 | 4.14 | 4.03 | 3.94 | 3.86 | 3.80 | 3.70 | 3.62 | 3.51 | 3.43 | 3.34 | 3.26 | 3.21 | 3.14 | 3.11 | 3.06 | 3.02 | 3.00 |
| 15 | 4.54 | 3.68 | 3.29 | 3.06 | 2.90 | 2.79 | 2.70 | 2.64 | 2.59 | 2.55 | 2.51 | 2.48 | 2.43 | 2.39 | 2.33 | 2.29 | 2.25 | 2.21 | 2.18 | 2.15 | 2.12 | 2.10 | 2.08 | 2.07 |
|  | 8.68 | 6.36 | 5.42 | 4.89 | 4.56 | 4.32 | 4.14 | 4.00 | 3.89 | 3.80 | 3.73 | 3.67 | 3.56 | 3.48 | 3.36 | 3.29 | 3.20 | 3.12 | 3.07 | 3.00 | 2.97 | 2.92 | 2.89 | 2.87 |
| 16 | 4.49 | 3.63 | 3.24 | 3.01 | 2.85 | 2.74 | 2.66 | 2.59 | 2.54 | 2.49 | 2.45 | 2.42 | 2.37 | 2.33 | 2.28 | 2.24 | 2.21 | 2.16 | 2.13 | 2.09 | 2.07 | 2.04 | 2.02 | 2.01 |
|  | 8.53 | 6.23 | 5.29 | 4.77 | 4.44 | 4.20 | 4.03 | 3.89 | 3.78 | 3.69 | 3.61 | 3.55 | 3.45 | 3.37 | 3.25 | 3.18 | 3.10 | 3.01 | 2.96 | 2.89 | 2.86 | 2.80 | 2.77 | 2.75 |

Source: Reprinted by permission from *Statistical Methods*, 4th edition, by George W. Snedecor, © 1946, Iowa State University Press, Ames, Iowa.

TABLE 4 (Continued)

$n_1$ degrees of freedom (for greater mean square)

| $n_2$ | 1 | 2 | 3 | 4 | 5 | 6 | 7 | 8 | 9 | 10 | 11 | 12 | 14 | 16 | 20 | 24 | 30 | 40 | 50 | 75 | 100 | 200 | 500 | ∞ | $n_2$ |
|---|---|---|---|---|---|---|---|---|---|---|---|---|---|---|---|---|---|---|---|---|---|---|---|---|---|
| 17 | 4.45 8.40 | 3.59 6.11 | 3.20 5.18 | 2.96 4.67 | 2.81 4.34 | 2.70 4.10 | 2.62 3.93 | 2.55 3.79 | 2.50 3.68 | 2.45 3.59 | 2.41 3.52 | 2.38 3.45 | 2.33 3.35 | 2.29 3.27 | 2.23 3.16 | 2.19 3.08 | 2.15 3.00 | 2.11 2.92 | 2.08 2.86 | 2.04 2.79 | 2.02 2.76 | 1.99 2.70 | 1.97 2.67 | 1.96 2.65 | 17 |
| 18 | 4.41 8.28 | 3.55 6.01 | 3.16 5.09 | 2.93 4.58 | 2.77 4.25 | 2.66 4.01 | 2.58 3.85 | 2.51 3.71 | 2.46 3.60 | 2.41 3.51 | 2.37 3.44 | 2.34 3.37 | 2.29 3.27 | 2.25 3.19 | 2.19 3.07 | 2.15 3.00 | 2.11 2.91 | 2.07 2.83 | 2.04 2.78 | 2.00 2.71 | 1.98 2.68 | 1.95 2.62 | 1.93 2.59 | 1.92 2.57 | 18 |
| 19 | 4.38 8.18 | 3.52 5.93 | 3.13 5.01 | 2.90 4.50 | 2.74 4.17 | 2.63 3.94 | 2.55 3.77 | 2.48 3.63 | 2.43 3.52 | 2.38 3.43 | 2.34 3.36 | 2.31 3.30 | 2.26 3.19 | 2.21 3.12 | 2.15 3.00 | 2.11 2.92 | 2.07 2.84 | 2.02 2.76 | 2.00 2.70 | 1.96 2.63 | 1.94 2.60 | 1.91 2.54 | 1.90 2.51 | 1.88 2.49 | 19 |
| 20 | 4.35 8.10 | 3.49 5.85 | 3.10 4.94 | 2.87 4.43 | 2.71 4.10 | 2.60 3.87 | 2.52 3.71 | 2.45 3.56 | 2.40 3.45 | 2.35 3.37 | 2.31 3.30 | 2.28 3.23 | 2.23 3.13 | 2.18 3.05 | 2.12 2.94 | 2.08 2.86 | 2.04 2.77 | 1.99 2.69 | 1.96 2.63 | 1.92 2.56 | 1.90 2.53 | 1.87 2.47 | 1.85 2.44 | 1.84 2.42 | 20 |
| 21 | 4.32 8.02 | 3.47 5.78 | 3.07 4.87 | 2.84 4.37 | 2.68 4.04 | 2.57 3.81 | 2.49 3.65 | 2.42 3.51 | 2.37 3.40 | 2.32 3.31 | 2.28 3.24 | 2.25 3.17 | 2.20 3.07 | 2.15 2.99 | 2.09 2.88 | 2.05 2.80 | 2.00 2.72 | 1.96 2.63 | 1.93 2.58 | 1.89 2.51 | 1.87 2.47 | 1.84 2.42 | 1.82 2.38 | 1.81 2.36 | 21 |
| 22 | 4.30 7.94 | 3.44 5.72 | 3.05 4.82 | 2.82 4.31 | 2.66 3.99 | 2.55 3.76 | 2.47 3.59 | 2.40 3.45 | 2.35 3.35 | 2.30 3.26 | 2.26 3.18 | 2.23 3.12 | 2.18 3.02 | 2.13 2.94 | 2.07 2.83 | 2.03 2.75 | 1.98 2.67 | 1.93 2.58 | 1.91 2.53 | 1.87 2.46 | 1.84 2.42 | 1.81 2.37 | 1.80 2.33 | 1.78 2.31 | 22 |
| 23 | 4.28 7.88 | 3.42 5.66 | 3.03 4.76 | 2.80 4.26 | 2.64 3.94 | 2.53 3.71 | 2.45 3.54 | 2.38 3.41 | 2.32 3.30 | 2.28 3.21 | 2.24 3.14 | 2.20 3.07 | 2.14 2.97 | 2.10 2.89 | 2.04 2.78 | 2.00 2.70 | 1.96 2.62 | 1.91 2.53 | 1.88 2.48 | 1.84 2.41 | 1.82 2.37 | 1.79 2.32 | 1.77 2.28 | 1.76 2.26 | 23 |
| 24 | 4.26 7.82 | 3.40 5.61 | 3.01 4.72 | 2.78 4.22 | 2.62 3.90 | 2.51 3.67 | 2.43 3.50 | 2.36 3.36 | 2.30 3.25 | 2.26 3.17 | 2.22 3.09 | 2.18 3.03 | 2.13 2.93 | 2.09 2.85 | 2.02 2.74 | 1.98 2.66 | 1.94 2.58 | 1.89 2.49 | 1.86 2.44 | 1.82 2.36 | 1.80 2.33 | 1.76 2.27 | 1.74 2.23 | 1.73 2.21 | 24 |
| 25 | 4.24 7.77 | 3.38 5.57 | 2.99 4.68 | 2.76 4.18 | 2.60 3.86 | 2.49 3.63 | 2.41 3.46 | 2.34 3.32 | 2.28 3.21 | 2.24 3.13 | 2.20 3.05 | 2.16 2.99 | 2.11 2.89 | 2.06 2.81 | 2.00 2.70 | 1.96 2.62 | 1.92 2.54 | 1.87 2.45 | 1.84 2.40 | 1.80 2.32 | 1.77 2.29 | 1.74 2.23 | 1.72 2.19 | 1.72 2.17 | 25 |
| 26 | 4.22 7.72 | 3.37 5.53 | 2.98 4.64 | 2.74 4.14 | 2.59 3.82 | 2.47 3.59 | 2.39 3.42 | 2.32 3.29 | 2.27 3.17 | 2.22 3.09 | 2.18 3.02 | 2.15 2.96 | 2.10 2.86 | 2.05 2.77 | 1.99 2.66 | 1.95 2.58 | 1.90 2.50 | 1.85 2.41 | 1.82 2.36 | 1.78 2.28 | 1.76 2.25 | 1.72 2.19 | 1.70 2.15 | 1.69 2.13 | 26 |
| 27 | 4.21 7.68 | 3.35 5.49 | 2.96 4.60 | 2.73 4.11 | 2.57 3.79 | 2.46 3.56 | 2.37 3.39 | 2.30 3.26 | 2.25 3.14 | 2.20 3.06 | 2.16 2.98 | 2.13 2.93 | 2.08 2.83 | 2.03 2.74 | 1.97 2.63 | 1.93 2.55 | 1.88 2.47 | 1.84 2.38 | 1.80 2.33 | 1.76 2.25 | 1.74 2.21 | 1.71 2.16 | 1.68 2.12 | 1.67 2.10 | 27 |
| 28 | 4.20 7.64 | 3.34 5.45 | 2.95 4.57 | 2.71 4.07 | 2.56 3.76 | 2.44 3.53 | 2.36 3.36 | 2.29 3.23 | 2.24 3.11 | 2.19 3.03 | 2.15 2.95 | 2.12 2.90 | 2.06 2.80 | 2.02 2.71 | 1.96 2.60 | 1.91 2.52 | 1.87 2.44 | 1.81 2.35 | 1.78 2.30 | 1.75 2.22 | 1.72 2.18 | 1.69 2.13 | 1.67 2.09 | 1.65 2.06 | 28 |
| 29 | 4.18 7.60 | 3.33 5.42 | 2.93 4.54 | 2.70 4.04 | 2.54 3.73 | 2.43 3.50 | 2.35 3.33 | 2.28 3.20 | 2.22 3.08 | 2.18 3.00 | 2.14 2.92 | 2.10 2.87 | 2.05 2.77 | 2.00 2.68 | 1.94 2.57 | 1.90 2.49 | 1.85 2.41 | 1.80 2.32 | 1.77 2.27 | 1.73 2.19 | 1.71 2.15 | 1.68 2.10 | 1.65 2.06 | 1.64 2.03 | 29 |
| 30 | 4.17 7.56 | 3.32 5.39 | 2.92 4.51 | 2.69 4.02 | 2.53 3.70 | 2.42 3.47 | 2.34 3.30 | 2.27 3.17 | 2.21 3.06 | 2.16 2.98 | 2.12 2.90 | 2.09 2.84 | 2.04 2.74 | 1.99 2.66 | 1.93 2.55 | 1.89 2.47 | 1.84 2.38 | 1.79 2.29 | 1.76 2.24 | 1.72 2.16 | 1.69 2.13 | 1.66 2.07 | 1.64 2.03 | 1.62 2.01 | 30 |
| 32 | 4.15 7.50 | 3.30 5.34 | 2.90 4.46 | 2.67 3.97 | 2.51 3.66 | 2.40 3.42 | 2.32 3.25 | 2.25 3.12 | 2.19 3.01 | 2.14 2.94 | 2.10 2.86 | 2.07 2.80 | 2.02 2.70 | 1.97 2.62 | 1.91 2.51 | 1.86 2.42 | 1.82 2.34 | 1.76 2.25 | 1.74 2.20 | 1.69 2.12 | 1.67 2.08 | 1.64 2.02 | 1.61 1.98 | 1.59 1.96 | 32 |
| 34 | 4.13 7.44 | 3.28 5.29 | 2.88 4.42 | 2.65 3.93 | 2.49 3.61 | 2.38 3.38 | 2.30 3.21 | 2.23 3.08 | 2.17 2.97 | 2.12 2.89 | 2.08 2.82 | 2.05 2.76 | 2.00 2.66 | 1.95 2.58 | 1.89 2.47 | 1.84 2.38 | 1.80 2.30 | 1.74 2.21 | 1.71 2.15 | 1.67 2.08 | 1.64 2.04 | 1.61 1.98 | 1.59 1.94 | 1.57 1.91 | 34 |

Table of critical values (upper row: roman type; lower row: bold type) indexed by degrees of freedom.

| df | | | | | | | | | | | | | | | | | | | | | | | | |
|---|---|---|---|---|---|---|---|---|---|---|---|---|---|---|---|---|---|---|---|---|---|---|---|---|
| **36** | 4.11 | 3.26 | 2.86 | 2.63 | 2.48 | 2.36 | 2.28 | 2.21 | 2.15 | 2.10 | 2.06 | 2.03 | 1.98 | 1.93 | 1.87 | 1.82 | 1.78 | 1.72 | 1.69 | 1.65 | 1.62 | 1.59 | 1.56 | 1.55 |
|  | **7.39** | **5.25** | **4.38** | **3.89** | **3.58** | **3.35** | **3.18** | **3.04** | **2.94** | **2.86** | **2.78** | **2.72** | **2.62** | **2.54** | **2.43** | **2.35** | **2.26** | **2.17** | **2.12** | **2.04** | **2.00** | **1.94** | **1.90** | **1.87** |
| **38** | 4.10 | 3.25 | 2.85 | 2.62 | 2.46 | 2.35 | 2.26 | 2.19 | 2.14 | 2.09 | 2.05 | 2.02 | 1.96 | 1.92 | 1.85 | 1.80 | 1.76 | 1.71 | 1.67 | 1.63 | 1.60 | 1.57 | 1.54 | 1.53 |
|  | **7.35** | **5.21** | **4.34** | **3.86** | **3.54** | **3.32** | **3.15** | **3.02** | **2.91** | **2.82** | **2.75** | **2.69** | **2.59** | **2.51** | **2.40** | **2.32** | **2.22** | **2.14** | **2.08** | **2.00** | **1.97** | **1.90** | **1.86** | **1.84** |
| **40** | 4.08 | 3.23 | 2.84 | 2.61 | 2.45 | 2.34 | 2.25 | 2.18 | 2.12 | 2.07 | 2.04 | 2.00 | 1.95 | 1.90 | 1.84 | 1.79 | 1.74 | 1.69 | 1.66 | 1.61 | 1.59 | 1.55 | 1.53 | 1.51 |
|  | **7.31** | **5.18** | **4.31** | **3.83** | **3.51** | **3.29** | **3.12** | **2.99** | **2.88** | **2.80** | **2.73** | **2.66** | **2.56** | **2.49** | **2.37** | **2.29** | **2.20** | **2.11** | **2.05** | **1.97** | **1.94** | **1.88** | **1.84** | **1.81** |
| **42** | 4.07 | 3.22 | 2.83 | 2.59 | 2.44 | 2.32 | 2.24 | 2.17 | 2.11 | 2.06 | 2.02 | 1.99 | 1.94 | 1.89 | 1.82 | 1.78 | 1.73 | 1.68 | 1.64 | 1.60 | 1.57 | 1.54 | 1.51 | 1.49 |
|  | **7.27** | **5.15** | **4.29** | **3.80** | **3.49** | **3.26** | **3.10** | **2.96** | **2.86** | **2.77** | **2.70** | **2.64** | **2.54** | **2.46** | **2.35** | **2.26** | **2.17** | **2.08** | **2.02** | **1.94** | **1.91** | **1.85** | **1.80** | **1.78** |
| **44** | 4.06 | 3.21 | 2.82 | 2.58 | 2.43 | 2.31 | 2.23 | 2.16 | 2.10 | 2.05 | 2.01 | 1.98 | 1.92 | 1.88 | 1.81 | 1.76 | 1.72 | 1.66 | 1.63 | 1.58 | 1.56 | 1.52 | 1.50 | 1.48 |
|  | **7.24** | **5.12** | **4.26** | **3.78** | **3.46** | **3.24** | **3.07** | **2.94** | **2.84** | **2.75** | **2.68** | **2.62** | **2.52** | **2.44** | **2.32** | **2.24** | **2.15** | **2.06** | **2.00** | **1.92** | **1.88** | **1.82** | **1.78** | **1.75** |
| **46** | 4.05 | 3.20 | 2.81 | 2.57 | 2.42 | 2.30 | 2.22 | 2.14 | 2.09 | 2.04 | 2.00 | 1.97 | 1.91 | 1.87 | 1.80 | 1.75 | 1.71 | 1.65 | 1.62 | 1.57 | 1.54 | 1.51 | 1.48 | 1.46 |
|  | **7.21** | **5.10** | **4.24** | **3.76** | **3.44** | **3.22** | **3.05** | **2.92** | **2.82** | **2.73** | **2.66** | **2.60** | **2.50** | **2.42** | **2.30** | **2.22** | **2.13** | **2.04** | **1.98** | **1.90** | **1.86** | **1.80** | **1.76** | **1.72** |
| **48** | 4.04 | 3.19 | 2.80 | 2.56 | 2.41 | 2.30 | 2.21 | 2.14 | 2.08 | 2.03 | 1.99 | 1.96 | 1.90 | 1.86 | 1.79 | 1.74 | 1.70 | 1.64 | 1.61 | 1.56 | 1.53 | 1.50 | 1.47 | 1.45 |
|  | **7.19** | **5.08** | **4.22** | **3.74** | **3.42** | **3.20** | **3.04** | **2.90** | **2.80** | **2.71** | **2.64** | **2.58** | **2.48** | **2.40** | **2.28** | **2.20** | **2.11** | **2.02** | **1.96** | **1.88** | **1.84** | **1.78** | **1.73** | **1.70** |
| **50** | 4.03 | 3.18 | 2.79 | 2.56 | 2.40 | 2.29 | 2.20 | 2.13 | 2.07 | 2.02 | 1.98 | 1.95 | 1.90 | 1.85 | 1.78 | 1.74 | 1.69 | 1.63 | 1.60 | 1.55 | 1.52 | 1.48 | 1.46 | 1.44 |
|  | **7.17** | **5.06** | **4.20** | **3.72** | **3.41** | **3.18** | **3.02** | **2.88** | **2.78** | **2.70** | **2.62** | **2.56** | **2.46** | **2.39** | **2.26** | **2.18** | **2.10** | **2.00** | **1.94** | **1.86** | **1.82** | **1.76** | **1.71** | **1.68** |
| **55** | 4.02 | 3.17 | 2.78 | 2.54 | 2.38 | 2.27 | 2.18 | 2.11 | 2.05 | 2.00 | 1.97 | 1.93 | 1.88 | 1.83 | 1.76 | 1.72 | 1.67 | 1.61 | 1.58 | 1.52 | 1.50 | 1.46 | 1.43 | 1.41 |
|  | **7.12** | **5.01** | **4.16** | **3.68** | **3.37** | **3.15** | **2.98** | **2.85** | **2.75** | **2.66** | **2.59** | **2.53** | **2.43** | **2.35** | **2.23** | **2.15** | **2.06** | **1.96** | **1.90** | **1.82** | **1.78** | **1.71** | **1.66** | **1.64** |
| **60** | 4.00 | 3.15 | 2.76 | 2.52 | 2.37 | 2.25 | 2.17 | 2.10 | 2.04 | 1.99 | 1.95 | 1.92 | 1.86 | 1.81 | 1.75 | 1.70 | 1.65 | 1.59 | 1.56 | 1.50 | 1.48 | 1.44 | 1.41 | 1.39 |
|  | **7.08** | **4.98** | **4.13** | **3.65** | **3.34** | **3.12** | **2.95** | **2.82** | **2.72** | **2.63** | **2.56** | **2.50** | **2.40** | **2.32** | **2.20** | **2.12** | **2.03** | **1.93** | **1.87** | **1.79** | **1.74** | **1.68** | **1.63** | **1.60** |
| **65** | 3.99 | 3.14 | 2.75 | 2.51 | 2.36 | 2.24 | 2.15 | 2.08 | 2.02 | 1.98 | 1.94 | 1.90 | 1.85 | 1.80 | 1.73 | 1.68 | 1.63 | 1.57 | 1.54 | 1.49 | 1.46 | 1.42 | 1.39 | 1.37 |
|  | **7.04** | **4.95** | **4.10** | **3.62** | **3.31** | **3.09** | **2.93** | **2.79** | **2.70** | **2.61** | **2.54** | **2.47** | **2.37** | **2.30** | **2.18** | **2.09** | **2.00** | **1.90** | **1.84** | **1.76** | **1.71** | **1.64** | **1.60** | **1.56** |
| **70** | 3.98 | 3.13 | 2.74 | 2.50 | 2.35 | 2.23 | 2.14 | 2.07 | 2.01 | 1.97 | 1.93 | 1.89 | 1.84 | 1.79 | 1.72 | 1.67 | 1.62 | 1.56 | 1.53 | 1.47 | 1.45 | 1.40 | 1.37 | 1.35 |
|  | **7.01** | **4.92** | **4.08** | **3.60** | **3.29** | **3.07** | **2.91** | **2.77** | **2.67** | **2.59** | **2.51** | **2.45** | **2.35** | **2.28** | **2.15** | **2.07** | **1.98** | **1.88** | **1.82** | **1.74** | **1.69** | **1.62** | **1.56** | **1.53** |
| **80** | 3.96 | 3.11 | 2.72 | 2.48 | 2.33 | 2.21 | 2.12 | 2.05 | 1.99 | 1.95 | 1.91 | 1.88 | 1.82 | 1.77 | 1.70 | 1.65 | 1.60 | 1.54 | 1.51 | 1.45 | 1.42 | 1.38 | 1.35 | 1.32 |
|  | **6.96** | **4.88** | **4.04** | **3.56** | **3.25** | **3.04** | **2.87** | **2.74** | **2.64** | **2.55** | **2.48** | **2.41** | **2.32** | **2.24** | **2.11** | **2.03** | **1.94** | **1.84** | **1.78** | **1.70** | **1.65** | **1.57** | **1.52** | **1.49** |
| **100** | 3.94 | 3.09 | 2.70 | 2.46 | 2.30 | 2.19 | 2.10 | 2.03 | 1.97 | 1.92 | 1.88 | 1.85 | 1.79 | 1.75 | 1.68 | 1.63 | 1.57 | 1.51 | 1.48 | 1.42 | 1.39 | 1.34 | 1.30 | 1.28 |
|  | **6.90** | **4.82** | **3.98** | **3.51** | **3.20** | **2.99** | **2.82** | **2.69** | **2.59** | **2.51** | **2.43** | **2.36** | **2.26** | **2.19** | **2.06** | **1.98** | **1.89** | **1.79** | **1.73** | **1.64** | **1.59** | **1.51** | **1.46** | **1.43** |
| **125** | 3.92 | 3.07 | 2.68 | 2.44 | 2.29 | 2.17 | 2.08 | 2.01 | 1.95 | 1.90 | 1.86 | 1.83 | 1.77 | 1.72 | 1.65 | 1.60 | 1.55 | 1.49 | 1.45 | 1.39 | 1.36 | 1.31 | 1.27 | 1.25 |
|  | **6.84** | **4.78** | **3.94** | **3.47** | **3.17** | **2.95** | **2.79** | **2.65** | **2.56** | **2.47** | **2.40** | **2.33** | **2.23** | **2.15** | **2.03** | **1.94** | **1.85** | **1.75** | **1.68** | **1.59** | **1.54** | **1.46** | **1.40** | **1.37** |
| **150** | 3.91 | 3.06 | 2.67 | 2.43 | 2.27 | 2.16 | 2.07 | 2.00 | 1.94 | 1.89 | 1.85 | 1.82 | 1.76 | 1.71 | 1.64 | 1.59 | 1.54 | 1.47 | 1.44 | 1.37 | 1.34 | 1.29 | 1.25 | 1.22 |
|  | **6.81** | **4.75** | **3.91** | **3.44** | **3.14** | **2.92** | **2.76** | **2.62** | **2.53** | **2.44** | **2.37** | **2.30** | **2.20** | **2.12** | **2.00** | **1.91** | **1.83** | **1.72** | **1.66** | **1.56** | **1.51** | **1.43** | **1.37** | **1.33** |
| **200** | 3.89 | 3.04 | 2.65 | 2.41 | 2.26 | 2.14 | 2.05 | 1.98 | 1.92 | 1.87 | 1.83 | 1.80 | 1.74 | 1.69 | 1.62 | 1.57 | 1.52 | 1.45 | 1.42 | 1.35 | 1.32 | 1.26 | 1.22 | 1.19 |
|  | **6.76** | **4.71** | **3.88** | **3.41** | **3.11** | **2.90** | **2.73** | **2.60** | **2.50** | **2.41** | **2.34** | **2.28** | **2.17** | **2.09** | **1.97** | **1.88** | **1.79** | **1.69** | **1.62** | **1.53** | **1.48** | **1.39** | **1.33** | **1.28** |
| **400** | 3.86 | 3.02 | 2.62 | 2.39 | 2.23 | 2.12 | 2.03 | 1.96 | 1.90 | 1.85 | 1.81 | 1.78 | 1.72 | 1.67 | 1.60 | 1.54 | 1.49 | 1.42 | 1.38 | 1.32 | 1.28 | 1.22 | 1.16 | 1.13 |
|  | **6.70** | **4.66** | **3.83** | **3.36** | **3.06** | **2.85** | **2.69** | **2.55** | **2.46** | **2.37** | **2.29** | **2.23** | **2.12** | **2.04** | **1.92** | **1.84** | **1.74** | **1.64** | **1.57** | **1.47** | **1.42** | **1.32** | **1.24** | **1.19** |
| **1000** | 3.85 | 3.00 | 2.61 | 2.38 | 2.22 | 2.10 | 2.02 | 1.95 | 1.89 | 1.84 | 1.80 | 1.76 | 1.70 | 1.65 | 1.58 | 1.53 | 1.47 | 1.41 | 1.36 | 1.30 | 1.26 | 1.19 | 1.13 | 1.08 |
|  | **6.66** | **4.62** | **3.80** | **3.34** | **3.04** | **2.82** | **2.66** | **2.53** | **2.43** | **2.34** | **2.26** | **2.20** | **2.09** | **2.01** | **1.89** | **1.81** | **1.71** | **1.61** | **1.54** | **1.44** | **1.38** | **1.28** | **1.19** | **1.11** |
| **∞** | 3.84 | 2.99 | 2.60 | 2.37 | 2.21 | 2.09 | 2.01 | 1.94 | 1.88 | 1.83 | 1.79 | 1.75 | 1.69 | 1.64 | 1.57 | 1.52 | 1.46 | 1.40 | 1.35 | 1.28 | 1.24 | 1.17 | 1.11 | 1.00 |
|  | **6.64** | **4.60** | **3.78** | **3.32** | **3.02** | **2.80** | **2.64** | **2.51** | **2.41** | **2.32** | **2.24** | **2.18** | **2.07** | **1.99** | **1.87** | **1.79** | **1.69** | **1.59** | **1.52** | **1.41** | **1.36** | **1.25** | **1.15** | **1.00** |

Row labels (both left and right margins): 36, 38, 40, 42, 44, 46, 48, 50, 55, 60, 65, 70, 80, 100, 125, 150, 200, 400, 1000, ∞

TABLE 5    Percentiles of the $\chi^2$ distribution*

| n. (d.f.) | P=.99 | .98 | .95 | .90 | .80 | .70 | .50 | .30 | .20 | .10 | .05 | .02 | .01 |
|---|---|---|---|---|---|---|---|---|---|---|---|---|---|
| 1 | .000157 | .000628 | .00393 | .0158 | .0642 | .148 | .455 | 1.074 | 1.642 | 2.706 | 3.841 | 5.412 | 6.635 |
| 2 | .0201 | .0404 | .103 | .211 | .446 | .713 | 1.386 | 2.408 | 3.219 | 4.605 | 5.991 | 7.824 | 9.210 |
| 3 | .115 | .185 | .352 | .584 | 1.005 | 1.424 | 2.366 | 3.665 | 4.642 | 6.251 | 7.815 | 9.837 | 11.345 |
| 4 | .297 | .429 | .711 | 1.064 | 1.649 | 2.195 | 3.357 | 4.878 | 5.989 | 7.779 | 9.488 | 11.668 | 13.277 |
| 5 | .554 | .752 | 1.145 | 1.610 | 2.343 | 3.000 | 4.351 | 6.064 | 7.289 | 9.236 | 11.070 | 13.388 | 15.086 |
| 6 | .872 | 1.134 | 1.635 | 2.204 | 3.070 | 3.828 | 5.348 | 7.231 | 8.558 | 10.645 | 12.592 | 15.033 | 16.812 |
| 7 | 1.239 | 1.564 | 2.167 | 2.833 | 3.822 | 4.671 | 6.346 | 8.383 | 9.803 | 12.017 | 14.067 | 16.622 | 18.475 |
| 8 | 1.646 | 2.032 | 2.733 | 3.490 | 4.594 | 5.527 | 7.344 | 9.524 | 11.030 | 13.362 | 15.507 | 18.168 | 20.090 |
| 9 | 2.088 | 2.532 | 3.325 | 4.168 | 5.380 | 6.393 | 8.343 | 10.656 | 12.242 | 14.684 | 16.919 | 19.679 | 21.666 |
| 10 | 2.558 | 3.059 | 3.940 | 4.865 | 6.179 | 7.267 | 9.342 | 11.781 | 13.442 | 15.987 | 18.307 | 21.161 | 23.209 |
| 11 | 3.053 | 3.609 | 4.575 | 5.578 | 6.989 | 8.148 | 10.341 | 12.899 | 14.631 | 17.275 | 19.675 | 22.618 | 24.725 |
| 12 | 3.571 | 4.178 | 5.226 | 6.304 | 7.807 | 9.034 | 11.340 | 14.011 | 15.812 | 18.549 | 21.026 | 24.054 | 26.217 |
| 13 | 4.107 | 4.765 | 5.892 | 7.042 | 8.634 | 9.926 | 12.340 | 15.119 | 16.985 | 19.812 | 22.362 | 25.472 | 27.688 |
| 14 | 4.660 | 5.368 | 6.571 | 7.790 | 9.467 | 10.821 | 13.339 | 16.222 | 18.151 | 21.064 | 23.685 | 26.873 | 29.141 |
| 15 | 5.229 | 5.985 | 7.261 | 8.547 | 10.307 | 11.721 | 14.339 | 17.322 | 19.311 | 22.307 | 24.996 | 28.259 | 30.578 |
| 16 | 5.812 | 6.614 | 7.962 | 9.312 | 11.152 | 12.624 | 15.338 | 18.418 | 20.465 | 23.542 | 26.296 | 29.633 | 32.000 |
| 17 | 6.408 | 7.255 | 8.672 | 10.085 | 12.002 | 13.531 | 16.338 | 19.511 | 21.615 | 24.769 | 27.587 | 30.995 | 33.409 |
| 18 | 7.015 | 7.906 | 9.390 | 10.865 | 12.857 | 14.440 | 17.338 | 20.601 | 22.760 | 25.989 | 28.869 | 32.346 | 34.805 |
| 19 | 7.633 | 8.567 | 10.117 | 11.651 | 13.716 | 15.352 | 18.338 | 21.689 | 23.900 | 27.204 | 30.144 | 33.687 | 36.191 |
| 20 | 8.260 | 9.237 | 10.851 | 12.443 | 14.578 | 16.266 | 19.337 | 22.775 | 25.038 | 28.412 | 31.410 | 35.020 | 37.566 |
| 21 | 8.897 | 9.915 | 11.591 | 13.240 | 15.445 | 17.182 | 20.337 | 23.858 | 26.171 | 29.615 | 32.671 | 36.343 | 38.932 |
| 22 | 9.542 | 10.600 | 12.338 | 14.041 | 16.314 | 18.101 | 21.337 | 24.939 | 27.301 | 30.813 | 33.924 | 37.659 | 40.289 |
| 23 | 10.196 | 11.293 | 13.091 | 14.848 | 17.187 | 19.021 | 22.337 | 26.018 | 28.429 | 32.007 | 35.172 | 38.968 | 41.638 |
| 24 | 10.856 | 11.992 | 13.848 | 15.659 | 18.062 | 19.943 | 23.337 | 27.096 | 29.553 | 33.196 | 36.415 | 40.270 | 42.980 |
| 25 | 11.524 | 12.697 | 14.611 | 16.473 | 18.940 | 20.867 | 24.337 | 28.172 | 30.675 | 34.382 | 37.652 | 41.566 | 44.314 |
| 26 | 12.198 | 13.409 | 15.379 | 17.292 | 19.820 | 21.792 | 25.336 | 29.246 | 31.795 | 35.563 | 38.885 | 42.856 | 45.642 |
| 27 | 12.879 | 14.125 | 16.151 | 18.114 | 20.703 | 22.719 | 26.336 | 30.319 | 32.912 | 36.741 | 40.113 | 44.140 | 46.963 |
| 28 | 13.565 | 14.847 | 16.928 | 18.939 | 21.588 | 23.647 | 27.336 | 31.391 | 34.027 | 37.916 | 41.337 | 45.419 | 48.278 |
| 29 | 14.256 | 15.574 | 17.708 | 19.768 | 22.475 | 24.577 | 28.336 | 32.461 | 35.139 | 39.087 | 42.557 | 46.693 | 49.588 |
| 30 | 14.953 | 16.306 | 18.493 | 20.599 | 23.364 | 25.508 | 29.336 | 33.530 | 36.250 | 40.256 | 43.773 | 47.962 | 50.892 |

*For larger values of $n$, the expression $\sqrt{2x^2} - \sqrt{2n-1}$ may be used as a normal deviate with unit variance.

Source: Taken from R. A. Fisher, *Statistical Methods for Research Workers*, 14th Edition, 1970, published by Oliver and Boyd, Edinburgh. Reproduced by permission of the author and publishers.

TABLE 6  Critical values of Spearman's rank correlation coefficient

| $n$ | $\alpha = 0.10$ | $\alpha = 0.05$ | $\alpha = 0.02$ | $\alpha = 0.01$ |
|---|---|---|---|---|
| 5 | 0.900 | — | — | — |
| 6 | 0.829 | 0.886 | 0.943 | — |
| 7 | 0.714 | 0.786 | 0.893 | — |
| 8 | 0.643 | 0.738 | 0.833 | 0.881 |
| 9 | 0.600 | 0.683 | 0.783 | 0.833 |
| 10 | 0.564 | 0.648 | 0.745 | 0.794 |
| 11 | 0.523 | 0.623 | 0.736 | 0.818 |
| 12 | 0.497 | 0.591 | 0.703 | 0.780 |
| 13 | 0.475 | 0.566 | 0.673 | 0.745 |
| 14 | 0.457 | 0.545 | 0.646 | 0.716 |
| 15 | 0.441 | 0.525 | 0.623 | 0.689 |
| 16 | 0.425 | 0.507 | 0.601 | 0.666 |
| 17 | 0.412 | 0.490 | 0.582 | 0.645 |
| 18 | 0.399 | 0.476 | 0.564 | 0.625 |
| 19 | 0.388 | 0.462 | 0.549 | 0.608 |
| 20 | 0.377 | 0.450 | 0.534 | 0.591 |
| 21 | 0.368 | 0.438 | 0.521 | 0.576 |
| 22 | 0.359 | 0.428 | 0.508 | 0.562 |
| 23 | 0.351 | 0.418 | 0.496 | 0.549 |
| 24 | 0.343 | 0.409 | 0.485 | 0.537 |
| 25 | 0.336 | 0.400 | 0.475 | 0.526 |
| 26 | 0.329 | 0.392 | 0.465 | 0.515 |
| 27 | 0.323 | 0.385 | 0.456 | 0.505 |
| 28 | 0.317 | 0.377 | 0.448 | 0.496 |
| 29 | 0.311 | 0.370 | 0.440 | 0.487 |
| 30 | 0.305 | 0.364 | 0.432 | 0.478 |

Source: "Distribution of Sums of Squares of Rank Differences for Small Samples," E. G. Olds, *Annals of Mathematical Statistics,* Volume 9 (1938). Reproduced with the kind permission of the Editor, *Annals of Mathematical Statistics.*

# Index

239